OSSNORTHEAST

Loving Mr Spock

of related interest

The Complete Guide to Asperger's Syndrome
Tony Attwood
ISBN 978 1 84310 495 7

Asperger's Syndrome
A Guide for Parents and Professionals
Tony Attwood
Foreword by Lorna Wing
ISBN 978 1 85302 577 8

Asperger Syndrome and Long-Term Relationships
Ashley Stanford
Foreword by Liane Holliday Willey
ISBN 978 1 84310 734 7

Alone Together
Making an Asperger Marriage Work
Katrin Bentley
Foreword by Tony Attwood
ISBN 978 1 84310 537 4

An Asperger Marriage
Gisela and Christopher Slater-Walker
Foreword by Tony Attwood
ISBN 978 1 84310 017 1

Aspergers in Love
Maxine Aston
Foreword by Gisela Slater-Walker
ISBN 978 1 84310 115 4

Asperger Syndrome and Adults... Is Anyone Listening?
**Essays and Poems by Spouses, Partners and Parents of Adults
with Asperger Syndrome**
Karen E. Rodman
Foreword by Tony Attwood
ISBN 978 1 84310 751 4

Asperger Syndrome – A Love Story
Sarah Hendrickx and Keith Newton
Foreword by Tony Attwood
ISBN 978 1 84310 540 4

Loving Mr Spock

Understanding an Aloof Lover – Could It Be Asperger's Syndrome?

Barbara Jacobs

Jessica Kingsley Publishers
London and Philadelphia

This edition published in the UK
by Jessica Kingsley Publishers 2006
116 Pentonville Road
London N1 9JB, UK
and
400 Market Street, Suite 400
Philadelphia, PA 19106, USA

www.jkp.com

Published by Michael Joseph 2003
Published by Penguin Books 2004

Copyright © Barbara Jacobs 2006
Printed digitally since 2010

The right of Barbara Jacobs to be identified as author of this work has been asserted by her in
accordance with the Copyright, Designs and Patents Act 1988.

British Library Cataloguing in Publication Data
A CIP catalogue record for this book is available from the British Library

ISBN 978 1 84310 472 8

Contents

Foreword

Can you fall in love with someone who has Asperger's Syndrome? The answer is yes, you can, and many people do, but when you fall in love with that aloof, intelligent, kind and idiosyncratic person, whose behaviours and emotions are confusing, you probably do not know he or she has Asperger's Syndrome. Barbara Jacobs, the author of *Loving Mr Spock*, is a very successful advice columnist. She is remarkably intuitive and insightful in her ability to read another person's thoughts and feelings. She knows the social conventions and etiquette and is an expert in social and emotional communication. She is a compassionate, mature and maternal person. These are exactly the characteristics needed and sought by a partner with Asperger's Syndrome. Why is there mutual attraction between someone with Asperger's Syndrome, who has limited social understanding and empathy, and someone with advanced abilities in these areas? The answer becomes apparent as you read *Loving Mr Spock*.

When Barbara met Danny, she immediately recognized that he was not a typical young man and certainly not her equal in terms of social understanding. She describes him as the kind of man you would not obviously fall for. However, he was the handsome stranger who captivated her heart and released from within her powerful maternal and protective instincts. Barbara and Danny found that they had many interests in common and she initially found his childlike characteristics charming and endearing. Danny found in Barbara his mentor, social interpreter and someone to mother and father him.

The story of their relationship is written in the style of a conversation between the author and the reader as though you are best friends. Barbara discovers Danny's diagnosis after she fell in love with him, and her journey of exploration, of a parallel universe inhabited by those similar to Mr Spock, who prioritize logic and facts over emotion and intuition, is a fascinating and entrancing story. The reader will become knowledgeable in the nature of Asperger's Syndrome, not only from reading about Barbara's observations, insight and experiences but also from reading her review of the academic literature and the quotations from other adults with Asperger's Syndrome. She has also conducted a small survey of couples where one partner has Asperger's Syndrome to compare experiences, and provide a list of resources for more information and support.

While Barbara became Danny's mentor, she needed her own mentor to guide her through the relationship that so dominated her thoughts and emotions. However, she travelled alone, and her travel journal, this book, is a guide that will be valued by those who have travelled, or are about to travel, the same path and come to love someone with Asperger's Syndrome.

Those who have Asperger's Syndrome will also value *Loving Mr Spock*. The story is inspiring in that the person with Asperger's Syndrome may think that there will be no one outside of his or her family that will love, accept and admire them. Yet such individuals can be extremely attractive to those at the opposite end of the social understanding and empathy continuum. The relationship can be mutually beneficial. However, there are some characteristics of Asperger's Syndrome that can test the understanding and patience of a saint. Barbara has to try to adjust to very different expectations in a relationship. She clearly loves Danny deeply, but can she cope with aspects that bewilder her and challenge her expectations?

Loving Mr Spock is a mystery and adventure story that is fact, not fiction, and similar stories are being experienced everywhere. Barbara is very brave in revealing her inner thoughts and experiences. She has a purpose: to provide a unique insight into the mind of the person she fell in love with – a man who has Asperger's Syndrome. Perhaps you know someone who has fallen in love with a person with Asperger's Syndrome?

Dr Tony Attwood

Preface

This is the story of a specific relationship I had with a specific man. In the course of that relationship I noticed a pattern of behaviour that puzzled me, and eventually I found an explanation for this entire pattern. Asperger's Syndrome.

But please tread cautiously through these pages. Many behaviours of the 'typical bloke' have some similarities with Asperger's Syndrome, and the condition can't be attributed to every oddball you may meet, of whatever gender. It's always best to seek diagnosis if you feel that someone close to you displays the traits which I describe.

Nor is Danny representative of all Aspergers. As I say repeatedly in the book, all Aspergers have different balances of skills and deficits, and each has their own individual personality, and particular ways of coping with those skills and deficits.

And this is a very personal account, and therefore can't be regarded as typical. I've concentrated on those people who experienced relationship difficulties which shed light on my own, but I know many Aspergers who are in happy and successful long-term relationships, and I sought their advice too.

I hope that in looking carefully at those who are other-wired, I may help others think more carefully about the factors common in all relationships, and the adjustments each person has to make, some of which may be unexpected.

Most of all I wanted to tell you about Asperger's Syndrome itself, and to raise awareness of this mysterious and poorly understood condition, which can be so subtle that it may be mistaken for a psychological rather than a neurological condition.

Throughout the book I've referred to those who suffer from Asperger's Syndrome as 'Aspergers'. This may give offence to those who don't like to be described by their condition. It would have been more considerate to have referred to 'people who suffer from Asperger's Syndrome', but that's too long-winded and formal for a book of this nature. So I apologize in advance.

I've also used the terms Asperger's Syndrome and High Functioning Autism interchangeably, whereas most experts would make a subtle distinction between the two. I've chosen not to.

Finally, this is not a book written by an expert. It may appear that I've over-generalized at times. Some experts might argue with some of my definitions or the weight I give to different 'treatments'. But this is my particular view. It's my book.

And it's Danny's too. I'd like to thank him for giving me the insight to write it.

Acknowledgements

Thanks are due to all those who encouraged, helped, contributed and gave permissions, including the National Autistic Society, Cambridge Autism Research Centre, the World Health Organization, the American Psychiatric Association, A/S Partners and Debbie, Karen Rodman, John Muggleton, Kevin Phillips, Larry Arnold, George Handley, Jane Meyerding, Joel, the estate of Marc Segar, Brenda Wall, Wendy Lawson, Donna Williams, Matthew Belmonte, Leneh and Ian, Anna, David, Roger N. Meyer, Mark Koontz, Simon Baron Cohen, Tony Attwood, Tony Hazzard, Phyllis Phillips, Lorna Wing, Christopher and Carina Gillberg, Steph Ebdon, Steve Jones, and Debi, Katie, Stephen, Christopher, David and Andrew Evans.

1 The Handsome Stranger Syndrome

Danny wasn't the kind of man you would obviously fall for.

When I first saw him he was perched on a stool at the pool-side bar of my hotel behind a large glass of white wine. Even at a first cursory glance I decided that he was someone who didn't merit a second. He was short, his legs too muscular, he was hiding behind a tacky pair of plastic sunglasses and, what's worse, he was wearing a rugby shirt over his shorts. I have a low tolerance for rugby players.

It was the early summer of 1997. I was staying in a seaside village in southern Spain on my last day of a working vacation, writing a piece for the *Daily Mail* about single vacations and the mature woman. Danny was a thirty-something window salesman, a rugby player, a man with a private and almost unheard-of problem. And me? Well, I'm not supposed to have problems of my own. I'm an advice columnist.

I'd struggled up along the winding route from the beach to the small family-run hotel, tanned, happy, out of breath. The holiday had given me the chance to indulge my own hobby too – wine-tasting. There was a wonderful local gin I'd discovered. I'd have that with a large spritz of tonic on the rocks as a pre-shower aperitif, then change, and treat myself to the mixed fish grill at the smart restaurant opposite the hotel. I'd sample a glass of chilled white Rioja wine with my meal, and have a sherry-based warmed Spanish brandy with my espresso. It was a wine-buff's gentle and genteel farewell to Spain. Then I was due for an early night before the midday flight the next day.

But there was Danny, sitting watching from behind his plastic glasses, desperate for attention. My attention. As I talked to and laughed with one or two of the other guests I'd befriended, sitting around the straw-roofed bar while the sun set, he continually butted into the conversation. I thought him gauche and rude. A nerd. We glared at him. He smiled broadly. That's the trouble with Asperger's Syndrome men. They don't know the rules of conversation, and they don't know when they're not wanted.

Persistent, unfazed, he asked me about the restaurants in the village and, as politely as I could, I gave him a rundown of them. When he asked me where I liked to eat, I pointed out the fish restaurant. I thought little of it at the time, and didn't include him in the goodbyes I said to the others as I went up to change, nor acknowledged his presence when I came back down in my terracotta silk trousers and white T-shirt past the bar. He hadn't registered with me except as a very small irritant.

But, after I'd sat down at the restaurant terrace table overlooking the distant sea and harbour lights, ordered my meal and that glass of white wine, I saw him again, and my heart sank as I realized he was headed straight for my table. I really didn't want to have my evening interrupted. I put on my sunglasses and tried to hide.

He'd changed from his rugby shirt at least. He wore beige checked cotton trousers with a cheap blue silk shirt which had breast pockets with button-down flaps. I wondered who would find that package attractive, and who would be the lucky girl to get landed with him that night.

It turned out to be me.

And yes… I'm long past being a girl, and no… he certainly *wasn't* my type.

The last thing I wanted to do was share a meal with a man who looked like a Staffordshire bull terrier puppy. I'd met men like him before, I thought. But, actually, I had never met a man anything like him before. Not ever.

He told me he was buying my meal. I refused as frostily as I could. He should have realized that he was intruding on a privacy I wanted and enjoyed. Anyone who could read my tone of voice and body language would have been frozen stone cold, as most are when I adopt my ice-maiden role. Yet he laughed as if I had said something to encourage him. Strange. My party-trick Medusa voice had never provoked that reaction. I took off my sunglasses to see if I could make out what his face was doing. It was just crumpled into blank laughter. There wasn't even a reaction to my quizzical look. I didn't know it then, but this skewed emotional response that we've all encountered at some time is typical of those with Danny's problem – Asperger's Syndrome. Those with the condition can't read body language, tone of voice, or verbal clues. And their responses are all wrong too. They almost try too hard.

Asperger's Syndrome? Like most women, I wouldn't have had any idea what it was: that is before I met Danny. If you'd asked me – and I'm supposed to know about unusual conditions – I might have made a wild stab in the dark and guessed that it might be some sort of genetic dysfunction, a metabolic problem, perhaps, or something to do with the digestive tract. Never would I have guessed that it's a complex neurological disorder.

The truth is that it *is* complex, and very common, and largely undiagnosed in adults. It touches all our lives. It's so widespread that someone you know, someone in your family, someone you work with, is likely to be an Asperger. You might even know two or three. And if you're particularly attracted to intelligent, fascinating men with fine features and an idiosyncratic child-like personal style, you might even fall in love with one of them...

Just as I did.

'I'll order us a bottle of wine then,' he said, and, with total authority, picked up the wine list, frowned impressively, and in fluent Spanish ordered what I knew to be the best wine on the list. He had made karmic connection with my own consuming interest. Serendipity. 'And I'll have what she's eating,' he added.

The waiter left. Danny turned the full Monty of his radiant cross-toothed smile on me, and said, 'Know what I'm going to do? After this meal I'm going to take you round this town, get you pissed out of your head, then take you back to the hotel and shag you.'

I spluttered. No one had ever said anything so funny to me before. It was so direct and uninhibited – typical Asperger talk. As a way of grabbing my attention, he couldn't have tried harder. But there were other reasons for my splutter. One was that he was a lot younger than I was, the other that, following two painful relationships, I'd decided on celibacy, and had spent the previous ten years not even thinking about romance or attraction, let alone the unsung glories of the Saturday night shag.

'I've been celibate for ten years,' I said, after the splutter.

He gave me a quick sidelong glance, then – sidelong glances being an Asperger trait as most find it almost impossible to maintain eye contact with a stranger – 'What a waste,' he said, softly and sadly.

I'd never quite thought of it like that. I'd always been recklessly hot-blooded (when I wasn't being icily distant with strangers) and the decision to clear out relationships from my life had been taken quite logically. I'd been busy, working hard, seeing my son through university, treating myself to another degree course. I hadn't wanted distraction or another heartbreak. And the softness of his reply, with the sudden realization in me that it *had* been a waste, broke through some of the barriers.

He'd managed, in two brief exchanges of almost monosyllabic bluntness, to produce the two emotions which fuelled my entire existence – humour and compassion. But the compassion I now felt was for myself. There had been no one around in my life to tell me what I should have told myself during the last ten barren years, and here was a total stranger, a giant child, hitting two nails on the head, one after the other. And the strange thing was that there was no hidden agenda in that last remark of his, no attempt at manipulation or pressing his invitation to a meaningless bonk. It was an observation, that was all, uttered with brutal honesty. His opinion. Unasked for. Par for the course for Aspergers.

So what exactly *is* Asperger's? It might help if I tell you that it's sometimes called HFA or High Functioning Autism, and autism is something we've all heard of. The autistic person lives in his or her own mind, a logical mind, a mind full of wonder and movement, excitement and stimulus, fixation and sensation. Autistic people can't easily connect with others, as they don't see other people as having thoughts and feelings as they do. They exist in a self-protective bubble of their own reality, mapping the patterns they see.

On the high functioning end of this, the autistic spectrum, are Aspergers (AS), affectionately known as 'aspies', with high intelligence, wanting to be friends and lovers, but with little idea of how to do either. Unlike conventional autistics they are geared to think rather than feel. Thankfully, they have a desperate child-like eagerness to learn. Asperger's Syndrome was only identified as a diagnosis for schoolchildren in the late eighties. Anyone over the age of twenty-five could be Asperger and undiagnosed, just like Danny. We, and they, have no way of knowing. We just think them a bit 'different'. But that problem with eye contact can be an indicator.

'I'm old enough to be your mother,' I said, finally.

He squealed. I noticed, later, that he squealed quite a lot. Adults don't usually squeal, especially not adult men, but Asperger men can. They make a lot of the noises that other people repress or grow out of. The squeal was in his head so it came out of his mouth without touching the sides. 'How old do you think I am?' he asked.

I looked at him properly for the first time. He had a very round head, small searing blue eyes, close-cropped curly black hair, tiny circular ears, a neat nose, and a perfectly sculpted mouth and chin which should have been in Carrera marble and signed with an Italian master's name. He had a lovely face – which I hadn't even noticed until then – almost like a tiny porcelain baby doll. But there were specks of grey in his dark curls.

'Thirty-two,' I guessed.

He looked deflated, and made the noise of a punctured cushion.

'Hmmmmm,' he said. 'You're right. No one's ever right about my age. They always think I'm much younger than I am.'

'Snap,' I said, hoping he'd take the hint.

Strangely, he didn't ask me, so I didn't tell him my age. I expected him to, and in the normal course of conversation that would have been the next bead on the thread. This conversation was already a broken string of pearls. Best to let them lie where they fell, I decided. There's always something special in the unpredicted, and eccentricity in anyone fascinates me. Both of the men in my life had been excitingly unconventional.

I watched him eat, making small appreciative noises like a hungry puppy, little growls and lip smacks, almost private noises of delight in the food and the wine.

Of course I know now. Aspergers have no hang-ups about age. They literally don't mind the gap. In fact, they can sometimes unconsciously seek out someone older who can guide and help them to make sense of the world. They have no problems with cultural difference either, and because of their linguistic idiosyncrasies often find themselves most comfortable with those who don't speak their language, and therefore don't notice the degree of bluntness and literality they employ. Their straight talk comes not from the 'let's cut the bullshit' book of social graces, but from their lack of any in-built social graces. They have to learn social graces by copying. Living in a world where others are interesting, but not as interesting as their own thoughts and feelings, communication isn't dominated by what might be the right thing to say. They don't even know that there are right and wrong ways of saying things.

We spent most of that night talking. I thought him sweet if very strange. If I am unconventional, and I am, he was off the scale. He had the face of a cherub, the focused intelligence of a professor, and the social skills and emotional maturity of a three-year-old. It was clear that despite his brashness he was tender, clinging to the memory of his divorced wife, whom he described as the best friend he'd ever had. They'd been school sweethearts, married at nineteen, and she'd walked out one day, never to return, when he was twenty-six. He was still grappling with the impossibility of under-standing why. She had taught him so much, he said. He admired her logicality.

Despite his naiveté and bluntness, his thinking was clear, logical and impressively intelligent, and despite his disreputable sales job, he was honest (apart from the odd unbelievable transparent exaggeration), cultured, well-read, with a keen appreciation of music, art and theatre. He spoke eruditely about Mozart's 'Magic Flute', which I'd once produced on stage.

And, of course, there was wine. We spoke at length about that; the extent of his knowledge, memory and expertise amazed me. I wondered why he hadn't looked for a job in the wine trade.

'I'd like that,' he said. 'Before wine I wanted to be a marine biologist.'

'You did?'

'Yes. I know everything there is to know about whales. Ask me any question. Go on…' He paused. 'And before that it was dinosaurs. I know everything about every dinosaur that ever lived, and when exactly each one died out.'

'And now wine?'

'And now wine.'

We left it at that, and I left for the airport the next morning, without any idea of his surname, where he lived, or who he lived with. It was one of those holiday madness meetings which had collided with one of my zany moments, and zaniness is one of the attributes I'm famed for.

He had made me laugh, that was all, I kept telling myself.

And he'd intrigued me.

No, it was more than that. I kept thinking how odd it was that I'd met someone whose consuming passion was the same as mine, and wondering why and how that could have happened in the scheme of things. Was it Fate? He knew even more about wine than I did, although I'd been studying it for years.

The passion to learn all there is to know about one subject after another should have alerted me to the possibility of Asperger's Syndrome. Compulsive factual knowledge is a factor in diagnosis, but I had never heard of it, so how could it? I just thought, that's what children do, have those obsessions about dinosaurs, and whales and…whatever. But children grow out of it. Aspergers never tire of their serial fixations, until they move on to the next. But the facts stay with them. Their rote memory is astounding.

After a week or so, I found I couldn't get him out of my mind. It wasn't so much the memory of his child face which kept returning, but the memory of his voice, the strange sounds he made, the flat pragmatic way he spoke, his mischievous sense of humour, and this vulnerability, an almost feminine vulnerability which made me want to protect him and care for him, which was plainly stupid as he was a rugby player and well able to look after himself.

And then I realized. It wasn't exactly vulnerability, it was innocence, something I'd lost, and needed to recapture. With him that night I had played at being a kid again, and talked like a kid. He had never got into that boring stuff that many men can get into – the full psychoanalysis ('your problem is…'), and the confessions of a justified sinner ('call me abusive, but I just wasn't ready to commit at that stage…'). I couldn't let Danny's breath of fresh air go. It had blown away all my adopted media cynicism. I didn't know what I was letting myself in for.

Believe me, loving an Asperger is not simple rocket science about women from Venus and men from Mars, but about loving a beautiful pretender from a parallel universe. We don't even share a common language as the same words may be interpreted and used differently, literally, without nuance, by an Asperger. This is the language of the open-minded child – tactless, without agenda.

Asperger's is a neurological disorder, not a disease. As it's not something you can catch, it's not something you can take medication for; it's not something that can be cured. Neurology is about wiring in the brain. These men and women don't share our wiring systems, that's all. *We* are wired to put relating to others as our top priority. Aspergers are hard-wired to an internal system where facts and self are the true reality. They really can't help being what we might judgementally identify as egocentric and fixated. They function without pretence. This is basic intelligence. It's binary without the complementary unit. Log on and link up, if you dare. Prepare to be disabused of any intuitive tricks your media-frenzied upbringing may have taught you. Lose the convoluted salsa dance of courtship and romance, secret motivations, concealed hints, emotional blackmail, word-gloss. Meet Mr Spock.

So you can ditch your self-help books. To date, there is no manual for loving the Asperger, nothing that helps route into their heads and their hearts. Until now. This is a guidebook to understanding. It starts with a rugby player and window salesman called Danny, who initially didn't attract me at all, but who turned my world into a PlayStation.

★ ★ ★

I traced him. It wasn't too difficult. I knew where he had played rugby, I knew what position he had played. I phoned the local paper, where the editor – who doubled up as the reporters, the advertising manager and the sports editor – promised to phone me back the following day with a name and address.

He called, as promised, the next day. 'I've got good and bad news,' he said.

'You can't get his name?'

'Oh, I've got that,' he laughed. 'Danny Wheeler. Well known around here, a bit of an oddball. No, the bad news is that I can't get an address for him. Apparently he arrives from a different place every day.'

'Serial bonker?' I asked.

'That kind of thing. Yes. But I've got his work address, if that's any use.'

It was. I telephoned Harrods, asked them to send him a bottle of the Gran Reserva Rioja we'd shared, with a message, 'Rioja 'n' Roll', and my address and phone number. We were back in touch. There were many times after that when I wished I'd left the innocence in Spain, instead of inviting it, with all its childlike tantrums and incomprehensible behaviour, into my world.

But, on the other hand, I hadn't underestimated how he would fill my life with sunshine either. His laughter, his hedonism and his ability to take life head on and misinterpret it so joyously were deliriously infectious. He brought out everything that I know is best in me: my eccentric spontaneity and my own childlike wonder. He came to visit me, and we had the craziest weekend of my life. We drank an outrageously expensive bottle of wine in the dark, sitting outside the back door of my flat, after a day when, by showing him the wonders which appealed to me, I rediscovered my city.

There was a crazy night when we giggled and couldn't sleep because he kept telling me this hysterically funny story without a punchline. It was like a sleep-over or school camp. He said, in his blunt, straight way, 'I liked that. I was happy,' when he left, waving his small hand.

'Nobody,' I remember thinking, quoting Cummings, 'not even the rain, has such small hands.'

Then, without warning, he went away to Turkey for a week, and didn't come back. He decided at the airport to stay another week, so that's what he did. I had an American friend of mine, a wild journo with attitude, phone his office to check out what had happened to him, and they told her. She pretended to be some girl he'd invited over to the UK. 'He's always pulling stuff like this,' they told her. 'He won't get away with it for much longer. He needs to sort himself out. He's for the chop.'

He returned, phoned me after he'd landed and, instead of apologizing for disappearing, was just full of excited squealing stories about what he'd done, and how he'd talk his way out of it at work. I ended up laughing with him.

'And I'm coming to see you next weekend, if that's all right with you?' he chuckled. But he didn't arrive because he went out drinking the night before he was due to set off and woke 24 hours later. He was already roller-coastering through my emotions, and my plans, and didn't seem to realize.

But then impulsive, hyperactive Aspergers like Danny are deficient in social responsibility. The thought that someone may be waiting for them, want to reach or see them, or might be worried, never occurs to them. For all Aspergers it's the here and now, the mood of their very own moment, that takes them forward on their strange life course. They are, therefore they do. Danny was an extremist. He did what he wanted to do, maniacally, then fell into an almost catatonic trance. There was little middle ground where we could just be, and be together.

It was a hot and cold, all or nothing, on–off relationship by telephone and delayed visits. There were times when he'd turn off his mobile and not answer the phone in the cottage he shared with his elderly father. Sometimes his father would answer finally and say, 'I can't get him out of bed. Haven't seen him all week.' Danny explained to me later that it was something he did when depressed. He called it 'hiding', and said that he should never have sold his fishing rods, because he used to hide by going fishing, but now he had to hide by staying in bed. It all seemed perfectly logical to him, but maintaining a long-distance friendship, which was sporadically more than that, with a grown man who thought it logical to remain incommunicado and firmly embedded for 72 hours at a time, was difficult.

Now I know why he hid like that. Life to an Asperger is a series of strategic decisions at every moment of every day. Danny always had to think what to do next. He would have to run a thorough investigative internal dialogue before he could face a decision, a meeting, before he could read or answer a letter, instead of just knowing, instinctively, as the rest of us do. It was like having to turn back to the beginning of the reference book in his head and work through it, instead of being able to home in on a well-thumbed page, or read the index.

Nothing came naturally. He had to work things out. He had also to keep running reality checks – is this my route? How do I know? What are the signposts I'm familiar with? And please don't move anything! This incessant theorizing, having to route everything through the brain instead of relying on intuition, means that he was in a constant state of alertness and anxiety. No wonder he had patches of eczema all over his body. No wonder he had to carry a nebulizer for his asthma. No wonder he had to get away from it all.

By this time he had lost his job, as he'd been prosecuted for drink driving. That, too, was inevitable. He'd many times phoned me, furry with drunkenness, from his mobile, as he drove to find a bed for the night. He made little sense at those times, but was warm, his defences down, bursting with affection and desperate to urinate, which he sometimes did, slewing the car to a halt, while he was still on the phone. Aspergers have few physical inhibitions. His phone calls could also be inconsequential. He once spoke to me for an hour on a drive home, merely giving me a commentary on his driving and the things he saw out of the car window. What he rarely chose to talk about were emotional issues. He seemed confused and flustered by them, although keen to tell me that he wanted to talk about them to me, for some reason which he could never identify.

His behaviour, although fascinating, was erratic. I started blaming this on his binge drinking, then began to wonder if I had it wrong, and if the binge drinking was itself a symptom. There was no discernible pattern which I could work out in his mood swings, although I thought I had made allowance for the fact that he was trying to run a business he had set up, without a car, in the rural area where he lived. Was this bipolar disorder? Manic depression? Well, no, actually, it was Asperger's Syndrome.

After the loss of his sales job – you can't have a sales job without a driving licence – he'd decided to sell windows on his own account, using his old firm's suppliers and a friend of his as the installer. To me it seemed like a recipe for disaster. He had few executive skills, despite his almost savant reading of spreadsheets and accounts. He took to riding through country lanes to visit clients on a bicycle he hadn't used for years. Yet he was upbeat about this when he chose to be. He phoned once, laughing irrepressibly, to tell me how he had fallen from his bike in a gale force wind: 'And I went right over the hedge, on to my head! Got a big gash!'

'Wasn't it painful?' I asked.

'No! I'm always breaking my fingers or my wrist, or getting injured in rugby. It's nothing! I never feel pain!' he boasted. It registered on me as stoical.

But this is yet another characteristic of the condition – a high tolerance of pain and temperature in certain individuals. It's called hyposensitivity in sensory integration, a failure to feel things that most people would be pained by. It's balanced in the syndrome by hypersensitivity to some sensory stimuli. Some things hurt too much. Some things hurt less than they should. Each Asperger has his or her own painful sensitivities, and his or her own unfeeling pains.

Then there was the time six months after we met when I went to stay, close to his home, for a week at the seaside. He could be improbably callous for one who was basically sweet-natured, if eccentric; another symptom of the Asperger wiring system. I was about to find out just how callous he could be. It was my birthday week, and the plan was that for the week he would move into the rented cottage with me. We enjoyed every moment of the planning. I'd given him a shopping list, and he was there at the station to meet me, then picked up boxes of groceries at his father's house. He helped me move in, made a log fire, lit candles, but announced after the meal that he had to go out, promising to be there in the morning. Next day he called to say he couldn't come as he was going to watch a rugby match on television with his business partner, but I should phone his partner's house at five and we'd go out for the night.

I called. He wasn't there, and hadn't been there. I called his home. There was no reply. I called again and again, until at seven his father answered and said he'd just got up and gone out to the pub. I packed all the things he had brought, took them in a taxi to his father's house, and left them on the doorstep. Danny didn't phone again. I spent that entire week on my own, in a strange place, but planned to have a meal alone, if necessary, on my birthday. Finally I managed to get hold of Danny. He'd been 'hiding' again, angry that I had returned his things. He was grumpily apologetic, and agreed to meet for my birthday meal.

At the restaurant, as we drank the expensive bottle of vintage Krug I bought, and shared a wonderful meal, he was his old cheerful self, apart from the odd moments when I tried to bring up the question of why he'd left me alone. I knew his warning signals and backed off. At the end of the evening I booked a cab.

'Will you come back to the cottage with me?' I asked.

He shook his head, sadly. 'Got a job in the morning. Have to get to it early, so I'd better go home,' he said.

'I'll give you a lift back in my cab then,' I smiled.

'OK,' he agreed.

He came out with me, saw me to my seat in the cab, then closed the door on me.

'I'm going for a drink with my friends now,' he said, and ran away into the night grinning malevolently, as I was driven away from him.

I was stunned. How could any grown man behave like that? It was the action of a naughty defiant toddler throwing an unsignalled tantrum. And my adult skills couldn't cope with it. I cried all night, the night of my birthday.

I didn't know then about his ability to mimic happiness when he was feeling desolate. He, like most Aspergers, was a social actor, modelling and scripting, rather than being able to vent naturally. He just assumed a posture in social situations. He had been more unhappy than I'd realized, felt more threatened and anxious, but had adopted a role of being cheerful. He'd pressed a smile on his lips and it had stayed there, by default. It's the way most sociable Aspergers operate, copying and imitating what they work out as best practice, and it's how they get through difficult meetings, the conventions of the workplace, or the locker room. They role-play. His repressed anxiety and anger had finally got the better of being on his best behaviour. He'd flipped. And he'd crushed me in the process.

I cursed him that night, and the next day, all the way back home on the train, throughout the seven-hour journey. That was it, I decided. It was finally all over. He was obviously seriously sick. For weeks I pondered on what his illness or dysfunction could be, then wrote the whole thing off as a bad job. I wouldn't even think about him again, I decided. But I did. And when he phoned, two months later, crying over some business crisis he was facing, I couldn't let him down. It seemed I was the only real friend he had. 'You're so logical,' he wept. 'You're the only one who can understand! I need you! You're intelligent!' Logic is understanding, for Aspergers. Forget emotion. Forget intuition. Forget, if you can, love as we know it. Just be there. Always. With your brain cells flashing the come-on signals. It's really attractive, apparently.

'He's useless,' my friends said. They were furious that after the birthday débacle, which I'd relayed to anyone with a telephone and email, I was back in touch with someone who was, variously, according to them, a loser, a loony, a manipulative little nerd, a stupid no-brain, and, according to my best friend from over the road, an abuser.

'You do realize that you're in an abusive relationship,' she said. She has always scored high on the judgemental scale on which I never register. I can't do judgements. I keep them, and my shoelaces, flapping. I like open-ended endings.

'It's not a relationship…' I argued. Did you notice the neat side-step from judgement?

'You can say that again,' she agreed.

Whoops.

It was impossible to convey to any of them why I was doing this. Only one friend had a good word to say. 'He's the unattainable. He's the only person you've ever met that you can't understand, and he wouldn't want your real understanding even if you gave it to him. You've found something more complex and screwed up than yourself, and you can't put a name to it, and it bugs you.'

He was the only one who came close to the truth. It isn't easy to talk about something as subtle as 'innocence'. Not these days. Not to media people – which most of my friends were. But then this friend was a former mental health patient, despite being a media star. I listen to those who've been there, done that, got the humanity.

And the truth was that I *did* want to put a name to it. Could it be a form of schizophrenia? I wondered.

I'd queried that, noting the way he talked to himself, or sometimes smiled to himself because he'd just told himself a joke, which he wouldn't share. Then there was the fact that he occasionally called himself 'he' instead of 'I'. He appeared to get confused about where I finished and he began. If he thought something, he immediately imagined I'd thought it, by some weird process of telepathy, I supposed. But I think it was more that boundaries, when we were close, weren't very clear to him. Asperger again. Theory of Mind stuff, which I'll explain later.

But I didn't know that. And, because I didn't know, I went through agonies, hearing these discords, wondering whether I should tell him, and wondering what I could do to protect myself from finding out that I couldn't help him any longer.

Then one day I watched him as he stood in my kitchen – typically wearing only his boxer shorts, not feeling the chill on the cold winter day, standing reading the newspaper which he had spread on a work surface. He was standing strangely, supporting his weight on one foot while the other leg was turned in at the knee and resting on the toes. His elbows were drawn in, his hands hanging limply downwards. Very camp, I thought. And did I say I am not judgemental?

But I had seen that awkward gauche stance before, I knew I had. And I'd also seen someone flapping their hands in the same way he did, wriggling their short fingers in a similar fashion. I couldn't remember where or when, but the image was printed on my mind, now overlaid with Danny's peculiarly twisted position. Where? When?

He left the next day before I realized where and when I had seen that. It had been almost thirty years previously. I'd worked during my summer holidays, once, aeons ago, teaching at a summer camp for children with behavioural difficulties. One of the boys had stood like that, and I'd asked why, and been told.

Autism.

I remembered.

I had a name.

I telephoned the National Autistic Society, and spoke at length to an adviser. I answered all his questions, offered some further examples of Danny's behaviour, and he was certain.

'It looks like HFA or Asperger's Syndrome,' he said. This was 1998. Asperger's was a very new, very raw, diagnosis.

'Explain!'

'HFA is High Functioning Autism, the top end of the autistic spectrum. It's a neurological condition,' he said. 'Some identify it as Asperger's Syndrome, more or less the same thing, but only recently publicized.'

'Is it curable?' I asked, shakily. I was almost crossing my fingers for this to be something that could be sorted by a course of medication, a session with a psychiatrist, a bit of surgery.

'No,' he said. 'It's a lifelong condition, possibly genetic, lots of research going on right now. There are one or two interventions that are showing success, usually with young children. And it can be managed. Most Aspergers are just thought of as a bit eccentric, and make it in the real world, just about. They haven't any real concept of what other people are all about, but they genuinely like being what they think of as sociable, although they get it all wrong most of the time. Think of your average geek, and you've got it about right, a geek who makes social blunders and can't communicate properly, but doesn't realize it.'

'And what about relationships? Do they do those?'

He paused. 'Many of them are in relationships. Some are married. We really don't know all that much about relationships, because we don't know all that much about adult Aspergers. It's a newly diagnosed condition, and we're really mostly dealing with children. There must be huge numbers of them, though. Huge numbers. Look, I'll send you some information and a checklist,' he said.

It arrived, but I already knew the telephone diagnosis was correct, even before I'd started checking off the characteristics on the list. Danny checked out on 80 per cent of the characteristics of autistic spectrum disorder. This was serious. Even I knew that. I telephoned his strange brusque mother to find out about his childhood, although I didn't tell her why. Yes, she said, Danny had had problems at school. He behaved badly, was bullied, didn't join in properly with the other children; he had his routines and woe betide anyone who ever tried to change them. And he'd been referred to the school psychiatric service.

'And they said?'

'Just that he'd grow out of it.'

'Right,' I said, understanding at last. Of course he hadn't grown out of 'it'. And what else did that huge wad of information tell me? That because of the genetic component, there may be other Aspergers within the family. So that explained the brother, a computer boffin, who disappeared for days and lived in his car. And, of course, that explained the sharp-tongued oddity whom he called, stiltedly and formally, as is common in some Asperger cases, 'Mother'.

She collected fossils, and displayed them, just as Danny collected and displayed empty wine bottles. Collecting and displaying are known Asperger traits. She'd given up everything at one point to live in another country, on a whim – that 'right here, right now' action of the totally self-absorbed – and was infamous for her sharp tongue, wild behaviour and her rigid rules. She had married and given birth to Danny in her very late thirties, and had later walked out, completely uprooting the boys, Danny and his younger, more passive and compliant brother, and taken them halfway across the country. It sounded about right for impulsive versions of Asperger's, his mother's version. Danny's version.

So – what to do, now that I knew the worst?

I had two choices, and each would destroy what I'd come to think of as 'us'. There had never been an 'us' in the conventional sense, just a wild free spirit which was answerable only to itself, and a 'me' that recognized how special that was. He had grown dependent on that recognition.

I could sever the bond. It was unspoken anyway. Everyone told me that it would never work out, and I'd been headstrong enough to think I could bring it all to a happily ever after. No chance. This was a life sentence for Danny, and I didn't want to watch him play his self-destructive game any longer, not if I wasn't going to win.

There was nothing I could do for him. This crazy style of his that I'd found so appealing, but which had broken me over and over again, wasn't going to change. All he wanted from me was my logic and equivalent intelligence. He'd never, ever, understand that I had a passion for his strangeness and wanted him to love me back.

It didn't matter. We could both live without the childish mutual fascination. That was best.

Yes, that was the way to deal with this. Just let it be. Let it go. I'd had enough accidental pain. But could I? Could I really leave him? Without explanation?

Or, did I take a gamble that if I told this pocket genius with the sweet unforgettable face and voice about Asperger's Syndrome, it just might help both of us survive, albeit more distantly and more dispassionately?

But events took the decision out of my hands.

It was early summer, only a year since we'd first met. Danny was on his annual trip to Turkey, while I agonized over sharing my knowledge about Asperger's Syndrome with him.

He'd visited Turkey originally with his business partner, who had a house in a rural village. Danny, a sun-lover like myself, had taken to the country and in his inimitable fashion made friends with many of the locals. In particular, there was the son of the widowed owner of the local hotel. Danny called him 'my twin', humorously, as Mehmet was well over six feet tall and towered over him. The two of them enjoyed all-night raki-drinking sessions, and shared childish mimed jokes and a brotherly relationship. So I knew that my Asperger innocent abroad was safe and among friends, even when he didn't return after a week as planned.

He'd done it before. But when the week turned into more than a fortnight, I did start to worry. I was busy recording a television show, a great distraction from my impatience to make a decision about my future with an Asperger man. The fact that I hadn't heard from him though kept intruding into my nights, when high on the adrenalin of performance I'd try to sleep, but could think of nothing but the words I'd read about autism, Asperger's, partnership, mentoring…

'Can Asperger people make happy and successful long-term relationships with those without the disorder?' I'd read in one of the books I'd bought.

The answer had been yes, where there was deep understanding on the part of the non-Asperger partner. I fulfilled that criterion. It helped if the two shared a common interest. Wine fulfilled that one. And especially if the Asperger partner sees the other as a mentor. That was our relationship in a nutshell.

But what about the mentor? Where did the mentor find support? That was my problem, as it's a problem for many who suspect or know that they have an Asperger partner. Could I work as hard communicating and facilitating in my private life as in my professional life? Partnership isn't supposed to be hard work, is it?

I began to read the stories of women who had done just that, taught and learnt some valuable lessons from their Asperger partner. Some stories lifted me. Some made the task seem an endless uphill battle.

Then he phoned.

I could hardly believe it was him. Communicating had never been his strong point – Asperger number one hang-up – and this time he was ringing on his mobile from Turkey. I laughed, delighted.

'Oooooh,' he said, that familiar little involuntary sound which frequently prefaced his most outrageous confessions. 'I've been very silly.'

Silly. My heart sank. In typical Asperger fashion, Danny selected childhood words for the most complex emotional crises. Silly had been the word he used when he phoned me after a night in police custody, after his drink-driving offence.

'What?' I asked, hardly daring.

'I got engaged,' he said.

Everything stopped.

'And?' I could think of nothing. I was desolate. He would never realize how this was hurting me. 'Do you love her?'

'Yes,' he said.

His voice went on and on now, words punctuated with little squeals, accidental grace notes, becoming higher and higher as his excitement spilled over. I died, emotionally.

It was Mehmet's sister, Fatima. He'd shown me a photograph of her once, a sweet doll-like girl, looking much younger than her eighteen years. I'd have put her at twelve. She was beautiful in the way pre-pubescent girls are beautiful – reed-slim with huge baby-brown eyes and a gloss of dark hair. Danny had referred to her, echoing Mehmet's phrase, as 'little sister'. Now he said he loved her, as far of course as he understood that word.

'She reminds me so much of Heather,' he piped, and I knew immediately that I'd lost him. Heather, his ex-wife, was his icon.

'But she's not as clever as you!' he added. 'And I've told her that I can't live without you. I said you will be my wife, but Barbara will always be a part of me.'

He said it in that pragmatic way that brooked no argument. I would have laughed, again, at this perfect Asperger display of failure to identify emotional bonds or the responsibility they bring, but tears were running down my cheeks, so I couldn't manage it.

After the call had ended, I sat all night, the dead phone next to me, numb with pain. He had understood nothing. I had understood far too much.

I ran through Danny's engagement story again and again in my head, and each time the Asperger elements became clearer.

He'd said that he hadn't intended to fall for Fatima. They had been at a village dance, and afterwards had sat for hours on the wall outside the hotel while she'd told him she'd always loved him.

He was the handsome stranger. The effect worked world-wide.

The cultural differences would mean that his odd Asperger language, strange hand movements and eccentric behaviour had been placed in the category of 'foreign' rather than weird. I saw why she'd become infatuated with him. He was older, wealthy, so she thought, apparently worldly-wise – how wrong could she be? – yet his little-boy-lost looks and childish behaviour must have made him appear close to her own age.

And then there was his guiding principle of fairness. That had clinched it.

This is an odd paradox in the Asperger character. It's difficult to square a burning sense of what's right with what we characterize as robotic characteristics. If you can't empathize, how can you cry over injustice like starvation in Africa, imprisonment in the Third World, or despotic governments, as Danny did and as many Aspergers do?

But think of it this way, and the word 'think' is the clue – a sense of justice and fairness isn't emotional. Principles and ethics are rules. 'That's not fair!', a common cry from an Asperger, derives from a thought-out rigid view of the rule-book. Combine this with the world's habit of exploiting the innocent, and you realize that 'not fair' is a child's clear logic, without the cynical rule-bending we learn as we grow. Who says, 'It's not fair' when expected rulings aren't applied? The child, and the Asperger.

And 'not fair' came into play the next morning, Danny said. Fatima was waiting for him, bruised and sobbing. Mehmet had beaten her.

He'd beaten her for telling him, excitedly, that she'd confessed her love to the foreigner. It didn't matter to Mehmet that this foreigner was his friend. Or that nothing happened. To do this was shameful. Fatima had betrayed the family, he was head of the family, so he had beaten his sister, as he felt he was entitled to do. Mehmet applied the rules of his own culture.

But this wasn't in Danny's Rules of Life. So he'd freaked out violently, a regular occurrence in some Aspergers.

Experts call this 'Asperger meltdown'. It's like a Terrible Twos tantrum, a red mist, a loss of all reason. If you've ever seen this happen, you'll know exactly what I'm talking about. It's instant. In one of these sudden wild rages, Aspergers can do anything – bang their own heads against a wall or the floor, throw things around with superhuman strength, self-harm, or, far more rarely, attack someone. Danny had told me once about one of these episodes when he'd had to jump up to knock someone out, as his persecutor was a foot taller than he was. He'd broken all his knuckles in the attack, and still had uneven knuckles. The transformation from sweet child to rabid animal, Dr Jekyll to Mr Hyde, is terrifying to watch.

This time Mehmet was the object of his blinded sense of outrage. Danny floored him. It had taken four men to pull him off. Fatima had screamed and thrown her arms around him. Mehmet, when he regained consciousness, had ordered Danny off the premises, but by that time Danny had already left, after promising Fatima that he would marry her, that he would always protect her, that they were together, now, for ever.

That's the way the proposal had happened.

And he'd naturally phoned me, his mentor.

I know some of you will be scratching your heads, wondering what on earth he was doing phoning me about his proposal to another woman. It was, I agree, an odd position that I occupied in Danny's life. In many ways I'd taken over Heather's role. She'd taught him almost everything he knew about life. Ferociously intelligent, she'd been selected by him when he was only fifteen. He'd had his choice of the girls. Besides his exceptional good looks, his winning innocence and his infectious laughter, he was the school's star athlete.

Here he differs from many Aspergers, and this was the only one obvious part of the Asperger checklist which didn't fit Danny's profile. Most have dyspraxia, a medical term for clumsiness – you know, the typical ham-fisted geek. Most have an odd way of walking. Most can't catch a ball, or handle a pen, or ride a bike. Co-ordination is a major problem. And Aspergers don't learn the rules of games very easily, even if they have some skills.

Danny just happened to be very fast. Very slim, when young, he'd pumped most of his loner existence into running for miles and miles, driving himself to his physical limits. I've heard since of Aspergers who run marathons or hike for weeks through wildernesses as part of their need to put the social world at arm's length. Like many Aspergers, he felt little pain. Running until he vomited with exhaustion was a way of escaping into his own world. And when, at the age of twelve at a new school, he'd amazed everyone by demonstrating this skill, he became a hero. He broke the school record the first time he ever ran a race.

Danny's innate clumsiness was still evident in small ways – remember that stance that I'd noticed? His gait was more tip-toe than most, with more bounce in it, and his arm-swing was slightly unco-ordinated. That tip-toe walk and that unco-ordinated arm-swinging is a real pointer to Asperger's – you can spot it easily, once you know what to look for. He held pens badly. He couldn't do many simple DIY jobs, and hated having to tackle a home-improvement task. But he could drive a car, run like the wind, and play rugby, all skills he'd learnt. The school rugby coach had tamed him, the team had taught him how to co-operate, and, though his ball-handling skills were never very good, his speed was impressive. He'd found a niche for himself.

And Heather, he'd decided, would be the one to live in the niche with him. This is another Asperger pattern I've noted. Many Aspergers seem to choose intelligent partners, prioritizing intelligence above all else. Perhaps it's their way of finding their enabler, the one who smooths their way, performs an interpreter role for them in that frightening world of relating, and helps them formulate new rules. It may be an unconscious survival tactic. But, on the other hand, it's like with like, isn't it? Intelligence admires intelligence, Heather had given up her place at university after only one term to live with him – best friends, brother and sister, Hansel and Gretel. Their wedding photo, which he'd shown me, pictured two very small scared children, desperately holding hands.

'Mr and Mrs Pepperpot,' I laughed when I saw it.

'She was the only one I could ever talk to about myself,' he told me, 'until you. No one knows me like she knew me, and like you know me. I won't talk about myself to anyone except you. I don't trust anyone else. But I can tell you everything.'

And so he talked. He confided. All too much.

After his wild weekend binges he would phone to tell me the full details – how much he'd drunk, hazy memories of where he'd been, and who he vaguely recalled sleeping with. Yes. Danny's fidelity was in his mind. No one could get in there except me. But his body was anybody's.

Sex, he said, was meaningless. An act he rarely got anything from. But it was in the rules, which even before I knew about Asperger's I used to call

'Danny Rules'. Bedding someone was on the agenda every Saturday night. He faked that, too, every time, even with me.

Telling *me* that he'd fallen in love and was about to marry was just another of his Asperger takes on what a real relationship was all about – having enough confidence in someone to let them into everything you thought, and did, and I was the someone. The mentor role. Who'd have it?

Well, I'd had it. Right up to here.

If you think I was hurt past objectivity and understanding by the accidental cruelty he'd practised on me yet again, you've got it right. That was my emotional response. I've talked repeatedly with other Asperger partners about this inability of those of us who are wired for relationships to withstand the slings and arrows of those who aren't. My head understood, while my heart was broken. On the other hand I had the convenient logic to reason all this out in the light of my acquired knowledge of Asperger's Syndrome.

But so many of you, living with or loving an undiagnosed Asperger, don't even know that there *is* a reason – no, that there are galaxies of reasons – why the relationship can be heartbreaking. So let me tell you.

For Danny, and for Aspergers, the heart *is* the mind. It's that simple. All the rest is feeling. Feeling changes, minute to minute, day to day. It can be horrifically overwhelming to Aspergers in its impacts, but is ultimately just a confusing mish-mash of sensory and sensual impressions which they can't do anything about. They receive but can't process sensory information without an enormous effort of will and reasoning, so they have to let it all happen. Essentially they're passive, like televisions turned on and tuned in to three hundred or more channels at the same time. Just what do you take in? What do you respond to? How do you filter out what you don't want? When spoilt for choice, you choose the programme that's on at the time. You stick with that.

The only constant for Aspergers is what their minds have selected, then and there. Their reality is their personal immediate need, because everything else can be just too much to bear. And too much to process for meaning.

To understand Danny, I had to act like Danny. I had to react logically, for his sake, select the necessary bytes, and bin the overload if I could.

I reorganized my life. Some of this was serendipitous. I'd been offered two television series – one in London, one in Glasgow. And I had signed up for my own radio show, in Birmingham, every Sunday. Meanwhile, I dropped my guard and accepted two blind dates. What had I got to lose? Both of them worked out wonderfully. By the time Danny returned, my life was too full for him.

I went on, happily forgetting him. Sometimes he'd telephone on his travels between England and Turkey, to boast about some new rules he'd made for himself. Aspergers can boast in that open natural way that children do, proud of their achievements, giving themselves a pat on the back. He'd given up some of his wild binges so that he could save up for the house that Fatima's family insisted he bought in Turkey. It would cost him, he thought, no more than £3000. And he'd chosen to be celibate. This was a new experience for him. I laughed with him, encouraged him, and believed in him. Then, in the spring, after a silent spell, he phoned and asked if he could come to see me.

But, when he arrived, far from being able to share in his new happiness, I was shocked by his appearance. Something was wrong. I was still close enough to him to work that out. He sat opposite me in my kitchen, his stimming worse than ever.

Stimming? I learned that word when I found out about Asperger's, so let me share it with you.

Stimming is an Asperger constant. It's short for self-stimulation, a repeated set of gestures or sounds that seem to provide comfort or distraction from the sensory confusions in their inner world. Some Aspergers sniff their fingers, suck their thumbs, or rock. Some jerk a leg, or rub a piece of fabric. In Danny's case there were those involuntary sounds which escaped far more often when he was very anxious. They were stimming. And there was hair-tugging. He would select one of his close-cropped curls, and pull it, repeatedly, in counts of three. One, two, three (fast) – pause – one, two, three – twist – one, two, three. It had always intrigued me. Another was to bite a piece of fingernail off and suck it until it disintegrated. If you've seen an Asperger, you'll have noticed the stimming. It's unavoidable. The flapping hands, too, are part of it.

This time, he was doing all the stimming he could manage. The little humming sounds were more frequent than ever. Occasionally, he'd stop to scratch, his elbows and the backs of his knees, his thighs, where he usually had patches of eczema. Unusually, he was also scratching his chest and his back. Then suddenly he pulled off his sweater and T-shirt in a rage of scratching, and I saw that the whole of his upper body was covered in hives.

'Let me look at that,' I asked, and obediently as ever he undressed in an instant.

Every inch of his small body was blistered.

'What's up?' I asked.

'Pshttttttttt,' he said, eloquently, throwing his hands into another flap.

'It's an allergy,' I said.

He nodded. 'Father's dog.'

But of course it wasn't just his father's dog. The dog had been there all the time. This was a nervous reaction to stress, always a problem for Aspergers, who live their lives on constant overload, but this time even more noticeable than his usual asthma and eczema.

'What's really wrong with you?' I asked.

Between scratching bouts he told me.

'I'm going to Germany. I came to say goodbye.'

'Germany?!' I gasped. 'But I thought you were getting married?'

'It didn't work out. So I'm going to Germany to sell wine,' he chuckled, as his mood swung. 'Went out there for an interview last week! Commission only, but I'll be fine!'

Suddenly he was full of his latest adventure, the job in Germany, a country he'd never visited. He didn't even speak the language! There's endearing innocence and gullible innocence, but this was plain stupid.

In the short time I'd known him he'd got himself into some ridiculous situations. He'd lost his job, set up in business, and had now gone broke. All his money had been spent on the wild goose chases to Turkey.

Yes, it had all been a pipe dream, that Romeo and Juliet romance. Her mother had insisted Fatima would not leave Turkey, had asked for an expensive house for herself and another for her daughter, and, most importantly, Fatima herself had decided that she couldn't abandon her mother to move to a foreign country. Danny was regretful, in a shrugging kind of pshhhhhhttt way, but seemed relieved, too.

'Have you ever thought it might have been unrealistic?' I asked. Silly question to ask an Asperger. After all, what *is* real?

He looked at me from under his eyelashes, puzzled. It was obvious that the thought had never entered his head. To be fair, it hadn't entered mine, either. I'd listened and been carried away by his enthusiasm and my own positive thinking. In my rush to wanting him settled, married and happy, I'd discounted his Asperger's Syndrome.

Now I could see a pattern emerging.

Fatima had been a project, a source of stimulation, what he called 'adventures'. The business that he had set up was another stimulation, to motivate himself, an effort to create routines.

But as he told me about its failure, it became obvious to me that his own problems were the cause. He was owed money, but hadn't felt able to collect it – Aspergers, no matter how apparently sure of themselves, fear confrontation of any kind. He was being chased for non-payment to his suppliers, but had run away from that too. If he couldn't collect his debts or pay his bills, he was bound to fail, wasn't he? If he collected what was owed, his suppliers could be paid and he would be clear and free to start again. Any fool could work that out, let alone a mathematical wizard as he was.

'So what're you going to do about this money?' I asked.

He shrugged. 'I'm going to Germany, aren't I? When I get my driving licence back next month. They won't get me if I go to Germany, so I don't have to do anything.'

'Where's your common sense?' I wanted to yell at him. I wanted to shake him, preferably around the neck. I wanted to scream with frustration.

You'll know the feeling if you've ever dealt with an Asperger. But what was the point of asking him that? What was the point of blaming him for this child-view that I adored but which drove me to distraction?

He *had* no common sense. You might as well shout the same question at your three-year-old who runs out into the road on a whim, then tries to play catch with a speeding truck.

Common sense is an intuition about the best and safest way to operate in any given social circumstance. Most of us adults have it because we've been there, done that, and remembered what works and what doesn't, what hurts and what doesn't.

But Danny just flew by the seat of his Asperger's, mapping his way, stage by painful stage, through each new crisis, as if it was the first ever crisis of that kind, avoiding human contact if he could, running away if he couldn't. It was 'hassle' to him. He couldn't manage hassle, not even to save his bank balance.

He sat smiling, scratching and humming.

'Danny,' I murmured finally, plucking up the courage, 'you've got a problem.'

'Tell me about it!' he laughed.

'No, I mean a real problem…'

'Pshtttttt,' he giggled.

'You have Asperger's Syndrome.'

I'd said it at last.

'Whaaaat?'

I started to explain, bringing all the books and printouts I'd collected and placing them in a heap on the kitchen table. I read to him, aware that he didn't read very well. Like many Aspergers, he tended to see a document in parts, and had to concentrate very hard to edit, summarize or get the gist of anything.

Within no time at all, I heard his 'on' button engaging. It's the only way I can describe it – suddenly Aspergers tune in to what you're saying, internal and external distractions are put to one side, stimming slows. Contact is made. It's totally unlike the concentration you get from anyone else, because this is so unexpected. It's intense, and it's the closest thing I've ever felt to defining the word 'breakthrough'. Have you ever felt that? Music was playing in the background, but all I could hear was the power of his listening alertness to the words I was reading to him.

'Sheeeeeeeeeeeesh,' he murmured. 'It's me!'

'Yes.'

'I've always known I was different, but I didn't know it had a name!'

He was stunned, excited, desperate to know more. Every time I read out something new there'd be a sharp intake of breath or a quick nod or a rueful grin.

'Oooooooh,' he said, when I finally put the books and the papers to one side. 'I can learn more then? I mean, Heather taught me everything I know, but I can learn more! You can teach me! I'll listen to you. You can explain things to me.'

'Wouldn't know where to start!' I grinned.

But we started with Heather.

'Why did she leave you?' I asked gently.

He shrugged, 'Don't know.' It's the Asperger answer. Sometimes it's totally genuine.

They can feel the emotions of a crisis, but only know that it's hurting badly and don't quite know how to engage the ideas or the words to begin to identify and classify. Sometimes it's necessary evasion. They know this is a delicate area, and going into it is very frightening. But he was trying hard, I could tell. For months I'd been doing my radio phone-in, having to listen for the clues to the frightening things people didn't want to say, and I would listen to him, and he knew I wouldn't let it hurt more than it already had.

'She wanted to start a family, and I didn't. I wasn't ready,' he said. It was an explanation he'd given to me before, probably the only one he'd been able to come up with. His failure to understand the 'why' had undermined him for years. He knew it wasn't the right answer.

'But what happened on the day before she left? What made her walk out then?'

'Mmm.' He was thinking hard. He grabbed his curl and began to tug it ferociously. 'We had a flood in the night. In the house. She used to leave me lists of things to do.'

'Yes.' I smiled. He'd told me that. He'd told me that the lists sometimes included the instruction 'Have sex'. He used to forget to do the most natural and intuitive things. Heather, without realizing, had hit on one solution to breaking Asperger self-obsession – make a list for them! They're obedient to instructions on paper.

'She was decorating. She did all the decorating. And on the list she'd said that I had to take the radiators off the wall, so I did. But I mustn't have taken them off properly, and all the water started pouring out in the night. She started yelling, and tried to make me get up and sort it out, but I couldn't.'

'Why?'

'I was tired. I had to sleep,' he huffed, as if it was the most natural thing in the world and that I was an idiot for not understanding. 'I told her that. So she cleaned it up.'

'And she left next morning and never came back?'

'Yes.'

'Can you understand why now?'

'No,' he said tearfully.

It took me ages to explain. Cause. Effect. The Last Straw Effect.

'You see,' I said finally, 'it was your Asperger problem. You decided that sleeping was what mattered, because it was all that mattered to you, just then. It was the most important thing. But she doesn't have your kind of wiring. For her, and for most people, what mattered was what would happen if someone didn't stop the flood.'

He shook his head, perplexed. But I left it with him, knowing that in time he'd think that through. There are no instant results with Aspergers.

'Oooohhhh!' he said, flapping his hands again then clutching his head. 'System overload! System overload!'

I burst into laughter, and hugged him. We'd found a code!

'System overload!' became our 'stop' word from that moment.

I don't know whether you know much about SM? No, nor did I until I had to interview some sado-masochists on a television show. But one of the things that I liked was that they have a stop word for when things get too much. It cuts down the need for explanation and brings an end to whatever's going on at the time.

And 'system overload' was such an appropriate code for those moments when Aspergers just can't take in any more information. My Spock chose it, and I can't think of anything more suitable, so I'm passing it on for you to use, if you have to.

When I say Spock, don't get the wrong idea. I choose the name to describe the prioritizing of logic and fact over emotion and intuition, but I don't want you to think that all Aspergers are humourless and dull. In fact, all Aspergers are different, as all they share is this different wiring system like the Spock stereotype. But they're each unique in personality. Danny was sunshine and laughter, mischief and madness, and I couldn't understand, once we'd shared his secret, how I'd been able to do without him for months.

He was back to stay.

It took us both by surprise, because it happened so subliminally. He started to spend more time visiting while he was waiting to get his driving licence back so that he could go to Germany. I didn't bother to tell him that I thought Germany was a dream, another adventure that would inevitably go wrong. It was obvious, though, that something drastic had to happen to put routine and hope back into his life.

One weekend he amazed me by inviting me down to stay with him. I hadn't been to his town since that last time, my birthday, which we both wanted to forget. This time was special. There was an event in town, a dinner and ball, and he'd chosen me to partner him, an honour indeed.

There were a few surprises in store for me.

I knew that he lived with his father in a cottage that had been renovated, and I'd called once at the front door. I'd never been inside before. What I saw shocked me. It was squalid. I really couldn't see how he could have lived there. The floors were bare, uneven concrete, covered in puddles of dog urine. One bedroom was completely uninhabitable. There was a new extension with a bathroom and kitchen, but none of the work had been completed. Only his bedroom was decorated – by an ex-girlfriend, he told me.

'How can you live in this?' I asked.

He burst into tears. 'I have to!' he said.

Yet he'd earned huge sums of money in ready cash, squandered it, and had never thought to call the workmen back after four years to complete the unfinished job? Aspergers' avoidance and passivity is sometimes difficult to understand. He'd put up with his sordid existence because it was easier than organizing refurbishment.

But perhaps my greatest concern was his total misreading of his social status. He'd referred often to all his friends at home. How wrong! True, he did have a friend – his business partner, a huge man with huge charisma. But in reality he was protector rather than friend, and obviously selected for that job. And the owner of the local hotel where the dinner was held was friendly enough, and protective too. He shared Danny's love of wine.

I saw immediately, though, that if he'd been able to read faces and body language he would have understood that he was held in total derision. What I was reading, all evening, was that he was regarded as the local patsy, like so many Aspergers: too easily parted from his money, too strange in his behaviour for anyone to understand or trust. He and I had been seated in the back corner of the room, well away from the movers and shakers of that small community of which he thought he was a member. Then I was recognized, and we were rescued and space made for us. He hadn't even realized that he had been placed where he would be hidden.

'He's not much liked, is he?' I asked one of the wives.

She sneered. 'He's the town drunk. I don't know what you see in him, someone like you.'

'He's peculiar. He walks away in the middle of conversations and disappears,' her husband added. 'You never know where you are with him. I've been in the bar when he's wandered in wearing just his boxer shorts. He's got no idea how to behave. We put up with him though. He used to be a great rugby player. Fast on the wing.'

My heart went out to him – lovely, sweet, confused Danny, bright as a sunbeam, convinced he was among friends, buying drinks for all these people who despised him. If there were sides to take, I was on the side of the Asperger.

Perhaps I was too much on his side. Perhaps it showed. Perhaps I was drawn to overwhelm with empathy someone who had none. Perhaps his oddness touched and resonated with my unconventionality, my defiance of social convention – even though, unlike him, I knew the unwritten rules I sometimes broke.

Perhaps…

And perhaps if I hadn't been so shocked by the starkly contrasting worlds we lived in, I wouldn't have allowed myself to make one of the worst decisions I've ever made.

It was the following weekend. He was staying with me. We'd been to the wedding of the couple who lived in the flat above mine, then to a gay club on the invitation of the gay taxi driver who drove me to my radio show each week. It was a wild and exciting night out, and all the more wild and exciting for me to see the genuine happiness Danny took in being among people for whom anything goes.

When we returned home we were both fuzzy and giggling. I grabbed food from the fridge and we sat eating with our fingers.

Suddenly, he started to cry. Huge silent tears coursed down his face.

'What is it?' I asked. 'What's wrong?'

He flapped.

'Oh,' he said, as if it was an explanation, 'I cry. Take no notice…'

Inappropriate behaviour, crying when he should have been laughing. Asperger's. It gets to me every time.

'It's just that I remembered you said you had a row with your mother last week, and that's made me angry, and I want to protect you,' he sobbed. 'I want to protect you all the time. I never want you to be away from me.'

Yes, I know this is crazy. Here's a man who can't even look after himself believing that he can be my minder. Just bear with it, and remember this is an Asperger talking. This is his fantasy position. In his mind, he is Superman right now. He's overwhelmed with emotion which he can't identify, so everything is jumbled, but intense, and so heartrending that I guarantee you'd have been crying with him and not knowing why, any more than he did.

'I love you so much,' he said through his tears. 'I've always loved you. Even when I was with Fatima it was you I loved. Only you. I want to be with you for ever. I don't want to be with anyone else for the rest of my life.'

I was stunned. I was touched. I was almost lost for words of my own.

'So what do you want to do?' I stammered.

'I don't want to impose,' he said, and that almost made me laugh with its strange 'good manners' formality in the middle of this heartfelt declaration.

'You want to move in here with me?' I asked.

Stupid question. Very, very stupid. I hadn't lived with anyone but my son for twenty years, and I certainly shouldn't have invited this complex person in. I knew he was more than I could cope with. He wanted a solution, and it should never have been me.

'Yes,' he whispered.

'OK,' I said.

Sixty indications of Asperger's Syndrome

Not all these characteristics will be noticeable in all Aspergers. But all of them were evident in Danny, and all of them are known characteristics of Asperger's Syndrome.

You can use this to mark Asperger characteristics in someone you know, as a fairly rough or general guide. Remember, this is an indication only. It isn't a diagnostic tool.

Characteristic	Very evident	Somewhat evident	Not evident
1. Logical and factual			
2. Immaturity of looks and behaviour			
3. Failure to wait for cues to be 'invited' into conversation			
4. Small neat features, round head, round ears			
5. Difficulty with eye-contact – fleeting glances or hard gaze			
6. Poor dress and colour sense			
7. Direct and blunt language			
8. Inability to read body language or tone of voice			
9. Serial interests or factual obsessions			
10. Rigid and receptive habits – life by 'the rules'			
11. Inappropriate emotional response			
12. Egocentric			
13. Involuntary 'noises'			
14. 'Odd', 'strange', 'eccentric' or 'loner'			
15. Innocence and vulnerability			
16. Tolerance of age or culture gaps			
17. Needs 'space' and can cut off contact, disappear, or sleep for long periods			
18. Can be impulsive and therefore unreliable			
19. Dyspraxia, clumsiness, sometimes very subtle – odd gait, odd stance, gauche hand movements			
20. There can be 'meltdowns' – tantrums caused by frustration			

Characteristic

	Very evident	Somewhat evident	Not evident
21. No 'common sense'			
22. A keen sense of social justice – 'it's not fair!'			
23. Can need guidance and select a 'mentor' figure			
24. Usually someone in the near family who can be described as 'eccentric', 'fixed in their ways' or 'odd'			
25. Tendency to collect and display objects			
26. Often had difficulties at school, may have been bullied			
27. Unusual vocal tone – can be flat or high-pitched; speech can be fast, abnormally mumbled or garbled			
28. Reluctance to confide personal detail except to a chosen trustee			
29. A preference for solo sports and activities, often for endurance sports			
30. 'Stimming' – repeated set of gestures or sounds when under stress			
31. Marked passivity, even with an apparently impetuous and active personal style			
32. Sometimes residual difficulties with pronouns, describing himself as 'he' rather than 'I'			
33. Occasionally apparently 'callous' behaviour caused by a lack of understanding of the social conventions			
34. High tolerance for pain or extreme temperature, very low tolerance in other sensory areas, of some sounds, perhaps			
35. There is often high ability in some area – mathematics, computing, history, for instance			
36. Executive skills can be limited			
37. Sometimes problems with ego boundaries, i.e. where 'I' finish and 'you' begin			
38. Conversation can be 'commentary' rather than discussion			
39. Uninhibited, through inability to understand convention			
40. A high level of anxiety and sometimes allergic disorders like asthma, hayfever, eczema or urticaria at times of stress			
41. Has to consider each decision or action very carefully rather than intuitively			

Characteristic	Very evident	Somewhat evident	Not evident
42. Difficulty in filtering out unimportant information			
43. An ability to 'hyper-focus' on a task or an interest			
44. Childlike and literal sense of humour			
45. Great difficulty in becoming motivated – 'autistic inertia'			
46. Tendency to misinterpret words, or use them literally or differently			
47. Exaggerated fear of confrontation or others' anger			
48. Unrealistic expectations and inadequate forward planning			
49. Uncomfortable with emotional content in conversation			
50. An exaggerated flinching from casual touch			
51. Desire and ability to copy perceived 'correct' behaviour – 'social echolalia' – learning it by rote			
52. Strong response to music			
53. A tendency to be exploited without realizing it			
54. Avoidance of demands			

Scoring
Very evident – 2 points
Somewhat evident – 1 point
Not evident – 0 points

Add scores together.
A high score is over 60 points.
A high score is merely an indication of the possibility of a diagnosis of Asperger's Syndrome.

2 First Steps in a Parallel Universe

Let's leave Danny and me hanging over the precipice of commitment by our fingernails, while I fill in some landscape.

It's time to look at what Asperger's Syndrome actually is.

By one of those amazing patterned coincidences which many Aspergers love, in 1943 two Austrians, unknown to each other, discovered the same childhood disorder at the same time and called it by the same name.

One of those Austrians was Leo Kanner. He'd emigrated from his native country to the US where he established himself as a specialist in child psychiatry at the Johns Hopkins clinic. In 1943 he identified a type of disorder he'd seen in many children who were remote, had language problems, and seemed to have narrow interests and repetitive behaviour. He called it infantile autism, and saw it, correctly, as a disorder of development which affected many areas of their life and changed over time – a pervasive developmental disorder. This label, Pervasive Development Disorder, is still used in the US to describe the group of disorders to which autism belongs.

The other Austrian was Hans Asperger, twelve years younger than Kanner, who lived in Vienna and worked at the University Paediatric Clinic. In 1943, in a doctoral thesis published a year later, he outlined a previously undiagnosed condition in some of the young patients who had been referred to him. He called it autistic psychopathy. The symptoms he referred to were very similar to those Kanner had seen, although Asperger's cases were more sociable, had no delay in speaking, were rather less aloof, and were gifted with normal or higher than average intelligence. He described his autistics as 'little princes', drawing attention to their youthful good looks – handsome strangers?

The choice of the word 'autism' wasn't entirely coincidental. It was already in use in the observation of schizophrenia. It means social isolation. It's the 'boy in a bubble' behaviour of those who can't reach out and relate to others. Autism had been regarded as just a facet of early schizophrenia, childhood detachment. So autistics used to be diagnosed as schizophrenic, and still were until recently, although the other aspects of schizophrenia – delusion, hallucination and auditory hallucination – failed to appear.

Most of the Western world followed the English-speaking Kanner's description of autism. Although Kanner did mention that autism could be seen in children who had high intelligence and learned to socialize, slowly, what we think of as 'autism' is his picture of the silent, aloof child who, at some point in the first three years of life, seems not to develop social awareness and social responses, and can be seriously disabled by this. This type of autism is often now called 'classic' or 'Kanner's' autism.

In 1981 a British psychiatrist, Lorna Wing, in using the term Asperger Syndrome, drew the attention of fellow academics to Asperger's paper on autism, which was subsequently translated into English by Uta Frith. The translation of the paper led to further investigations of autism itself, and the dawning realization that autism was far more wide-ranging and complex than had originally been thought.

The idea developed that autism wasn't just a single specific developmental condition, but a huge spectrum from low-to high-functioning with different and observable levels of capabilities. And, because it's a developmental disorder, it can change in time, so a child who might be disabled by the condition at five may, by the age of fifteen, be more able to adapt and to relate to others.

It could even, if you think of it as a spectrum or a continuum, shade into normal but eccentric at the top end, couldn't it? Think about that. Let it sink in. Consider what implications that has, and how it may redefine our concept of the loner, the oddball, the recluse.

The fact that some autistic children were less incapacitated from the start is indicated by Kanner's term 'high-functioning autism'. But the discovery of Asperger's findings of a more verbal and socially adept group of children led, in the UK, to a diagnostic name being given to those at the top end of the spectrum – Asperger's Syndrome.

Debates still rage about whether high-functioning autism and Asperger's Syndrome are exactly the same and can be interchanged. I'm on the side that says they can.

In Asperger's Syndrome there isn't as severe a problem with language development as in classic autism. Language development in Asperger children is normal. And that makes quite a difference to how someone copes with the world. If you can use speech fairly well, you can, with a real effort of intelligence, which isn't lacking in Aspergers, use it to communicate with others and appear to be functioning normally.

We're getting to the real problem, aren't we? Asperger's Syndrome is so subtle that some experts say it can be even more disabling than classic autism. It can be a truly invisible disability, as it was in Danny's case. There's nothing to see. Aspergers just strike you as a bit odd. But it's so much more than that. That bubble is still there, even though neither the Asperger inside it, nor those who cluster outside, are aware of it.

Now, are you thinking what I'm thinking? Just check those dates. Before 1943, and allowing some leeway for the new diagnosis of 'autism' to gain recognition and then to be used in classifying some patients, what happened to those who were autistic? Before the 1950s were they just diagnosed as schizophrenic? And then think about the dates of Asperger's findings. In the UK they didn't become known until the 1980s, and diagnosis of Asperger's didn't come about until the early 90s. What happened to the most able people on the autistic spectrum? Did they just get on, get by, battling alone with a world they didn't ever feel a part of?

Yes, they did. And the overwhelming majority still do. It's an uphill battle for them and for everyone who loves them, befriends them, works with them, marries them and has their children.

The most chilling statement in the Medical Research Council Review of Autism Research, December 2001, is this one:

> Autism spectrum disorders may affect many more people than has generally been recognized. The prevalence of autism in the adult population is not known... Because autism was first described in the 1940s, little is currently known about the life course and old age in these individuals.

And little is currently known, either, about the life course of undiagnosed Asperger's Syndrome in people over the age of twenty-five. How can it be? Who diagnoses the adult and how? Which adults self-refer for diagnosis? Those middle-class adults who have some inkling of the disorder perhaps. Who has heard of Asperger's Syndrome? You'd have to have heard of it to begin to say, 'That could be me!' or 'That could be my partner!'

Invisible, unrecognized, Asperger's Syndrome adults give every appearance of being merely highly eccentric. There is always though the 'triad of impairments': three serious deficits, churning around just under the surface of the adaptations they make to life and love.

The most obvious is an impairment of social behaviour. Aspergers can and do develop an interest in other people, but they don't quite know how to belong. They don't use the accepted social cues – remember Danny just butting into my conversation, then inviting himself to sit at my table? Rules of social conduct in Aspergers have to be learnt painfully; they aren't instinctive, and don't come naturally as part of childhood observation and unconscious absorption of socially acceptable patterns.

Aspergers' social behaviour can be amusingly or infuriatingly inappropriate, like the husband of a woman I spoke to who had the unhappy habit of rising from the dinner table and, in front of the guests, lying down on the carpet and falling asleep. The dinner guest from hell.

Emotional inappropriateness falls into this category too – Danny crying when he should be laughing, or laughing at my frozen face and my request that he get out of my space. But his own space could be invaded by a gentle touch from which he flinched, involuntarily. Ironic? Yes, and sad.

All the emotions were there in Danny. I had no doubt about it, but this inappropriateness may be because there's no way to properly access them, recognize them as part of everyday communication, and then name them, and share them easily. Or even understand and communicate, to themselves, their own feelings.

Danny's emotional vocabulary was severely limited. He couldn't easily name what he felt. He understood anger. That was his biggest worry. He knew anger in himself and when he saw it in others he was terrified. He could never understand that my harmless anger could flare quickly then dissipate just as quickly. For him, anger itself was like a separate indestructible creature which could devour him whether he produced it or someone else produced it. It had taken him years to deal with his own anger, the total meltdowns I've told you about, the product of frustration and confusion. He knew those two emotions, as well. Frustration and confusion were his old friends although I never heard him name them once.

Tenderness was his greatest gift, although it lay beyond his recognition. It was the unconscious tenderness of a small child. Sometimes I could see it in his eyes, very briefly, when he wasn't exercising the conscious control he felt he needed to impose on all the emotional confusion that lay just under the surface.

Have you ever done marbling? You pour different coloured inks into a bath of oil, then settle a sheet of paper on the surface of the oil while tipping it gently back and forth. The inks are transferred on to the paper in glorious swirls. That's what Danny's emotions were like. Swirls of colour, without separation or definition, but all there with a kind of unfocused integrity of their own. And all nameless, chromatically.

I remember him sitting next to me while I answered the cries for help which came to me on my radio show, a problem phone-in. He sat very still, sucking, usually, on a piece of chewed nail, but his concentration, despite the blankness of his face, was absolute. Sometimes after a difficult call, he would touch my leg with the toe of his shoe to let me know that he had heard the call, heard my response, and that it had meant something. Once he whispered, 'You saved her life.'

Whoever that expert was who said that those on the autistic spectrum can't do compassion ought to be hanged by a rope of his own words. Danny could do it – he just didn't know what it was, what it was called.

The second feature of the triad is an impairment of communication. The most disabling aspect of this in Asperger's Syndrome is probably the failure to read body language, and the weakened ability to convey very much by their own body language either. Danny's gestures were invariably gauche. His fingers always seemed glued together. He pointed with his middle finger, although he pointed rarely, as attracting my attention to something wasn't a priority for him – he never, for example, ever called me by name. He had no idea how this diminished me.

And his face, although usually alive with laughter and giggles, would sometimes fall into total blankness. He didn't know how important it is for other people to take their cues from reading a face. And, of course, he himself refused eye contact until he trusted someone. When called upon to maintain eye contact, it was often a stiff gaze, almost a rude stare. At least, that's what we'd call it. To Danny it was just following the rules and trying to look at people. But he rarely knew what he was looking for.

And with this impairment goes an over-literal use and sense of what words mean. Wendy Lawson, an Asperger who I'll be quoting again, was misdiagnosed as schizophrenic at seventeen because of that. Her consultant psychiatrist asked her if she heard voices. She answered, literally, 'Yes'. She wasn't deaf. He asked her if she saw things. Sight-impaired, she replied that yes she did, although it was a problem.

He diagnosed her as having auditory and visual hallucinations and put her on anti-psychotic drugs for the next twenty-five years.

Many adult Aspergers have taught themselves about puns and irony and can have an endearingly fresh use of language. Although a woman I interviewed said that her Asperger husband 'never understood a word I said and always misinterpreted what I meant,' Danny's very high intelligence level enabled him to use his own literality as childlike but knowing humour.

This derived from his two-layered attitude to words. His basic inbuilt layer was totally literal. His self-taught and self-conscious layer was the way other people use words. Those two layers could interplay fascinatingly.

We were once talking about his father's ambition for him to go into the armed forces, as he'd done.

'But I wouldn't go in except as a General,' he assured me in his usual bombastic way.

'Not many job openings for Generals,' I replied.

Later that day, he was reading the paper, and, after thinking for a while, looked up at me with a cheeky grin.

'You lied to me,' he said.

'How?'

'You said there weren't any job openings for Generals. But it says here, in the job section, "General Vacancies!"' He laughed, and then, as he so often did, mouthed the words immediately to himself silently, repeating a joke of which he was very proud.

His language, delivered in his strangely high-pitched singsong tone, was also littered with echolalia – exact mimicry. Usually this was devoid of meaning. He would suddenly say something in another accent, using a form of words he'd heard on television. He would quote from nursery rhymes, or Doctor Seuss. I never knew why the phrase 'Green eggs and ham said Sam-I-am' meant so much to him that he said it at least once a week. The word 'egg' in any context would spark off that response in him.

Sometimes he would repeat my own words back at me. He could speak fluent French, except that it had no vocabulary or grammar. It was just a perfect linking together of nonsense in an impeccable French accent, often incorporating 'chamois leather', or 'shameez lezzerrrrr'. When he spoke to his Turkish girlfriend on the phone he used exactly the same broken English and the same soft tone she did. He had no idea how incongruous this sounded.

And the number of times I wanted to beg him to talk 'to' me not 'at' me was incalculable. Sometimes I'd just have to say, 'I'm here,' to remind him that conversation is not a monologue.

The third of the impairments is imagination. Aspergers, in common with all those on the autistic spectrum, have little imagination as children. Don't think of this in the conventional sense of storytelling though. It refers mostly to their inability to understand the existence of their own and others' mind-states. This is a very subtle issue. Every Asperger I've spoken to has a fertile fantasy life. Danny was always off, in his head, chasing baddies and putting the world to rights single-handedly. The problem seems to be in separating what is fantasy and 'let's pretend' from real life. Danny continually offered me rash promises which would have been better prefaced by the words, 'Wouldn't it be good if…'

Aspergers usually prefer fact to fiction. Danny's professorship in dinosaur taxonomy at the age of six made him prioritize this over the wishy-washy imaginative world of the spirit. He walked out of Sunday School when he discovered that there were no dinosaurs in the Bible. This proved to him that Biblical evidence 'wasn't true'. He's spurned Christianity since.

This impaired imagination gives them their fixations on facts and lists; rigid routines; strange, intensely focused interests; and repeated stimming; and also could be responsible for their focus on part of the object rather than the whole thing. I used to watch Danny's eyes as he tried to read a letter. His gaze would fall on one part, dart to another, then another. He seemed unable to read in a progressive linear way if he was anxious, and could never give me the gist of what he'd read.

Another problem, not prioritized in some of the diagnostic criteria, is clumsiness. Danny's odd stance comes under that heading. This isn't evident in classic autism where motor control is often quite exceptional, but Aspergers often have poor motor control, catch poorly, walk with an odd gait, and break things. In Danny's case that was usually the glass he was drinking from, but his clumsiness was rarely obvious. He drove a car well – his father had been a test driver – and he played rugby at county and schoolboy international level. But his ball-skills were always suspect.

So that's the overview of Asperger's Syndrome. Simon Baron-Cohen, the Cambridge-based autism expert, explains it perfectly when he says that there's little 'folk psychology' in the Asperger make-up, but there's a compensatory excess of the other non-emotional, non-empathetic, non-social side of the brain which he calls 'folk physics'. Asperger's is often called the 'engineers' disorder' as so many engineers, including computer engineers, seem to suffer from it. The ability to focus on parts rather than the whole, to persevere with a theory or task beyond normal limits, to work out how to take things apart and put them together, to understand and read circuits and patterns, is an invaluable part of scientific discovery.

But what on earth could cause these apparently random symptoms, or the clusters of other strange abnormalities, like heightened or depressed sensory alertness? Why should Danny be unresponsive to cold or pain, but would moan loudly in pleasure at the hairdresser when being shampooed? He was an embarrassment at every salon he ever went to. Why would he sometimes jump out of his skin at a sudden unexpected soft noise? Why was his palate fine enough to list all the ingredients in something he was eating or drinking? Sensory sensitivity, too much (hyper), or too little (hypo), can also be part of the Asperger bag of tricks as can something very strange called synaesthesia.

We've probably all had a momentary flash of that – it's sensory confusion. You hear a sound and think of it as a colour – have you done that? Even when you haven't partied for too long? Some Aspergers experience that often.

The *cause* of Asperger's is as yet unknown.

One thing is certain: there's a strong genetic factor. How do we know? Because many of the studies done on Asperger children reveal that there are other Aspergers, autistics, or 'Asperger traits' within the extended family in most cases. However, it's also likely that this isn't a problem with a single gene but that there may be several involved, and research is very close to identifying which ones they may be.

And here we come to a 'yes, but…'. Identifying the genes may be helpful but won't produce the whole answer, because the genetic factor may just make someone susceptible to developing Asperger's, or some other autistic spectrum disorder, but won't be the full story. Some 'trigger' could also come into play.

What that is seems to be preoccupying research scientists. Some thought in the past that it may be connected with what happens before or around the birth time. But that theory has now been tested and found to be suspect. The conditions surrounding pregnancy and birth may not be particularly relevant in autism. Scientists now believe that any pre- or perinatal problems, apart from viral infection like rubella in pregnancy, or genuine brain damage because of seriously traumatic birth, are probably caused by whatever caused the autistic spectrum disorder in the first place.

Other risk factors being assessed include the effect on pregnant women or their children of drugs (not likely), hormonal activity (which would explain why more boys than girls seem to be at risk of Asperger's) and carbon-monoxide poisoning of the mother (very unlikely).

Another is the presence of dormant viruses, particularly the measles virus, because there are very rare cases where this virus has persisted in a child's body for many years and finally erupted as a form of encephalitis, a brain inflammation which causes serious damage. This dormant virus theory, too, seems unlikely according to current research thinking.

The big headline story in the autism world is of course that there may be a connection between autism and the MMR (mumps, measles and rubella) vaccine. Gastro-enterologist Andrew Wakefield has identified the measles virus in the gut of twelve children with autistic spectrum disorders who were referred to a gastro-intestinal department of the Royal Free Hospital in London, and has coined the name 'autistic colitis' for this gut disorder and suggested that it may be caused by the MMR vaccine. In every subsequent test not only have these findings not been replicated, but no temporal link has been found between administration of the vaccine and a form of colitis thought to be associated with autism, including one study involving three million vaccinated children. Some experts, though, would like more research into the possibility of a connection. The link between Crohn's disease and autism – could the measles virus provide a clue to this? Many parents of autistic children, who insist that their child was developing normally until vaccination, would like some reliable research to be undertaken, by independent scientists, which would investigate Wakefield's tentative and so far unproven findings.

Much of the MMR concerns are anecdotal, conveyed by anxious parents, and their worries, in turn, have been whipped up into a frenzy by the media, and by internet websites, often dominated by the theories of alternative practitioners and cranks, especially from the US sites, keen to cash in on the frenzy. Without further research, anxieties will not be calmed, and the www charlatans will reap the profits of panic.

Another scare story about the cause of autism seemed to point a finger at mercury poisoning being the culprit. This lies in the realm of sensationalism. The only metal which is present in the blood of autistic children in amounts larger than average, according to current research, is lead, and the reason for this has yet to be ascertained. The UK MMR vaccine has never contained mercury, although it is present in the US MMR vaccine and in the UK vaccine for diphtheria, tetanus and whooping cough. Again, websites and message-boards carry confusing and confused messages for the parents of children on the autistic spectrum. The lunatic fringe, and some of it is very lunatic indeed, is alive and well and living on the World Wide Web, offering both attractive anti-establishment conspiracy theories and a panacea, at a price.

Work is still continuing on the theory that autistic spectrum disorders, like Asperger's Syndrome, could be triggered biologically. Batten's disease, another neurological condition like autism, can be diagnosed from a rectal biopsy, revealing its own connection with digestive processes. There are many other major research projects looking at a link between unusual gut flora and autism, one at candida (thrush) and autistic spectrum disorders and another, very hopeful, one relating to reduced phenol sulphation in those with autism. This theory is biologically plausible, but not yet proven.

A British research scientist, Paul Shattock, has always believed that autism could have a metabolic basis. He continues to test the theory that some foods aren't broken down properly in the gut and pass into the bloodstream and brain producing a morphine-like effect which may contribute development of autistic spectrum disorders. He believes that gluten and casein intolerance, or other factors, can lead to 'leaky gut', causing the bowel to release improperly digested peptides which act like opiates on the central nervous system, disrupting its functions. This could be a possibility.

And in that area, there certainly is a big story. It's the autism equivalent of Lorenzo's Oil. Prepare to suspend all disbelief as this story is true and quite amazing.

It's about a US couple, Gary and Victoria Beck, from New Hampshire whose son, Parker, was showing all the classic symptoms of autism. At three his language skills disappeared, he became aloof, didn't relate to them, had screaming fits, sleep disturbances and he developed serious diarrhoea which continued for two years. His parents were at their wits' end. Then one day they took him to have his pancreatic function assessed at the university hospital, where a doctor performed an endoscopy.

Three days later Parker slept through the night for the first time for two years. His behaviour settled. His diarrhoea stopped. A week after that Victoria was called to look at him as he happily read aloud some flash-cards with his home tutor although he'd been virtually mute since the autism symptoms began. He said words he'd never said in his life.

Neither she nor Gary could understand what had happened. The child was miraculously returning to normal. They worked out that this must have something to do with the endoscopy procedure he'd had. They phoned the hospital and demanded to know exactly what had been given to the child in the endoscopy.

Secretin.

It's a hormone derived from pigs and used to produce a bicarbonate release in the pancreas. They eventually managed to persuade the hospital to give Parker another secretin infusion and, yet again, his progress was astonishing.

When the hospital refused to co-operate further, saying that secretin wasn't licensed for this purpose, Parker stopped improving but didn't regress. Finally the Becks found another doctor who agreed to give regular infusions, and the rest is rainbows! One totally normal son. And other parents who managed to obtain infusions then reported similar results in their own children.

Unbelievable, isn't it? Well, yes, according to many researchers in the field of autistic spectrum disorders. In the UK, there is the typical British scepticism about anything not backed up by academic research and peer review. Is it just a Hollywood storyline? Could be. But it does have that essential feel-good factor which we all love.

I'll come back to this story later, but now let's look at brain function and autism. It's a neurological disorder, so research into where exactly brain defects can be seen is very important.

There have been several investigations into the brains of those with autistic spectrum disorders. One has mentioned that head circumference is larger in autistics, which is for me a very interesting finding. After I first met Danny I made some notes about him. These included 'abnormally round large skull, with very round ears'.

No, I don't make notes about everyone I meet, and these notes weren't detailed, only about six or seven quick reminders of the most fascinating eccentric I'd ever met, but that skull stuck in my memory. As did his round ears. So when I read that Temple Grandin, a woman who is herself a high-functioning autistic, and who's written several books about her experiences as an Asperger, wrote 'all autistics have round ears' I was quite spooked. I even searched through all my scraps of paper to find the original note.

Larger skulls, however, even when they include additional brain weight as autistics' skulls so often do, don't necessarily imply any brain disorder, do they?

The only defects found in the Asperger brain that statistically stand up to scrutiny are that there is often some developmental abnormality seen in the inferior olive, which is part of the brain stem, and there's a reduced number of Purkinje cells.

Purkinje cells? There's an entire website devoted to a fan club for these brain cells, because they look so beautiful – strange how people develop these odd fascinations. It makes me wonder whether there are Aspergers working in all branches of science. Basically Purkinje cells are brain neurons which limit overload and help control coherence. A reduction in them would be perhaps inevitable in a condition where overload is a constant feature.

Other facts about brain involvement in autism are that PET (positron emission tomography) and MRI (magnetic resonance imaging) scans show that there is low activity in the part of the brain which is thought to control complex planning, and some abnormality in the limbic system, which processes emotional and social information. Much as expected really.

Less expected, perhaps, is that there seems to be a connection between autism and epilepsy, with a third of those with autistic spectrum disorders eventually developing epilepsy. It's curious. One night I watched Danny having an epileptic seizure in his sleep. I thought that was because of what he happily called 'boozin'', his binge alcoholism. Maybe not.

But we still haven't arrived at a conclusion as to what 'causes' Asperger's Syndrome, have we? And in the light of the fact that scientists haven't been any more successful at deciding what exactly is the starting point for those strange behaviours we identify as autistic spectrum disorders, we should not be embarrassed by our failure. Autism research is still in its infancy.

Something that might help, although it won't explain causes, is psychological theory. What it will do, I guarantee, is to help you understand how to put all these symptoms together into a neat package. It might help you, as it's helped me, and Danny, and others, to work out how to see, and therefore, maybe, how to burst that bubble.

The most helpful tool, I think, in understanding autistic spectrum disorders (ASDs) is Theory of Mind.

You see, ASDs are difficult to understand because we're always working back from an observed set of behaviours to possible causes, unlike most illnesses or disorders where we know the cause and are simply looking for cures for the symptoms or behaviours stemming from it.

So, to understand Asperger's, we look at behaviour, and we think of the brain. The link between brain and behaviour is mind.

We all have mind. But Aspergers and others on the spectrum don't realize that we do, at least not as early as other children.

Mind is a set of beliefs and desires and knowledge that is individual to each of us but it is something we know we have. By the age of about four, most of us can play let's pretend. We know that if we pretend something, create a belief about something, we can keep that separate from the real world around us. We have developed mind.

We can 'make believe' that a mud pie, as we make it, is something nice to eat, and shape it like a cake, but we have enough sense to only 'pretend' to eat it. You can pretend something that isn't a physical reality (your cake isn't edible although you pretend it is), and you can believe something that isn't true. And that understanding is what helps us to realize that other people may have different beliefs from us. Sometimes it means that we may know the truth but someone else doesn't, and we actually *know* that the two mind-sets, beliefs and understandings are different. It's a huge milestone in child development.

To discover whether a child has developed an understanding of mind and mind-states, a test, the Sally Anne test, is used. The following story, illustrated or animated, is shown and narrated to children. Can you answer the tester's question?

There are two dolls, Sally and Anne. Sally has a basket. Anne has a box. Sally puts a marble in her basket, then leaves the room. Anne then reaches into Sally's basket, takes the marble, and puts it into her own box. Sally comes back into the room.

Where will she look for her marble? That's what the tester asks.

The answer is, of course, in her basket, because that's where she left it, so that's what she 'thinks'. This answer is given by children over four, and by Down's syndrome children of eleven with a mental age of three. But no

Asperger child with a chronological age of less than eleven, despite a mental age at least equivalent to that, gives the right answer.

The answer Aspergers give is, 'She'll look in Anne's box.'

Why? Because that's what they saw. They know it's there. They can't understand that Sally didn't see what happened and won't have a clue about the theft. And they can't understand the notion of other mind-states, what someone else might think or believe.

And if you ask one of the very few older Aspergers who eventually get the question right, 'What does Anne think that Sally thinks?' ('second order Theory of Mind') they're completely lost. Flummoxed. Even Asperger adults capable of doing complex calculations in their heads can't work that one out, although they could perhaps write you a computer program that would save the universe from nuclear winter.

I've spoken to two exceptionally intelligent Aspergers, both with IQs in the genius range, both with additional 'savant' (abnormally gifted) skills. Both of them failed the Sally Anne test in their twenties. And neither of them, despite their intellectual brilliance, several years on, can tell me what Anne thinks that Sally thinks, a question I, and most of you, would have been able to answer at five years old.

One of them told me, 'Listen, I was 18 before I knew other people were *real.* It blew my mind.'

How scary is that?

This means that Aspergers find it really difficult to imagine that someone else has a personal, unique set of beliefs, desires and knowledge – that someone else has the reality of an individual mind, or even that they themselves do. They just don't see the differentiation which each of our minds gives us. The connection between brain and behaviour is not within their understanding.

Can you see what problems that causes? It's a question to ponder. Be careful. Thinking about this will make your brain hurt. A lot.

Just think of this as an example. Danny, at thirty-four, told me very seriously, as a way of congratulating himself for being clever, 'I've really tried hard with my Christmas present-buying this year. You know what I did? I thought about what each person might actually want, and then bought it!'

Phew. Bear in mind that this was the man I saw doing an internet high-intelligence test and scoring 142 IQ, as I'd expected. He did the number patterns faster than I've ever seen them done. In fact he raced through the entire test, at times a little carelessly, as he realized afterwards when, typically, he argued that the test was wrong and he was right.

Yet here he was, grown up, affectionate, sensitive and caring, apparently, and unable until that moment to get to grips with the notion of what present-buying is all about, something that most children get their heads round at about seven.

If you think of Asperger's Syndrome as being a set of symptoms arising from a lack or a delay of 'Theory of Mind' it really will help you work out why we say that Aspergers are 'differently wired'.

Another helpful theory is the CC (Central Coherence) theory. Central coherence is the way we non-Aspergers put information together to form meaning. We can take what we need from the information around us and choose what's important and what isn't. We can edit, and generally process, getting out of our life the things that make most sense, and putting everything else on the back burner.

Aspergers have weak central coherence. All the bits of things that are happening all the time come at them in the same form, at the same speed, the same level of importance. Birdsong, a television blaring, drinking a glass of wine, someone on the phone, all that goes on as it does in all our lives simultaneously at times. We tune out what's not important, like the birdsong maybe, we turn the television down, we sip the wine but don't savour it while we listen to what the person on the phone is saying. If the person on the phone is trying to sell us something, we might turn the television louder to drown out the droning predictable salesmanship on the phone. We take meaning from layers and we always know which layer to concentrate on.

Aspergers see the detail rather than the picture, and this detail can confuse, because where's the sense in it? If the layers are equal in importance and meaning, as they often are to Aspergers, how on earth do they manage to take it all in? They don't. They cut it all out, finally. They blow a fuse. They have to, as all of us would if we couldn't get that birdsong out of the television sound and the sales pitch.

They have wonderful rote memory, but what use is that in a practical application which demands that you select for meaning?

Let me illustrate this. Before I took my English Literature exam at 15, my mother, who was very impressed by my memory for words, made me learn by heart two of the set texts – the poetry of Keats and Shakespeare's *Merchant of Venice*. Even she realized that it was probably beyond me to learn *The History of Mr Polly* by H.G. Wells.

So there I sat in the exam, with my head full of poetry, and whenever I wanted to put a quote in my essay, I had to start from the beginning and work through the poem or play to find it. Can you imagine having to find a line in Portia's mercy speech by going back every time to 'What news on the Rialto?'

I was exhausted, and what I'd done was totally irrelevant to the process of essay writing. I didn't even finish the exam. I think my mother had weak central coherence and wanted to pass it on to someone who might be able to do something with it.

Consider this too. Central coherence is vital to all forms of relating, whether it's personal or professional. If you've ever had a conversation with one of those people who starts, 'It was a Tuesday, no, I'm telling a lie, it must have been a Thursday, because that's the day the post arrives at 7.15 not 7.30, as Mrs Green at the craft shop closes on a Thursday, and the postman's always exactly quarter of an hour early because he doesn't have to deliver her post until the next day, well, anyway, where was I?', you've either met an Asperger, or my mother.

Or perhaps if you've tried to ease a difficult situation with someone who keeps saying, 'I don't know'…

'Is anything the matter?'

'I don't know.'

'You're very quiet. Have I said something to upset you?'

'I don't know.'

'Was it something that happened at work?'

'I don't know.'

…then you were probably trying to talk to Danny or another Asperger.

Danny, at those times, was trying to sift through information about his emotions, identify them by name and discover the reason for them. He genuinely didn't know. He was searching for meaning, a process he had to do consciously and work at it. Instant response at times of tiredness isn't something that someone with weak central coherence can do. Remember 'system overload'? That's what you get without Theory of Mind and Central Coherence. You just can't do multi-tasking without a method of prioritizing, editing, selecting, and understanding what's important to you, the task, and others.

Hubert Cross, a forty-seven-year-old US Asperger, discovered both theories, Central Coherence and Theory of Mind. There is a joyous Road to Damascus feeling about the immense difference this made to his life, as he writes on his website (www.rogernmeyer.com/Hubert_Cross/Asperger's_ Syndrome_and_Making_Sense_July_2002.htm):

Asperger's Syndrome and Making Sense

Can you imagine what it is like to *spend a lifetime of confusion, not understanding anything about anything that has to do with people, and being unaware of your predicament?*

I spent forty-five years of my life not understanding anything about anything that had to do with humans. It was not until I read about autism and 'mindblindness', in particular, about three years ago, that I began to *make some sense* of the world.

The world of humans constantly presents you with small little puzzles. A normal person constantly takes these pieces and puts them together. When the normal person reaches old age, he has thousands or even millions of solved little puzzles. I am finding now that all I have is millions of disconnected puzzle pieces that I never put together to *make sense* of anything...

The idea behind all this is that the human brain can *consciously* do only one thing at the time, but unconsciously it can do, and does in the case of a normal person, a surprisingly large number of things at the same time. When the brain modules or mechanisms that are in charge of unconsciously doing all those things does not function, it is not possible to compensate doing them all consciously *at the same time*. (One at a time, it can be done and I have done it.) From this is that I get an idea about the very large amounts of modules and mechanisms that must be compromised in Asperger's Syndrome.

Hubert hits the nail on the head. Aspergers can function by learning and then by consciously working things out. What they don't have is the secret language of instinctive understanding that no one ever teaches us but which we pick up by watching and interpreting at an unconscious level.

Who teaches us what a raised eyebrow means, for instance? Two raised eyebrows? Can you ever remember having to go through a conscious process to learn to pick up and identify nuances of emotion expressed by tiny facial gestures? Who taught you to know the difference between love, liking, sexual attraction, and caritas? Who taught you selection procedures?

'I love you,' Danny said.

'And what does that mean for you?' I asked.

He thought for a long time.

'I feel safe,' he said.

It was the best he could do in his world of confusion. The very best.

One final theory worth considering is the theory of weak Executive Function. I've left this to last, because this is a very subtle problem for the Aspergers I know.

Executive function, thought to be very poor in those on the autistic spectrum, concerns the activities of planning, modifying plans according to feedback, shifting between different kinds of behaviour, and rejecting behaviours that just don't work in sorting out what the next stage in your plan might be. Many Aspergers do struggle with keeping their business, both personal and professional, in order. They also have great difficulty in shifting their attention from one task to another, and in altering their behaviour.

However, some features of executive function enable intelligent Aspergers to modify their behaviour patterns, although not instinctively.

They do it by purely strategic and conscious effort. It's slow. It demands almost superhuman efforts of concentration, but it's possible.

They see eventually where their behaviour isn't working, and they try something else, even though this means that they may have to try to be adaptable, which is extremely hard for them. They're as flexible as they could possibly be in the purely dogged working out of what's the best way to operate, and this is where the normal or higher than normal intellectual ability comes into play. When Aspergers question themselves about why something didn't work they do seem capable (by painstakingly modelling their behaviour on those they see as successful) of turning things around. Although some issues, like cause and effect, and attention-shifting, remain very difficult.

This is where Asperger imitations come in. I've mentioned echolalia before. It's the talent of mimicry, saying what someone else says, exactly, although perhaps without any communicative intention.

Aspergers who succeed in modifying their traits often do this by social echolalia, imitating what they see as the best (most rewarding) way of reacting to other people. They understand. They can plot paths which involve adaptation. It's like a game of chess, which many Aspergers play very well. Danny told me, 'I can always work out what the next move is,' when referring to a business deal.

He could sometimes. Most of the time even. But if the move was emotional, irrational, it threw him, and he'd have to rethink. He could be wildly impulsive, following the immediacy of what he felt and making a rash move, but he couldn't work out that other people, too, might do that, and it would confuse him.

Is there any way out of the Asperger confusion? Is there any cure for the condition?

No.

Simple as that.

Neurological conditions are imprinted on the system. They just won't go away with a pill or an injection.

But let's not forget what Asperger's is. It's a developmental disorder, and that means that it changes with time and over time. If there are cases, and there are, as I've said, of the same child being diagnosed autistic at five, and Asperger at fifteen, there are conclusions to be drawn. The most obvious is that although the child has an autistic spectrum disorder which won't disappear, he or she can adapt so well with the help of mentors that they may function successfully and happily. Many of the children being diagnosed at present, because they'll have the advantage of special educational strategies put into place over the last five or ten years, will be better socially adjusted when they become adults. The future looks a lot brighter.

And now, let's go back to the secretin story. It has all the ingredients of a great drama, but it also has the ingredients of an interesting medical intervention.

Before we start on the possible aids to autism by the use of secretin, it's worth looking at the disputes behind the scenes of this narrative. Remember we left the Beck family rejoicing in the behavioural development of their son, Parker? Remember that he was refused further infusions by the doctor who had initially administered the secretin? The plot thickens.

Unknown to the Beck family, the university doctor, harassed by the family, who saw this as a treatment for autism and wanted him to investigate further, secretly took out a patent on the secretin treatment. At the same time, according to the family, he was refusing to administer any more infusions as, quite correctly, he said that the hormone was not sanctioned for such an intervention.

So perhaps it was slightly hypocritical of him to apply to have this recognized as a treatment, and under his name? The story became a cause célèbre. Eventually the rights in the patent devolved to Victoria Beck rather than the doctor, but then there was another crisis. The company which had originally produced secretin, Ferring, by grinding up imported pig intestines to extract the hormone, was overwhelmed by demand.

The secretin 'magic wand' story had taken the US and the rest of the world by storm. Quacks started appearing in the get-rich structure of the Internet, promising secretin injections for thousands of pounds, some supplying sugar water.

Ferring was working at the edge of its capacity, and there had to be another source of secretin. This was provided by a tiny company, Repligen, which began, with the blessing and patents of Victoria Beck, to produce a synthetic version of secretin.

Why did Victoria Beck allow this small company to have rights over her own discovery of the hormone? Because the founders of the company, Nancy LeGendre and her husband Walter C. Herlihy, had used secretin on their own daughter, a seven-year-old autistic, Lillian. It had changed her life, they said.

And what is fascinating about the results of the tests which followed is that the head of the Autism Research Institute in the US, Bernard Rimland, used secretin on his own forty-three-year-old autistic son. The result? His son, after one infusion, became suddenly less tuned-out, more aware of what was going on around him, responsive to his mother and her welfare. He had never been so socially aware. Rimland is a supporter of the secretin cause.

The trials continue on secretin.

The case is as yet unproven.

But let's think of the implications. If secretin, a hormone involved in the digestive process, is providing improvements, even in adults with Asperger's Syndrome, could it possibly be that the digestive system is a key to helping those on the autistic spectrum?

And, if that's so, could Paul Shattock, who has always been at the forefront of the debate on whether ASDs connect with gut dysfunction, have a response to the call for more research into the 'leaky gut' hypothesis?

He has. It's dietary intervention. According to Shattock and his team at the University of Sunderland, the key to lessening the symptoms of ASDs is to eliminate casein and gluten from the diets of people on the spectrum. Casein is found in dairy products. Gluten is found in grain products, most specifically wheat. With the help of this dietary intervention and other adjustments, Donna Williams, author of *Nobody Nowhere*, reclaimed her life from autism.

Shattock's message, contained in a paper called 'The Sunderland Protocol', struck a chord with me.

'The Sunderland Protocol' suggests cutting out all dairy and grain from the diets of anyone on the spectrum, as a first step to improvement of symptoms. It calls this a 'Ceasefire', the first stage in damping down 'the bullets of the warfare of autism'.

Why did the paper have such a powerful effect on me? It's that it corresponded exactly to my own experience with Danny.

I have mild lactose intolerance. Although there have been times when I've craved a milkshake, I've always been very ill afterwards. Give me a Stilton sauce, and I'll show you the plumbing in my bathroom. I've had Irritable Bowel Syndrome all my life; at any rate, since I took the Advanced Neurotics course in what not to eat. Bread and milk and cheese are all off limits for me. I eat them only when I sense that I can, and that's very rarely. Sandwiches make me bloat. Since I limited them, severely, I've had fewer problems.

So since the time when Danny started visiting, I've been eating and drinking only what I can tolerate easily. Basically it's a Mediterranean diet without the croissants or baguettes, and Danny, being Danny, and anxious to model himself on me, said that this was exactly his choice of food, too – lots of vegetables and fruit (although I avoid apples and some citrus fruits), lots of fish, chicken, some lamb, masses of olive oil, garlic, herbs, new potatoes, and some eggs, black Earl Grey tea, black coffee.

Every time he came to visit he said, 'This is what I eat too!'

Oh yes?

Danny was actually a secret hamster. While eating and enjoying the food I prepared, and, for the first time in his adult life, losing some of the patches of eczema that plagued him, when left to his own devices he would stock up on the junk he craved.

He'd return from the supermarket with hunks of cheese, squashy bags of double chocolate chip muffins and cartons of clotted cream. He'd buy and consume pints of milk while driving.

He insisted, in time, on returning to his happy burger habit at the end of a drunken binge night. Although I'd bought him chicken for his middle-of-the-night fridge raids, he'd cover it in mayonnaise. And when we returned from my radio show he'd shout for what he always called, lispingly, 'chippy chippy chip chips', which he'd collect from the chip shop and bring home hungrily to slather in mayonnaise too.

When he cooked for me he'd make floury sauces and gravy and hated it when I snobbishly referred to it as canteen food. It's too heavy for my taste.

As his old habits returned, so did his eczema and so did his old behaviour. It could have been an inevitable consequence of settling down and trying less hard, but I wonder, now, if the food played any part in that?

It's worth considering.

Paul Shattock says that the effect of removing dairy products produces very fast results: improvements in behaviour can be seen within two or three days for children, and within a fortnight in adults. With the removal of wheat, barley, rye and oats the effects take longer to kick in, perhaps as much as a year. On his programme he expects that all adults will see their autistic symptoms easing significantly over a period of two years.

He then suggests testing for allergies to other foods – eggs, tomatoes, avocados, aubergines, red peppers, soya and corn in particular – perhaps by following a supervised elimination process.

At the same time, checks should be made on candida (yeast) infections, and sugar may be limited, or an anti-fungal prescribed. Oil of Evening Primrose is a recommendation as a supplement on the Protocol.

And there's another strange thing recommended – baths in Epsom salts. I don't know if you've ever tried an Epsom salts bath, but it is truly delicious, producing a soothing velvety water. I love it. The reason for this recommendation is that sulphates in the body may be limited in autistics and Epsom salts (magnesium sulphate) can be absorbed through the skin to rebalance the deficiency. Danny always took showers, but I'm sure he wouldn't have objected to being rubbed down with a handful of Epsom salts while showering.

So there's the Protocol, in pared-down form, and of all the suggested interventions for Asperger's, I'd certainly consider trying it. What appeals to me is that it's practical and simple, although I can imagine that for many adult Aspergers it would be difficult to give up their ritualistic eating routines – like the Asperger husband who eats only corn chips and dips – for the sake of something that may not give immediate results. On the other hand, it's better than self-medicating with alcohol, which was Danny's way through his depression.

Depression is the most serious side-effect of living on the autistic spectrum. It's what's known as a co-morbidity, existing alongside Asperger's, and shares its place with epilepsy as being the most common co-diagnosis of adults with the syndrome.

It's not difficult to work out why.

The knowledge that you're different is as much a curse as it is a blessing, and if that difference can't be communicated easily, can't be appreciated by your peers, can't be easily helped, can't be escaped from except in sleep, and at times seems to serve no useful purpose, then sometimes there will be a gaping black pit into which you sink.

Danny's depression was a back-beat to his Hymn to Joy. He told me once that on holiday a Greek girl had plundered her limited vocabulary to describe him and said, 'I have found the word for you. You are the fun.' He was. And that's what made his periods of dark despair all the more frightening. He would curl in a foetal position, unable to move, racked with silent pain.

The statistics for suicide in adult Aspergers are amazingly high – 6 per cent.

Part of this may be due to the lives they've had to live, undiagnosed, bullied, misunderstood. Many have been exploited – they're emotional children in a very sadistic adult world. Few have been able to find a suitable outlet for their idiosyncratic talents. Most are employed at far below their capabilities. Some fail to complete their education.

And when crises occur they are ill-equipped, emotionally, to deal with them.

Danny had a major crisis, a breakdown, when Heather left him. He told me he cried for a month. Every day for a month. Every night for a month. His mother took him to the doctor who prescribed him tranquillizers which he threw away. He had a brief meeting with a counsellor, but walked out after five minutes. He never could talk to strangers.

'I went to the cliffs and decided I'd jump off,' he told me, 'but I didn't even have the courage to do that.'

It was his childlike sweetness which saved him. Two of Heather's girl-friends, seeing that he couldn't hold himself together, took him home with them, and made him sleep between them for a month, like a sick baby.

They fed him and let him sleep, and in time he recovered, driving himself to work again, playing the same song over and over again when he returned home. He would put his stereo on repeat, another feature of Asperger repetitive behaviours, and listen to 'Under the Bridge' by the Red Hot Chili Peppers.

'It's my song,' he always told me, but it was so inappropriate that I wondered how he, a country boy in the UK, could relate to a song about Los Angeles. I think it was the line 'I don't ever want to feel like I did that day' that made such a deep impression on him.

During the time I spent with Danny, part of the job I did for him was helping him to make sense of the cruel world, and ease his underlying depression. In a way, that's my profession, taking random emotional experiences and turning them into words to identify and share and understand.

It's what a writer does.

For Danny I became the membrane between the pictures in the right brain and the words he could interpret them with in the left, his personal corpus callosum. On the left, there was the logical, composed 'folk physics' of his world, but on the right the kaleidoscopic pictures were blurred and there seemed few natural connections between the two, or little reason to make the connections.

But that's why he needed me.

A short time after he'd moved in with me, I found that my favourite paring knife had gone missing. I eventually found it, hidden under some papers by the side of his bed.

'What're you doing with this?' I asked.

'It's for my cyst,' he said sheepishly.

He had a cyst at the base of his spine which came up painfully at times, and sometimes drained.

'I cut it,' he said. 'Sometimes I cut it.'

'Sometimes?'

'Every day.'

For once I didn't say anything. He'd heard enough of my radio calls to know what the problem was, and, after a pause, he showed the first real sign of brutal self-awareness he'd ever displayed.

'It's self-harm, isn't it?' he asked.

He finally knew about his urge to self-destruct.

Depression as a co-feature of adult Asperger's is well documented, and various treatments are suggested to deal with it so that it doesn't become a psychosis in its own right. There's also been a suggestion that anorexia nervosa could be an expression of autistic behaviour in women, a little-researched topic, but one which relates to the tendency to destructive behaviour and depression in those who are aware of their difference.

But I don't really think that it's helpful to concentrate on these difficulties because awareness of Asperger's Syndrome in the general public is what's needed for all of us to accept and work with what is, and can be shown to be, just a different and fascinating way of thinking and operating. The way forward has to be in understanding.

If we ask most Aspergers if they'd relinquish their unique view of the world, and would want to exchange AS (Asperger's Syndrome) for the NT (Neuro-Typical) mode of behaviour, most would refuse. Here's what one of them says:

I am twenty-seven years old and have been successful in a career other than computers (though I am a good coder and used to be in computers). I make my living buying and selling companies. How can someone with AS do this, with all the social interactions? Simple – my gifts are twofold. First, I am very good at seeing patterns in seemingly random data. For me, that translates into seeing the patterns of successful companies across industries. I can then generalize these patterns across other industries, and make acquisition decisions. This is all done via visualization; I can 'see' dynamical systems and the variables that drive success (or failure). I am also an exceptional negotiator. How? As someone with AS, I've spent my life learning how to 'read' people using conscious thought, based on my past experience of how people seem to respond, and on extensive reading (I read many, many books). After twenty-seven years of this I have become skilled at reading people. Unlike NT folks, this is a conscious effort and requires considerable energy, but it works and I can often 'see' things NT people would never see in negotiations. The only downside of this is that negotiations are absolutely exhausting for me. I think I do a good job of appearing 'normal' on the surface, but I am actually burning through incredible amounts of CPU cycles trying to read the other people. Being blessed with a high IQ (in the upper 160s or so) certainly helps, but I am still completely exhausted after even an hour of seemingly 'informal' conversations with people. I have to sleep nine to ten hours a night, and I often nap in the afternoons to make up for energy used. But, in those times that I am 'on' I can both see things nobody else sees, and I can read people – often better than even they can read themselves. For me, Asperger's is a *gift*. Given the choice, I would never want to be 'normal'. The world is a richer, more profound place for someone who can see the deeper patterns behind surface phenomena. Yes, I've suffered over the years for my lack of natural social skills. I've been confused about many things, and never had anyone explain to me that the world is different for me. I don't understand people and generally don't want to be around them. I've been the outcast and never really had friends. I've had to work incredibly hard to build social skills, or the appearance of these skills, that come so easy for NT folks. I'd have it no other way! Anyway, I wanted to share a success story of sorts. I've had my bad times and my good times, but I've been fortunate enough to use my Asperger's gifts to become very well off financially, which in turn enables me to shield myself from most social interactions that I need not engage in.

Can you see how this different wiring system does have compensatory advantages for both them and us? It must have. If it were a genetic fault rather than a genetic difference then natural selection would have meant it would have disappeared by now. And I make no apologies for stealing that idea from Simon Baron Cohen:

> ...the computer revolution in the twentieth century has created un-precedented opportunities for employment and economic prosperity for individuals with superior folk physics. This may have had positive effects on the reproductive fitness of such individuals, leading to an increase in the genes for AS/HFA in the gene pool... Our recent survey of scientists in Cambridge University showing increased familiality of autistic spectrum conditions is a first such clue that such effects may be operating.

So, the future looks hopeful, and it also looks a great deal more Asperger.

But you know what I find really strange? Even as I write, now, I'm finding that I'm looking back at my past to people I knew, and there are so many of them who obviously fell on the spectrum.

There was that boy in my primary school class. He, as I did, went to grammar school a year early. He smelt of mothballs, and had very little to say most of the time. He was odd, never joined in any games, used to sit spinning his pencil and watching it.

Our teacher made us give presentations to the class.

Mine was on chocolate. I'd sent to Cadbury's for information, hoping they'd send me some samples. Even at that age I had my eye on the main chance. So I had lots of colourful posters and bits of cocoa butter, things to pass round for everyone to share.

He, on the other hand, gave his talk on 'The Internal Combustion Engine', which he illustrated with a diagram on the board. It truly was the most boring monologue I had ever sat through, but he was all fired up with enthusiasm for pistons and valves and things that go whizz under bonnets.

And, do you know, he didn't even have the social sense to explain to the class of nine-year-olds that he was rattling on about a *car* engine. I only realized what he'd been talking about ten years later.

He's now Senior Lecturer in Astrophysics at some European university.

Then there was my ex-boyfriend.

My mother insisted I went out with him as he'd got a scholarship to Cambridge and was reputed to be very clever. He spoke only about history (his subject), Everton Football Club and the state of his bowels.

He'd say, as I opened the door, 'Before I come in I'll tell you what's wrong with me. My guts are playing up, I've got a headache and Everton lost.'

That was as far as we ever got as regards conversation.

But his face was similar to Danny's, with those extraordinary doll-like features and the sculpted jaw and the Hugh Grant lips.

He used to do lines from James Bond novels as his party piece. 'Bond's eyes were little fierce slits' was his favourite, and he'd screw up his eyes. It made little difference as he never looked at me anyway.

He had an eidetic (photographic) memory, a savant ability possessed by some Aspergers. He'd say to me, 'Name a book, name a page number, name a paragraph,' pointing at the pile of history books he was revising, and I'd select one at random, give him a page and paragraph number and he'd start reciting, word perfect.

One day he said, 'You're not my girlfriend any more.' He was at the end of his first year at Cambridge at the time. 'I've decided to go out with a man.'

The last I heard, he'd got his doctorate, he was married with two children, and was a top Whitehall civil servant.

If I had the time, and this wasn't Danny's story, I could go on listing Asperger childhood friends, people I worked with – including bizarrely the female radio presenter who was scared of telephones and couldn't talk to people unless she was on-air or in on-air mode – the partners of friends, almost every computer boffin I've ever met, the genius inventor I did a television show with, at least one of my university lecturers, and some of the sub- and copy-editors who've checked my work.

At the latest count these number over a hundred.

Now that you've read this chapter, perhaps you're doing the same, running a list in your mind?

Before you do, let me ask you to consider something while you're doing it. Aspergers are all different. They have a range of personalities, a range of talents and abilities; they are not peas in a pod.

Asperger's only defines certain behaviours within the autism spectrum. But individuality remains, as marked and as unique as in the NT world.

So, next, I'll show you what that means.

Asperger's Syndrome can be confused with...

ADD (Attention Deficit Disorder) – This diagnosis is often given to children who are easily distracted, are impulsive and restless. There is an alteration of the neurochemical systems in these children. It's a brain chemistry disorder with a strong genetic component. Some younger Aspergers may have ADD added to their diagnosis if the impulsivity is strong and they find it exceptionally difficult to concentrate and complete tasks.

ADHD (Attention Deficit Hyperactivity Disorder) – As above, but the restlessness is more marked and problematic.

Aphasia – A communication disorder where spoken or written words are poorly understood. This usually arises from a stroke or brain injury, a brain tumour, an infection or dementia.

OCD (Obsessive Compulsive Disorder) – Although at first this may seem similar to the repetitive behaviours and rituals seen in Asperger's Syndrome, OCD is totally different in quality. In Asperger's Syndrome the repetitive actions give pleasure and reassurance. In OCD they are intrusive and unwelcome, often very complex, and distressing. OCD usually first shows itself during late adolescence.

ODD (Oppositional Defiance Disorder) – Sometimes given as a co-diagnosis with Asperger's Syndrome in childhood, ODD is a tendency to refuse to do whatever is asked. There is marked defiance and a refusal to co-operate.

PDAS (Pathological Demand Avoidance Syndrome) – A pervasive developmental disorder. Children with this diagnosis are socially manipulative (unlike Aspergers), imitate socially inappropriate behaviour, and have an obsessive need to control others. They avoid any demands placed on them, are impulsive, have rapid mood swings, show no lack of imagination, and have some language delay. There can be some clumsiness.

SPD (Semantic Pragmatic Disorder) – This is another autistic spectrum disorder, which *some* consider is different from Asperger's as there is language delay, and the communication impairments are more noticeable. In SPD there's difficulty in interpreting language. It shares elements of the two triads of impairment as there are some problems in social situations, a preference for routines, and a lack of imaginative play, but these two impairments are not quite so serious as the language problem. Some may be diagnosed as High Functioning Autistic, some with PDD-NOS (see page 70).

Tourette Syndrome – Characterized by vocal or movement 'tics' which cause outbursts of 'involuntary' noises, sometimes loudly, and by facial or motor spasms which can seem similar to Asperger 'stimming'. However, in Tourette's, it's very difficult to control these sounds and movements. In Asperger's Syndrome, the sounds or movements give comfort. A few Aspergers are also diagnosed with Tourette's.

Asperger's Syndrome can include…

CAPD (Central Auditory Processing Disorder) – This causes problems in understanding and responding to spoken words. Although non-Aspergers can suffer from CAPD, it's very common in Asperger's Syndrome to various degrees. Some Aspergers find telephone conversations difficult because of this, but for most the problems arise when there's a face-to-face conversation, especially if it's stressful and instructions are being given. This makes dealing with authority figures and bureaucrats particularly difficult.

Dyscalculia – Literally number blindness, this can be a surprising deficit to find in Aspergers, who are reputed to be mathematically skilled and logical. However, because of the scattering of skills and deficits, some do have serious problems with numbers, and counting, which can make shopping very difficult indeed.

Dyslexia – Because of the communication impairments in Asperger's Syndrome, many have difficulty spelling, and a few may have difficulty understanding written words. This is, of course, a learning disability in its own right, but is more common in Aspergers.

Dyspraxia – The most common learning disability in Asperger's Syndrome, so common that one set of diagnostic criteria includes it specifically as a prerequisite of diagnosis. Sometimes known as 'clumsy child' syndrome, its effects range from obvious clumsiness to the more subtle awkwardness of gait, stance or hand movement. This distinguishes Asperger's Syndrome from classic autism. Autistics have notoriously good general and fine motor control.

Hyperlexia – Again, this skill can arise in those without a diagnosis of Asperger's Syndrome, and some believe that it is a spectrum disorder in its own right; however, it is far more common in Aspergers than in the general population. It's almost a savant skill in decoding the written word. Children with hyperlexia read at a very young age (anything from the start of their second year), read quickly, compulsively and accurately, but can't properly understand the meaning of what they read. They are 'rote readers'.

Prosopagnosia – Face-blindness, the inability to recognize someone by their facial features. It can be a socially disabling feature of autistic spectrum disorders (see Chapter 3).

SID (Sensory Integration Dysfunction) – Although this can occur in those outside the autistic spectrum, it's very noticeable in Aspergers. It causes either hyper (excessive) or hypo (deficient) responses to sensory stimuli in those on the autistic spectrum. It explains why a light casual touch can distress an Asperger, while pain can go unnoticed. There can be excessive dizziness, or none at all, even in activities like spinning round on the spot. Aspergers report sensitivities to some noises, none at all to others. Some fail to realize their own strength and slam doors without realizing. Breaking a glass that they're holding is another problem for some Aspergers, as is finding the correct pressure to apply when writing.

Asperger abbreviations

AC – Autistic Cousins. The name given to those with some autistic spectrum traits, even if insufficient for a diagnosis of an autistic spectrum disorder.

AS – Asperger's Syndrome, or those with Asperger's Syndrome.

ASDs – Autistic Spectrum Disorders, sometimes referred to as ASCs – Autistic Spectrum Conditions.

Aspies – A nickname for those with AS.

CC – Central Coherence. A function of mind which helps us to edit and select for meaning, and which is weak in those with Asperger's Syndrome.

DSM-IV – Diagnostic and Statistical Manual of Mental Disorders, American Psychiatric Association, 1994. The most commonly used set of diagnostic criteria for Asperger's Syndrome.

HFA – High Functioning Autism, or High Functioning Autistic.

ICD-1O – International Statistical Classification of Diseases and Related Health Problems (10th Revision) World Health Organization, 1993. Contains another set of criteria for Asperger's Syndrome diagnosis. Used worldwide.

NT – A Neuro-Typical, or someone who is not on the autistic spectrum.

PDD – Pervasive Developmental Disorder

PDD-NOS – Pervasive Developmental Disorder, Not Otherwise Specified. A common diagnosis in the USA, when there is evidence of an autistic spectrum disorder, but the symptoms are not specific enough to fit the criteria in the DSM-IV.

ToM – Theory of Mind, a psychological mechanism which is impaired in Asperger's Syndrome.

Names in Asperger's Syndrome history and research

Hans Asperger – Austrian psychologist, 1906–1980, who first described what is now known as Asperger's Syndrome in a doctoral thesis written in 1943, published in 1944.

Tony Attwood PhD – Author of *Asperger's Syndrome, A Guide for Parents and Professionals* (Jessica Kingsley Publishers, 1998), clinical psychologist, British, now living and working in Australia. Generally considered to be one of the world experts in AS.

Simon Baron-Cohen PhD – Cambridge (UK) academic at the forefront of autism research, author of *Mindblindness* (MIT Press, 1995).

Uta Frith – British professor and psychologist who translated Asperger's thesis in 1991 in her book *Autism and Asperger's Syndrome* (Cambridge University Press, 1991).

Christopher Gillberg – Swedish psychologist working at the University of Göteborg, whose diagnostic criteria for Asperger's Syndrome are thought to be the most comprehensive.

Leo Kanner – Austrian psychologist, 1894–1981, who emigrated to the USA where, in 1943, he published a paper defining autism.

Lorna Wing – Eminent British psychiatrist who first brought Asperger's work to the attention of the world in 1981, in 'Asperger Syndrome: a clinical account' (*Psychological Medicine 11*, 115–130).

3 Other-wired

Much as I'd like to do it for you, much as I'd like to do it for me, I can't wire either of us into Danny's autistic spectrum childhood.

What I can do, and what I'm going to do now, is to put you in touch with others on that glassy surface, and try to connect it with what I learned about Danny, whenever it's useful.

As I said, each Asperger is unique.

But, please, read on. I want to show you the rainbow. Absorb each colour, and draw your own picture. All of Danny's AS relatives, although they're only relatives in an abstract sense, will add to your full chromatic scale. When you've heard their stories, you'll be better able to appreciate Danny's own colour, tone and intensity of variant light.

We'll start with Marc Segar, author of *Coping: A Survival Guide for People with Asperger Syndrome*. He perfectly describes the world of the other-wired to those of us who are neurologically 'normal'. Marc began as a very confused, very clever little boy. He died tragically in a car crash when he was only 23. He'd already got a degree, and was starting work as a children's entertainer. Who knows what marvels he would have performed if he'd survived to knock us out of our complacency about what 'normal' means? He moved up the spectrum from autism to Asperger's Syndrome.

Along the way he developed a remarkable writing skill – clear, direct, sharply observant and beautifully interpretative of the experiences of his childhood and adolescence in an autobiography and guide book which everyone should read. He filters his experiences through the eyes of his older self, using that ferocious memory of events and sensory issues with which some Aspergers are particularly gifted.

> As far back as I can remember, I have had thoughts and ideas which, at the time, seemed to make me unique. In actual fact many of my earliest memories are theories I had about the world around me. Perhaps my earliest thoughts were about phonetics. Without actually knowing what 'phonetics' meant and probably not even knowing the alphabet, I was able to think to myself that 'P'

was a harder version of 'b' as was 'T' to 'd', 'K' to 'g' and 'S' to 'z'. This all worked reasonably well inside my own head, but at the time I was only four, an age at which apparently I wasn't even speaking yet except to express basic needs. However, I didn't know I wasn't speaking. I simply assumed I could.

Now, isn't that a surprising revelation?

His is an astonishing insight into the mind before communication starts. In Marc, everything was in place for speech, his head was full of it, but it wasn't coming out of his mouth. And just look at how he was *thinking* about the sounds, rather than the *meaning* of language.

Instead of speaking to others, he started speaking to himself in an internal monologue which he assumed others could hear. Can you see how that connects with the 'Theory of Mind' explanations in the last chapter?

It also throws light on the description of Asperger's by one expert as being 'extreme egocentricity'. Marc was the boy in the bubble.

But with his sister, Emma, two years younger than he was, he began to play ritualistic and repetitive games. Do these seem to lack imagination in the sense in which we use the word? Certainly it's not a familiar kind of imagination.

When my sister was approaching the age of two, this was probably when we first began to play together. Our games would usually involve a small number of characters or personas represented by dolls, teddies, other toys or even just objects. We would organize them into lines and bash them about a bit.

After seeing how indifferently I related to Action Man, my parents introduced me to Lego. Lego was the perfect toy for me. I used to spend whole days just making shapes and structures.

When I wasn't involved with friends, I would be doing lots of little projects on my own at home. For about two years I used to draw mazes. I also spent a lot of time making mixtures in coffee jars which included tea-leaves, grass and mud. I would leave them behind my bed and forget about them. When me and my sister were left in the absence of anyone else to play with, we used to string up dolls and teddies to the banisters, stick pencils in them, drown them and spin them round on a piece of string.

Emma and I moved on from torturing dolls and teddies and had begun building Lego colonies all over the house. We called our latest game 'punishing Hitler'. A Lego man with a moustache would represent Hitler and the rather grand and elaborate Lego city around him, with about twenty individual characters in it, would be constantly punishing him whilst having to defend their city against extra-terrestrial attack. They even had a colony in the garden which they would travel to in a small cabin which slid down a taut piece of string which led from the bathroom window to the trunk of the apple tree. The Lego game eventually drew to an end when I decided I was too old and grown up for it and this made Emma quite upset.

There's a noticeable development in these games from the simple lining up and displaying in the first versions of their joint play. Look at what was lined up too – not only dolls and teddies but 'even just objects'. Lining things up and displaying them, as I've said, is a common feature in Aspergers, and can remain long after childhood.

I've told you about Danny's wine bottles. His bedroom windowsill was lined with them, and when he came to stay with me he wanted to continue doing this. We made a pact. He could keep and display those which meant a great deal to him.

After three months the tops of my kitchen cabinets were covered in empty bottles, neatly aligned, about fifty or sixty of them. I threw them out one day. I'm sorry, Danny.

His mother, I told you, collected fossils. One AS child I heard of collects and lines up sweet wrappers. The choice of object seems to be fairly random.

But you'll also notice how in the games above there's what Hans Asperger himself chose to describe as 'malice' in his young patients, an urge, it might appear, to hurt and destroy.

We've come a long way from thinking of this as malice. To an NT the thought of 'torturing' dolls is slightly unpleasant, as we see dolls as cuddly representations of humans. But if you don't have a representation of what a human is, then this 'torturing' could be described as just experimenting with shape and form when objects are put into motion or drenched with liquid. Marc the adult carefully uses the word torturing to reflect what other children, or the NT world, might see in this game.

There's an intense curiosity here, not in what an NT might consider as play, rehearsing and mimicking human behaviour, taking the human form as 'mini me', but in the different type of imagination which asks, 'What would happen if…'

Finally the 'game' expanded to a complex representation of an entire world, not in humanistic terms, but in constructions and movement, containers and propulsion – the escape into the garden colony in a cabin along a piece of string, the invention not of a caring, sharing social creature, but of the engineer.

I hope that rings a bell. 'Engineer's disorder', remember?

It was both superbly inventive and consuming, one of those complex interests which Aspergers often adopt. Only when Marc began working on writing computer programs for his father's ZX computer, when he was still in early childhood, did his obsession with the Hitler game stop.

And you can see, too, can't you, that 'malice' by that time had been contained in more 'acceptable' expression? He chose to name his hate character after someone he'd realized could be identified as a 'baddie'. It was neuro-typically OK to attack Hitler.

Shapes, structures and patterns can absorb and fascinate. Marc drew mazes. He put things in jars to see what would happen, whether there'd be any structural change.

But any change would be one he'd controlled.

All Aspergers get tied up in repetitive behaviour. For some, this may mean that routes and patterns of day-to-day life can't be altered. Some AS children report serious panic if something in their environment is altered in any way. Children can go into meltdown if one of their neatly lined-up cars or dolls has been imperceptibly moved by a parent. For many, because they're hypersensitive, even changing their clothes is an issue.

Temple Grandin, a professor who designs animal handling equipment, was always anxious about feeling comfortable in her clothes. Some clothes were 'scratchy' to her, and she could hardly bear to wear them. Another AS you'll be meeting soon, Kevin Phillips, a 26-year-old from Barnsley, insisted on wearing his blue bobble hat and Wellington boots to school, and to bed…

Jane Meyerding, Programme Co-ordinator at a US university, had a similar problem, shared by her great-niece. Writing about a meeting with one of her sisters recently, she says:

> Her granddaughter started kindergarten, and for the first few days she refused to interact with anyone. When anyone approached her, even a teacher, she would 'close up like a flower' (my sister's words). After several days, this 'shyness' began to dissipate. That's when her mother (my sister's daughter) discovered that the child had taken to wearing her favorite bathing suit to school every day under her clothes. Fortunately she is the kind of mother whose reaction to something like that is, 'Whatever works!' She washes out the suit every night so her daughter can wear it to school the next day.
>
> That's exactly what my mother did for me when I started school, my sister tells me. As soon as she mentioned the clothes in question (a skirt and short jacket made of soft, soft cinnamon-colored corduroy), I could feel them immediately. A very happy memory for me (the clothes, not the school).

So why this insistence on rigidity, sameness, unalterable laws and rules?

I found this extract from an essay – 'Life Without Order: Literature, Psychology, and Autism' – by the brilliant young US polymath, Matthew

Belmonte, that I'd like you to read. Matthew, educated at Cornell, is a writer, computer expert and neuroscientist who now lectures and researches at MIT in the US and Cambridge University in the UK.

This is his explanation. Watch out for the last paragraph.

I got into science when I was a child because it offered me stability. I was always uncomfortable with any situation in which there was more than one right answer. I didn't want the responsibility of defining my universe; I wanted to discover what had already been laid out for me.

Science was my mother who would make all the choices for me and keep me safe from the horrible non-determination outside. In this respect I was very similar to my older brother. Neither of us could tolerate not being in control of our surroundings. We wanted some master plan, some canon, that would tell everything and everyone how to behave.

We were poorly disposed toward change, because it's so much more difficult to make sense of one's environment when it keeps slipping out of one's analysis. Things precarious or capricious – a newspaper hanging off the edge of the coffee table, furniture arranged at arbitrary angles instead of rectilinearly, items not stacked or lined up in order of decreasing size – were abhorrent to us.

The only solution in such a case was to attempt to fix the irregularity, or, if that were impossible, to leave the room and try to deny its existence.

In contrast, regular, repetitive events – the rise and fall of shadows under street lights, the rhythm of a twig caught in a bicycle wheel, water flowing in systems of pipes – were comforting because they gave us the power of prediction and control.

As we both grew older we diverged; this preoccupation with order began to dictate my behaviour less rigidly. I began to learn pragmatism and to accommodate wills and actions external to myself. I was still very shy with strangers, though, because people, especially people with whom one has no experience, are by far the most unpredictable elements of the universe, and the greatest threat to one's own control of it.

In the back of my mind always was the similarity in the ways in which my brother and I dealt with the world. I was a scientist. He was autistic. At times it became difficult, at least qualitatively, to tell the difference.

Sometimes you find a set of words that says it all. That does. Accurately, it draws the thin line between what we think of as genius, and what we think of as deviant or dysfunctional.

Both scientist and autist look for pattern. They need the familiar comfort of regularly, and therefore predictably, functioning parts and sequences.

The need to order existence is central to higher level thinking. If the world is chaos, then, if you're NT, you try to order it in your mind, and accept that others may contribute or may disrupt. You create theories and test them, with others, when you begin to trust.

If you can't get beyond chaos because you feel unable to control it, then you get stuck in pattern. Matthew's brother is seriously autistic and mute, and hasn't progressed, as yet, up the spectrum into AS.

So what is the AS child, who stares for hours into his favourite obsession, a washing machine, actually doing? Watching. Working out, and comforted by, the pattern. Fascinated by the sequence of sounds and movement. Making sense.

Do you remember Wendy Lawson? I mentioned her in the last chapter – the woman whose AS had been diagnosed as schizophrenia and who spent twenty-five years on medication for schizophrenia, totally the wrong medication for those on the spectrum. She now has a PhD and is an educationalist, lecturer and poet.

This is what she writes about the tendency of others to change things and even to change their minds:

> It was in 1996, when I was talking to Lawrie Bartak at Monash University, that I learnt the rule that people are allowed to change their minds! This new rule really helped me to cope with the fickleness of human nature. It also gave me an escape route for times when things happened, usually things beyond my control, that meant I had to change my plans. For years and years I lived with guilt and extreme anxiety just because things changed all the time.
>
> One of the best tools that we can equip our youngsters with is that of teaching them strategies to cope with change. One of those being that it is OK if things don't go exactly to plan.

Change

Change, change and more change,
Of context, place and time.
Why is it that life's transient stage,
Plays havoc with my mind?

You said, 'We'll go to McDonalds'
But this was just a thought.
I was set for hours,
But the plan then came to nought.

My tears and confused frustration,
At plans that did not appear,
Are painful beyond recognition,
And push me deeper into fear.

How can life be so determined?
How can change be so complete?
With continuity there is no end,
Security and trust are sweet.

So, who said that change would not hurt me?
Who said my 'being' could not be safe?
Change said, 'You need continuity'
In order to find your place.

For change makes all things different,
They no longer are the same.
What was it that you really meant?
All I feel is the pain.

Danny used to love Wendy's poems. He said she was writing about him too. And remember how important being safe was to Danny? This is why.

Change is one of the most difficult concepts for an Asperger to understand and to adapt to. This is because it takes them some time to move from one mind-state into another. They need preparation. We take it for granted that we can immediately adjust.

If I'm writing, and someone rings my doorbell, I'm none too pleased and may be curt with the woman who is standing on the doorstep determined to save my soul. It's a totally different mind-state, from tapping computer keys to being the unwilling victim of a soul-stealer. I feel preoccupied. But I can do it, just about. However grouchily.

What I noticed about Danny was that he couldn't. Ever. He had to get into a mode and stick with it. If I went into the room where he was working he'd not only jump out of his skin, but he'd glare at me with a totally blank face, which to me, NT and body-language reader that I am, meant that he was blanking me, throwing me out with a look.

He wasn't. He just had the greatest difficulty adjusting, making attention-shifts. Sometimes he was incapable of it. Adjusting to me, to sociability, meant a progressive series of wind-downs and -ups, all sequenced. It might take as much as ten minutes or more for him to go through this process. Sometimes he just didn't have the energy or the desire to make the adjustment at all.

But problems like these create havoc at school, which is the first real occasion that children are forced to move totally from the safety and familiarity of those few who understand them, and into the social and instructional world.

This is when any defects in relating, understanding language, and imagining – that triad of impairments, remember? – will be noted and selected for special attention by the NT world. It's when the real pain begins.

Even Marc Segar, obviously intellectually gifted, was baffling because of his strange habits:

> When I started school I had a teacher who took a sympathetic and open-minded approach. My classmates would accept me for who I was even though I spent so much time daydreaming and wandering over to the wrong side of the classroom while the teacher was reading a story. Even at that early age the other children could probably tell there was something wrong, despite the fact that I never suspected anything of the sort; and this was to be the case for a long time to come.
>
> What really seems to throw people is that they can't seem to understand that a six-year-old boy who knows all the planets in the solar system and who can already subtract three from five may not yet have worked out that it is inappropriate to climb in the dustbins during playtime or that it is naughty to chew up one's pencil and stare out of the window during a lesson.

A teacher who had been to an Asperger awareness conference was able to stop an AS child in her class wandering through the room during story-time. She placed a carpet tile of the child's favourite colour on the floor at the appropriate time each day. The child adopted the tile, and knew that this position was hers. It was her safe place. She never wandered again, and was able to listen to the stories with the others.

Kevin Phillips battled with the inevitable problems that Aspergers have with words. They just don't interpret metaphorical or idiomatic language as soon as most. They don't understand proverbs, folk sayings, little shorthand parental hints to prompt response:

> I remember being about seven years old and sent by my teacher to fetch a tube of glue from another class which was full. I walked in and received the object. 'Kevin, what's the magic word?' I was asked upon receiving it. I had never heard of this saying before and replied straight-faced 'Abracadabra'. The whole class erupted in hysterical and loud laughter. The teacher glared angrily at me obviously thinking I was trying to be smart. I was asked again and I said, 'It works'. She kept asking me for about half an hour until I finally said, 'Please'. I briefly became a hero with some of the boys who thought I was being rebellious or was trying to be a smart ass or a wise guy type. However, many of the other children thought frankly that I was dense and thick.

Kevin has come a long way in a short time. Like Danny, he's mastered the use of idiom and writes easily and naturally from the heart. His writing is a joy to read. There's this wonderful vitality and energy that bubbles out of him, an infectious humour that's supposedly lacking in Aspergers.

Kevin makes me laugh and cry with him.

I don't know how often I've read about Aspergers' limited use of language, the stilted quality, the formality of their speech and writing. Not true. The range you've already seen here must have convinced you of that. There's Jane's thoughtful, gentle prose, Wendy's wonder- and thunder-struck verses, Marc Segar's bright, sharp eyes. Aspergers who write well, write as well as NTs who do.

Writing is an expression of personality and, once language is fully grasped, Aspergers are as able as NTs to show who and what they are by their choice of style, and by their incomparable directness.

Larry Arnold also had language problems at school. Severely dyspraxic and dyslexic, although undiagnosed, he also suffered, rarely in Asperger's Syndrome, from dyscalculia, a problem with arithmetic, making sense of numbers. This became worse and worse throughout his schooldays until now, in his forties, this highly intelligent, possibly gifted, computer expert, photographer and musician is almost unable to calculate how much change he should have when he goes shopping.

Back in his schooldays, though, it was his sensory excitability, and that literal quality, which, as it did in Kevin's case, set him apart from the others:

> To the stories that were told in primary school I could see pictures. So vivid were these stories that I believed they were real and would cry openly at them. I had a strange belief system early in life which may have been due to literal thinking. I had an over-intensity of emotion and confusion about my feelings. I was also quick to anger and would have outbursts. These must have amused the other children because they would provoke me into these rages, where I would lash out wildly, and pick up whatever was to hand and throw it as hard as I could. Hard enough to break windows on more than one occasion.

Wendy Lawson was also confused by words:

> When I tried to talk to my peers, somehow my words only compounded the issue. My father once said to me, 'Make friends, Wendy.' I knew how to make a rice pudding, I even knew how to make my dog sit, but I had no idea how to make friends!

It's a problem that's persisted for her, too.

From January to June in 1997 I studied at a university in the UK. I was living in Halls. I was supposed to change one sheet on my bed every week. I didn't know how to do this (should I carry the sheet in a plastic bag, tuck it under my arm or what?). I didn't change my sheets for five weeks.

Then I saw another student taking a sheet to the laundry, so I did as they were doing. The laundry lady said, 'Top to bottom, dear.' I hadn't any idea what she was talking about so, as usual, I just smiled. It was several weeks later, after I had been taking my one sheet to the laundry, that I realized what she had meant. I helped my friend change the sheet on her bed. As we did so she said 'top to bottom' and placed the top sheet on the mattress, using the clean sheet as the top sheet under her quilt. 'Oh,' I said, 'is that what you are supposed to do?' I had simply been taking my top sheet off the bed and putting the clean one in its place. I hadn't changed the bottom one at all!!

Wendy calls this failure to completely understand the language of communication 'uneven skills'. Some call them scatter skills. I call it walking gingerly along the triad.

Wendy has scatter skills and deficits in language, still to some extent impaired. Yet, she's all the richer and more engaging because of it. The realizations that occur to her, and which she shares with us, make us think, too, about what we may be taking for granted.

We've also seen, in Marc Segar, and in Matthew Belmonte's breathintaking story of his connection with his autistic brother, skills of imagination, impaired. Now let's come to the hottest coals of all – and try this in your bare feet if you dare – impairments of social functioning.

You're going to have to stretch yourself to understand this particular impairment, as some of it is deeper than you could have imagined – NTs rarely have even to calculate social niceties.

For AS people, the navigation through the demanding social dramas of every day can be a white-knuckle ride.

One thing I noticed about Danny was a total contradiction between that initial impression of him as socially assertive and the passivity which lay just below the surface and was closer to his natural state.

It was almost as if life happened to him, rather than that he had any ability to modify what was occurring. He also used the language of passivity. According to him, girls 'seduced' or 'kidnapped' him. He was 'taken to the cinema'. Others, he said, 'got' him drunk. He told me once that after a boozy night out he'd found himself in a yacht moored off the coast of France.

It's hardly likely. He must have, at some stage in the wildness of the night in question, collected clothes, passport and money. His impulse to go with the flow, do whatever was suggested, agree to madness, was part of the impulsive passivity, and he almost wanted to deny that he exercised, or could exercise, any control over his actions and behaviour.

Or perhaps that's just my own cynical NT view of some of his behaviour. Perhaps he did see himself as just an object of play for others to manipulate? I used to tell him that he always took the easy way out. Perhaps I should have thought more carefully about what the alternative really was, for an Asperger.

I'm coming back, as you've noticed, to that point I was making about control of the environment being an integral part of the repetitive behaviours and rigid structures of the Asperger's world. The conditions on the triad aren't separate, but feed one into another.

If you want the predictable, but see only chaos, you have two choices.

One is to flow with the chaos like a stick in a stream, another is to work out the laws that govern the chaos, define, then select. That's the distinction that Matthew Belmonte describes.

You have two distinct ways of operating as an Asperger. There is no middle route. You make rules that you follow, which takes real conscious and painful effort, or you let yourself merely respond, which is the natural state of any human who started having to live without a Theory of Mind. Where as a child the entire world was chaos, once Theory of Mind is established, maybe Aspergers can see other people and their unpredictable ways as being responsible for the chaos they encounter wherever they go. So they tune out, or they make sense through rules.

Rules. Remember Danny's Rules? And you've heard about Wendy's discovery that you can change your mind, which she added to her rules? Wendy's Rules. Rules sort out the confusion, but it all takes time. Or you can ask someone you trust to give you the rules, ready-made.

In Marc Segar's case he felt shut out of the world of others, because he didn't quite understand what 'others' were:

Back at school I had a best friend, Ben, whose work was suffering as a result of his attempts to look after me. On the whole, people in the same class as me would casually defend me and look after me at playtime. However, when I chose to go running off in whatever direction pleased me, I was a sitting duck. I don't really know how the staff interpreted my funny rituals and habits but they would probably have classified me under the heading 'attention seeker'. It's actually quite strange the way in which I used to think of the staff. Myself, the other children and my parents were all people. However, teachers weren't people, they were teachers; and dinner ladies weren't people, they were dinner ladies. It is almost as if I thought of them as a separate species in the animal kingdom, beset with the role of looking after people.

Do you see how Marc's confusion comes down in part to a passive attitude? It's a case of 'what is happening to me, here?' And can you see how he's acquired a 'minder'? Where have you seen this before?

It's the caretaker/mentor/interpreter role that Asperger adults often need in their life, just as they did when they were children. It's Danny and me, isn't it?

Someone to watch over me, because I can't be trusted, and need externally imposed control, just in case I can't make up or work out the rules.

What's missing is the sense that NTs have of all being in this together, all equal, flowing easily between the roles of care-givers and takers, controlled or controlling, depending on the circumstances, making natural changes, fitting in where you see your chance.

Aspergers are marginalized by their own social behaviour, their innate lack of understanding about how to be in control when in the company of others, how to resist being controlled, and how to influence and participate in the course of social events of all kinds.

While many, at school, find a mentor or a protector, as Marc did, sometimes Aspergers are the obvious targets for bullies.

If you're odd and passive, you'll be picked on, unless you can find someone who'll help you out. Marc was picked on, for his gullibility. His passivity made him vulnerable.

> To the school tearaways I was a real object of interest. If they told me to do something, quite often I would do it, thinking I was being good and doing as I was told, not really knowing that it was against the school rules and it would get me into trouble. When they said 'Umm, I'm telling', I would immediately realize that I was breaking the school rules but that I didn't know about it at the time and that it was extremely unfair. I would respond to this injustice by saying, 'No, no, don't.'
>
> When I wasn't a target I was a reject. I remember how desperately I used to wish to be part of other children's games where the grass was always greener. I used to wish I could take a bag of marbles to school, join in with the game and come home with more, instead of always losing them all to little pirates and con-artists.

Sometimes, too, the possession of some special skill can mark you out as different. And we all know that Aspergers specialize in special skills and interests.

In fact, most conversational approaches that younger Aspergers make start with a, 'Did you know that... ?' This prioritizing of knowledge above all else is what made Hans Asperger call them 'little professors'.

If you look on a wonderfully zany Asperger website, the Institute for the Study of the Neurologically Typical (http://autistics.org/isnt), you'll see this ironically turned on its head. According to one of the authors, it's NTs who are obsessive about their consuming interest – other people. That's the real problem.

Jane Meyerding goes further. She offers some help to other Aspergers in establishing a degree of social conformity, getting on with the NTs in your life. Revelations about Jane's 'difference' here will shake any preconceptions you may have.

> I have noticed that most of the people around me (e.g. at work) seem to have a knack for collecting (and remembering) information about each other. It seems 'natural' for them to do so, and apparently it plays some part in their ability to 'network' with one another (the way socializing becomes a factor/tool in social, employment and political advancement).
>
> When I interact with people at work, I use scripts. That's the only way I have anything to say. There's no point in my asking them about themselves in the NT way, because I never remember answers to those kinds of questions. My brain seems to lack any storage capacity devoted to social trivia.
>
> The way I establish relationships is by beginning with a common interest. If I meet someone with whom I share an interest and we interact on that basis, eventually I will begin (over the course of time, measured in years) to accumulate bits of knowledge about them.

That rules of social behaviour have to be written in such detail to overcome the differences caused by ASD shows what a deep and pervasive disorder it can be.

Temple Grandin, in an interview with Oliver Sacks, famously described her position in the NT world as being that of an 'anthropologist on Mars'. Jane's account of the behaviour she adopts could almost have been written as a scouting report on Planet Earth and its mysterious inhabitants.

When social codes which come naturally to most of us have to be scrutinized, analysed and placed in this non-emotive language, in order to get by, it's no wonder that many Aspergers are exhausted by the effort of trying to be sociable.

Basically, as Jane says, their interest is in finding others who share their interests. This is not other people. This is not 'social trivia'. This is the essentials of whatever knowledge you have, and want to share. This is all that counts, ultimately. So you can forget about what she said to him, and what he said to her, and where that left both of them. You can forget about whether yours is a permanent relationship, or whether someone is passive aggressive because of childhood abuse. You can discount diet plans, too. And as for whether you can wear red lipstick with aubergine shoes, whether you can fiddle the tax system and get away with it, who cares?

That's magazine journalism for the mass market, and what does it matter when your Asperger life is predicated on the hard drive and the construction of a cantilever bridge, or some facts about British monarchs since 1206 or a discord in Mozart's 'Magic Flute'? These are the real AS consuming passions.

Marc's consuming passion was the solar system. He wanted to share his enthusiasm with everyone he met.

> I may have been unaware that there was anything wrong with me but the feelings of rejection I felt then were to crop up time and time again for years to come.
>
> Dr Elizabeth Newson came to visit us on one occasion when I was in my third year of schooling to try and determine what was wrong. She talked to me for an hour about my favourite thing, the solar system. Impressed with my knowledge of the subject, she suggested autism to my parents but with uncertainty. My parents replied with, 'Now try talking to him about something else.' On this note, my diagnosis was almost certain and my parents were worried at the prospect that I had an incurable social disorder, but were at the same time relieved that, finally, someone had shed some light on the problem.

Marc was luckier than most in getting a diagnosis at the age of eight. He was placed in a school for children with special educational needs, and was helped to overcome some of the more disabling characteristics of autism.

Contrast this with the fate of Kevin Phillips, who had the same symptoms, although perhaps not so pronounced.

You remember Kevin? He of the blue hat and Wellington boots and the Abracadabra? Kevin knew all the town's bus numbers by the time he was six. He was interested in town halls, churches and trains. When he was in primary school he'd go to bed at 8.31 precisely, every school night. Now, in his twenties, he has to get into the bath at exactly 9.30 on Sundays. As a child he watched an old movie on television and remarked what a sad world it must have been when it was all in black and white, and how lucky we are that the world is now in colour. He refuses to eat sandwiches with butter on.

Yes, some of you are saying, that takes me back, weren't we all like that as kids? Didn't we all say funny and silly things and have some strange beliefs? And everyone's got rituals and habits. We all have. I have.

Can you understand that it's exactly this belief which makes Asperger's Syndrome so difficult to detect and accept as a basic difference? This is why people like Kevin, undiagnosed until he was twenty-three, fall through the net of a caring society. It would have been easy, perhaps, for Elizabeth Newson to listen to Marc and decide he was just a gifted child with some funny ways and would grow out of them. She was, instead, his saviour. She didn't let him fall.

Danny slipped through the net, despite his school's psychiatric assessment, for the same complacent reasons. Just a funny little boy, that's all. Everyone knew he was strange. Some people were around when he climbed up on a wheeled clothes rack in Marks and Spencer's and took it for a scootering ride round the shop and round town. Everyone knew that he was the world expert on dinosaurs, that he wandered off out of school, that he was bullied, that at times his rages were so intense that he could damage himself and others, that he preferred to be with the girls in the school who looked after him rather than the boys, that he would wander off and disappear for hours. And no one caught him. He fell.

But Kevin's case, even allowing for the above rituals should have been so much clearer.

In 10 per cent of Aspergers there are savant abilities which go far beyond merely Danny's ability to run his finger quickly down an entire column of figures and add them up as he does so.

Kevin is very special indeed. He has a savant ability, as he explains here:

> If someone gives me any date between 1752 when the Gregorian calendar made its 12 day adjustment and 2100, I can tell them what day of the week that date fell on. I have been able to do this unconsciously since I was about ten years old. Even today I cannot explain how I do it. Some people have said to me that I have a special mathematical formula. This is untrue. I don't. After all, how many ten year olds are into mathematical formulas which enable them to calculate days of the week?!!
>
> For example ...
>
> What day of the week was 3 February 1914? This was a Tuesday.
>
> What day of the week was 5 January 1983? This was a Wednesday.
>
> What day of the week was 6 August 1830? Friday. What day of the week was 13 October 1776? Sunday. What day of the week will 11 July 2089 drop on? Monday.
>
> I find it very frustrating that I cannot turn this ability I have to any use. I wish I could turn some of my abilities into developing a suitable career and make money out of them. However, I don't want to go on television and become a walking, talking freak show. There must be some use I can put my abilities to somehow or somewhere. If you can think of any ideas or any careers where I could put them to use, or any ways I could make money out of them, could you please let me know.

There's far more to Kevin's calendar calculating skills than I've included here. If you'd like to read more about them, visit his website.

Savant abilities tend to cluster around the autistic spectrum, producing some of these unusual unconscious notes of pure ability which would defy most description. As Kevin himself says, it hasn't done him a lot of good. He is good at maths, but only some parts of maths – he can't do algebra for instance.

He just sees calendars. There's not a lot of practical use for that skill.

Kevin was bullied, too. And when one time it became too much for him, and he responded by flying into meltdown against a boy who had been harassing him for far too long, they were both punished, and suspended from school. Kevin, typically, is generous in his assessment of the other boy, understanding that he must have had severe behavioural problems. He is generous and understanding about most of the insults he had to bear.

> I remember on Thursday 8 June 1989 being told by another pupil who was in my class, 'Kevin, do you ever wonder why you are always in scrapes, are always getting into trouble and the sort?' To which I replied, 'No'. 'Well it is because you are so dumb. You make things so hard for yourself.' Looking back now, I have a reason for being 'dumb', I wonder what his excuse for being dumb was?

Exactly, Kevin. Along with the 10 per cent of Aspergers with special savant skills there is a proportion who have additional disabilities which seem to go hand in hand with the condition. I've already mentioned Larry Arnold's dyscalculia and his dyslexia. But it's the dyspraxia from which many suffer that can add to the pressure of school. If you're so clumsy that you have difficulty with skills like tying your shoelaces, it's unlikely that you'll ever be a school sports hero.

PE is one of the school subjects which Aspergers mention as their most hated. One Asperger woman says that she was always left until last when teams were chosen. With little awareness of how team games should be played and a gawky inability to catch or kick easily, it's hardly surprising that the humiliation of being noticeably different is compounded by ritual rejections every PE day.

This is powerfully described by a US Asperger, Joel, who was seen to be suffering in PE, and who was given 'help' for his problem.

> Also, in fourth grade, the school finally realized that I had bad coordination, balance, motor skills, etc. Apparently, it only takes five years for them to notice that I couldn't catch, write well, etc... Maybe they finally realized it wasn't just because I wasn't trying hard enough (that's what my PE comment

always was on my report card – Joel needs to work harder). (If I sound upset, this is probably the part that upsets me most.) I remember doing all sorts of assessments at this point for my motor skills and such. I don't think I did very well on most of them. Fortunately, they took me out of regular PE classes for a bit (although they decided to put me back into them after only a little while – something I wish they didn't do). I would also spend several hours a week working on these skills. I probably would have enjoyed that if they did it somewhere where I wasn't on display for the other students. We would do most of these activities in the hallway outside my classroom, so the other students just had one more thing to tease me about ('Joel can't catch a ball... Joel can't skip... Joel can't whatever else...').

How's that for helping you fit in with your peer group?

One of the most distressing problems faced by some Aspergers is prosopagnosia: face blindness. Some who suffer do so mildly in that they just can't easily remember a face from the past. Some are more seriously affected.

Jane Meyerding who suffers from it says:

> I am unable to remember people on the basis of having seen them several times. My brain lacks the ability to 'memorize' their faces, and it takes me a lot longer (than it takes non-face-blind people who can instantly memorize faces) to establish enough familiarity so that identifying details begin to stick in my brain.

Some Aspergers with this condition 'remember' by taking the 'essence' of a person, recalling general size, shape and one or two distinguishing features – hair, baldness, glasses, clothes.

But it is a truly anti-social problem to suffer from. Along with the oddity of the AS intonation, use of language, and problems in establishing eye contact, those with face blindness can be thought of as extremely rude when they don't recognize and acknowledge a schoolmate or a colleague. In one extreme case, an AS man found that he couldn't recognize his mother in the street. Joel suffers from this condition, too, and this added to his many confusions about how to get on with others when he moved up to junior high school.

> One of the hard things was that the school was much too big for my normal ways of recognizing people to work. In a class of twenty-five students, it was fairly easy to find ways to tell everyone apart and know who I was talking to. In junior high, there were eight hundred students, many of whom I would interact with in the halls, at lunch, in class, etc. I couldn't tell the students I knew from elementary apart from the students I had never met, so I even lost

the recognition of the people I knew, except for the few who were unique enough to be easily identified. It was also hard for me to learn who new people were. I could only give the names of a few of the people I ate lunch with during every day. I knew very few of my classmates. PE was the worst since we wore different clothes in PE than in normal classes (unlike elementary school, where we wore the same clothes in both normal and PE classes). I really couldn't recognize anyone in these classes. Obviously, this made things a lot more stressful for me and I felt a lot more isolated. I think this is when the most serious thoughts of suicide began.

And how can you possibly learn to interact with other people – or even define some rules about what certain facial expressions might mean – when you can't even 'see' the face itself? What is the point of looking, when you can't see? Unconsciously looking, as most of us apparently do according to anthropologists, for that widening of the pupils when someone you're smiling at is responding positively and fancies you – how do you ever fall in love if that never happens?

Jane, like the famously elective celibate Temple Grandin, chooses friendship rather than the overwhelming passion which can come from reading the frenzy of love in another's mirroring face and eyes.

Even Danny, child that he was, emotional learner-driver that he was, finally worked out that love is an intense face-to-face narrative, which you can learn to read and still not fear enough to drop the book and run away.

'Heather still loves me,' he told me confidently.

'How do you know?' I asked, and got an answer I didn't expect.

'Her eyes go all big when she looks at me,' he said.

Well done, Danny.

Joel, too, found a key to the NT world which helped him make it through the day at school. He discovered 'modelling' and 'scripting' – adopting acceptable behaviour and expressions which would fend off the difficulties he faced from his peers and his teachers.

There were other things going on, too, that made things more difficult. If I saw other kids laughing, and I didn't know why they were laughing, I would assume they were laughing at me. After all, they were usually laughing at me when I knew what was supposed to be funny. Anyone who thinks kids are basically nice has not lived through this kind of mental and physical torture.

My way of coping with this was to pretend that it didn't bother me, and to retreat back into myself. I got sick of trying to explain why I was upset to teachers who wouldn't do anything, so I would always smile, no matter what was happening. It seems people ask less questions of you if you smile than if you frown. I still remember teachers saying how nice it was that I always smiled. That was a horrible compliment. It proved that they didn't have any idea how I felt. They were complimenting my acting, not who I really was. It has taken a long time for me to learn how not to smile, but now my face is much more likely to express how I really feel inside. I couldn't let my real feelings be known in junior or senior high, though. It would have just given the other kids more ways of teasing me.

Does this remind you of Danny's smiles on the night of my birthday? I feel even more guilty now!

Marc Segar went further than merely adapting to get by. As confident as Danny, as capable, and more altruistic, he wanted to define the rules of behaviour, which he had so minutely studied and interpreted, so as to help others. He was very much aware of how the help he'd had, throughout his childhood, led to a degree of self-awareness and he wanted to communicate this to others.

I think of Marc as the future of Asperger's Syndrome, the child who is diagnosed early, who learns carefully, and becomes the responsible adult, capable of identifying the language of complex social relationships, and so entering, on tip-toe, the NT closed shop. His wonderfully eccentric approach would always have marked him out. It may also, we might have hoped, have marked him out as special – loved and accepted and admired for his innocent and incisive laterality.

Much as I loved, accepted and admired Danny's unique visions, to me he was always the alternative view. Something slightly weird. Someone who needed completion, and interpretation. Someone who needed Heather, or me, to exult in what he was. He was never quite whole, as Marc could have been, perhaps, had he lived.

Marc's autobiography concludes with a rule-book he wrote specifically for others on the autistic spectrum, 'A Survival Guide for People with Asperger Syndrome'. More rules? Really? Why do most of us not recognize life as a rule-book?

Because we're not other-wired.

Because all these things just feed into our system, effortlessly, and are taken as read by the majority. And how patronizing and smug is that?

You tell me.

In Marc's introduction, he writes:

When you have read this book, you might think that these are the rules to a rather silly game, but the game is life and the rules cannot be changed.

Whoops, Marc, yes they can! But the Asperger need for predicted situations and outcomes again predominates. I think that if I, or perhaps any other NT, were to write a Book of Life Rules, the first rule would have to be 'Be Flexible'. And there's the difference.

But Marc does make a good stab at setting out a rule book for those Aspergers whose anxiety and social concerns could be eased by a glimpse into some of the unwritten laws by which we live. How sad it is that they should need one.

This is his section on 'Distortions of the Truth'. Truth is always a huge issue for the moral and logical Asperger, and I can well understand why this has been put together in its very clear way. Some of us may describe it as defining the obvious.

But stop before you do that. And think. This is the world of the NT as defined through the eyes of an Asperger. It's not a very kind or pleasant world, is it? And yes, we really are as bad as this:

Sarcasm is when someone says one thing, but means the opposite. For example, in response to hearing someone burp, someone else might say 'how polite'. The easiest way of picking up on sarcasm is by listening to tone of voice. You may need to defend yourself against sarcasm at times and this will be covered in following chapters.

Not knowing the truth is a common reason why people might distort it.

A particularly nasty form of distorted truth is 'scape-goating'. This is setting up other people to take the blame for things which aren't their fault. What is even worse is having someone deliberately do something wrong for the sole purpose of getting you blamed for it. If this happens, you must first work out whether it is just a joke or whether it is a serious set-up. If it is serious, and if the blame successfully reaches you, you may need to somehow prove that the wrong doing was not your fault in which case you must tell the right people that you think you've been set up and stick to your word.

On the other hand, someone might quite innocently create a false truth for the mere purpose of fantasy play. This might apply to children pretending to be comic cartoon heroes, adults dressed up in costume pretending to be Father Christmas or someone who is acting in a play.

If someone asks you a question and giving them the true answer might upset them or cause embarrassment or unfair trouble to other people, you may decide to tell a 'white-lie' which is intended to avoid unpleasantness all round.

If you don't wish to lie, you might still want to withhold the truth. You might be keeping a secret for someone or you might be trying to keep yourself or others out of trouble. In this case, it may be sensible to avoid certain topics of conversation otherwise you might be forced into pretending not to know something, using awkward diversion tactics (which often involve humour) or even lying. Also, you may be expected to automatically know when something is to be kept a secret.

If someone tries to get a message across to you without hurting you, they might decide to drop a hint. The best example of this is when a man is chatting up a woman but she doesn't want to go out with him in which case instead of saying 'I'm not interested, go away' she might slip the words 'my boyfriend' into the conversation.

Sometimes it is possible to be misled by figures of speech (i.e. metaphors). For example, 'I'm over the moon' means I'm very happy. If figures of speech are a problem for you, they can be looked up in certain books, or you can get someone to teach some to you.

Sometimes someone might lie to you if they want something from you. The best example of this is a door to door salesman who wants your money. If he sells you a television which doesn't work then he would be conning you.

In conversation, it is not unusual for people to exaggerate. Someone who says 'I had about ten pints last night' might actually mean they only had five. People who exaggerate too much can be easily misinterpreted.

If someone says something which sounds offensive in the literal sense e.g. 'You ugly mug face', but with a laugh and a smile, then they mean it as a joke. You often need to pick up on this quite quickly.

Perhaps the most awkward kind of lies you encounter are teasing lies in which someone says something as a joke to see whether or not you believe them. If what they have just said is highly unlikely or people around them are trying not to laugh, they are probably teasing you. The correct response to this would be to laughingly tell them to p*ss off. If you show doubt as to whether or not they are teasing you, they may see it as a sign of vulnerability. Remember they are probably never going to admit that they are teasing you, no matter how seriously you ask.

People might start trying to persuade you to make a spectacle of yourself somehow. For example, they may ask you to do a dance or sing a song. Even if you can't see anything wrong with this yourself, it is important not to give in to them, no matter how persuasive they become. The correct response is the same as that for a teasing lie, only perhaps with a touch of anger. If you give in to such requests, you will probably become an all round target for other people's teasing. If you have already done this in the past, don't worry, just don't let it continue.

If ever joining in games like 'truth or dare' or 'strip poker' you could find yourself under even greater pressure to do something. In this case, it is often all right but you might be asked to do something which is completely 'out of order' in which case if people become too persuasive you might prefer just to leave the room. If they are true friends, they won't hold it against you for more than a day.

It must be remembered that not everyone is loyal to the truth. Also, many people select certain parts of the truth and reject others to their own advantages (e.g. in court cases).

If you need to find out whether or not someone is lying and you have a good reason for doing so, asking them questions might reveal faults in their logic.

That entire section is an indictment of our NT morality. It shows how complex and convoluted our rejections can be for the outsider, how we gang up, exclude, lie and mock in our efforts to conform to what we have decided is the norm.

So, if you were Asperger, would you want to retain your integrity, your valuation of your own (albeit scattered) skills, and opt out of the daily battle of being accepted by those whose brains are wired to be social creatures?

It's the paradox of Aspergers that they are inclined towards other people, despite constant rebuffs. A major characteristic is that Aspergers, unlike classic Kanner autistics, are sociable.

Yet the sociability, it seems to me, is parallel, rather than integrated. Just as an Asperger child will play alongside rather than with others, so Asperger adults retain this sense of being apart, but a part that is vital.

The ordeals that many of them go through on a daily basis to integrate their own sensory differences, to conform to rules they don't understand, to shift mind-states, to work out what words might actually mean, to attempt to see the 'big picture', to retain focus, to try to read expression and gesture, are never-ending.

Think of the worst day you had recently. It was probably one of those days when people and things got in your way, no one gave you a straight answer to a straight question, the phone kept ringing and people were just talking distracting gibberish, nothing was in the place it should have been in, someone let you down, your collar itched and you just ended up by losing it completely, or went out for a stiff drink, or flopped into bed, or got on the first plane out of here.

For Aspergers, every single day could be like that day.

'Why can't you do it, Danny?' I'd snarl at him.

'It's too hard,' he'd try to explain.

And then I'd launch into my usual nag about how he was always looking for the easy way out, and that some things are supposed to be hard, and that you can't go all through life just smiling and sleeping or running away.

How stupid was I?

The cumulative effort of living just got too much for him on a daily basis. He had to 'hide', turn the phones off, crawl under the duvet, or drink himself normal. His sensitivities to some of the things NTs find easy to withstand, and his lack of sensory reaction to other experiences, made each day scratchy and awkward, not exactly a minefield, but one protected by barbed wire through which he had to crawl.

Kalen, a Canadian Asperger, describes the sensory problems Aspergers can have to cope with:

> Sensory issues can also be hyposensitivities, where nothing gets in unless it is very loud or painful; synaesthesia, where one sense is perceived as another, or sometimes extreme fluctuations. They can affect any sense including proprioceptive (sense of one's body in space), and vestibular (movement). I am mostly hyposensitive with a few specific hypersensitivities.

Larry Arnold describes the pattern he fell into while at university in order to right the sensory disintegration which each day produced:

> I have an affinity with trees and I never sleep much. I would go out and about in the various woodlands around my university at night, and play my flute like the pagan god Pan, listening to the echoes which were particular to those locations and totally losing myself in the sound. I could make myself virtually invisible in the woods I knew so well. The university was close to where I was brought up. Other students never found who it was, out there, look as they might. They did not have my ability to travel through the woods in total darkness. I have since seen that other people on the Autism spectrum have felt an affinity to elfin kind, well, that is the nearest I came to it. Totally wild and free, you cannot beat it.

This is sensory integration at its best, moving through the darkness, accompanied by movement, smelling the breathing wood. I love it, empathize with it. But I don't actually need it, because I can say, 'Tomorrow's another day,' as a means of shrugging this day off, rather than as defining another looming test of character.

Jane Meyerding, in an essay 'Thoughts on Finding Myself Differently Brained', describes her own process as a need to 'decompress', which brings in aspects of Tourette Syndrome, a problem she shares with many Aspergers.

> After every social encounter, from interactions with co-workers on the job to political fundraisers to conversations with store clerks, I go through a period of what seems to be a kind of 'letting off steam'. I wait until I'm alone, and then, when I am able to relax my shell of control, I twitch and vocalize. My hands jump around, flying this way and that, or gesturing elaborately about nothing. Meanwhile, my voice speaks nonsense. I say 'my voice speaks',

because the words are involuntary. My conscious, deliberate mind is not involved. I don't know what I will say until I hear myself say it. Occasionally, I discover that I'm not as alone as I thought I was. The apparently deserted street is inhabited by a man crouching down to inspect the tire of his car, and I wonder for the rest of the day what he thought when this literally jerky middle-aged woman walking by all alone suddenly barked out, 'I don't love you.' Or 'elaborate retirement options'. Or 'thirteen purple penguins'. Or whatever phrase that non-voluntary portion of my brain happens to be using for decompression that day.

The Asperger wiring is taut. It's different. I needed to know about those differences in detail before I took Danny into my home. I was aware of them, of course, but not on this deep and disturbing level.

Humour and compassion, as I said, are my driving forces. Perhaps I should have geared them up more adequately. Perhaps I should have listened to other Aspergers telling their stories, first, so that I could have acknowledged the rich variety of the scattered skills, as well as the effort and anguish that living on the spectrum entails.

Here, then, are some of those stories. I only had to read them.

As you have.

Let's leave the last words of the chapter to the voice of George Handley, a 23-year-old, recently diagnosed Asperger who collects signed photographs, and writes poetry.

A doctor called Asperger that we'll call Hans
Had plenty to do and plenty of plans
To name a syndrome after himself
So that people like me weren't left on the shelf

Many years later thanks to Old Hans
People were diagnosed and they became his fans
Parents and doctors and teachers alike
Understood Asperger Syndrome just like riding a bike

They thanked Old Hans many years on
As the diagnosis kept going on and on
Lots of research does even more good
Just like the books of Tony Attwood

Hans Asperger is sadly no longer with us
But he did leave a lot so that he could give us
We thank him for making our lives so much easier
And I myself feel a whole lot pleasier*

*Pleased does not rhyme with easier

The AQ test

This is a test devised by Simon Baron Cohen and colleagues at the Cambridge Autism Research Centre in the UK. It is designed to measure what they call the AQ, or Autism Quotient, to show the extent of autistic traits in any adult. It isn't a fail-safe test, and isn't a diagnosis, but you may be interested in trying it as, along the way, you could get further insight into the Asperger world.

Just circle your preferred answer, then check the scoring at the end.

The team at Cambridge discovered in the first major trial of this test that the average score of a control group of NTs was 16.5 (my score was 14) whereas 80 per cent of those diagnosed as being on the autistic spectrum scored 32 or above.

Characteristic	Yes	No
1. I prefer to do things with others rather than on my own.		
2. I prefer to do things the same way over and over again.		
3. If I try to imagine something, I find it very easy to create a picture in my mind.		
4. I frequently get so strongly absorbed in one thing that I lose sight of other things.		
5. I often notice small sounds when others do not.		
6. I usually notice car number plates or similar strings of information.		
7. Other people frequently tell me what I've said is impolite, even though I think it is polite.		
8. When I'm reading a story, I can easily imagine what the characters might look like.		
9. I am fascinated by dates.		
10. In a social group, I can easily keep track of several different people's conversations.		
11. I find social situations easy.		
12. I tend to notice details that others do not.		
13. I would rather go to a library than to party.		
14. I find making up stories easy.		
15. I find myself drawn more strongly to people than to things.		
16. I tend to have very strong interests, which I get upset about.		
17. I enjoy social chitchat.		

	Characteristic	Yes	No
18.	When I talk, it isn't always easy for others to get a word in edgewise.		
19.	I am fascinated by numbers.		
20.	When I'm reading a story, I find it difficult to work out the character's intentions.		
21.	I don't particularly enjoy reading fiction.		
22.	I find it hard to make new friends.		
23.	I notice patterns in things all the time.		
24.	I would rather go to the theatre than to a museum.		
25.	It does not upset me if my daily routine is disturbed.		
26.	I frequently find that I don't know how to keep a conversation going.		
27.	I find it easy to 'read between the lines' when someone is talking to me.		
28.	I usually concentrate more on the whole picture, rather than on the small details.		
29.	I am not very good at remembering phone numbers.		
30.	I don't usually notice small changes in a situation or a person's appearance.		
31.	I know how to tell if someone listening to me is getting bored.		
32.	I find it easy to do more than one thing at once.		
33.	When I talk on the phone, I'm not sure when it's my turn to speak.		
34.	I enjoy doing things spontaneously.		
35.	I am often the last to understand the point of a joke.		
36.	I find it easy to work out what someone is thinking or feeling just by looking at their face.		
37.	If there is an interruption, I can switch back to what I was doing very quickly.		
38.	I am good at social chitchat.		
39.	People often tell me that I keep going on and on about the same thing.		
40.	When I was young, I used to enjoy playing games involving pretending with other children.		

Characteristic	Yes	No
41. I like to collect information about categories of things (e.g. types of cars, birds, trains, plants).		
42. I find it difficult to imagine what it would be like to be someone else.		
43. I like to carefully plan any activities I participate in.		
44. I enjoy social occasions.		
45. I find it difficult to work out people's intentions.		
46. New situations make me anxious.		
47. I enjoy meeting new people.		
48. I am a good diplomat.		
49. I am not very good at remembering people's date of birth.		
50. I find it very easy to play games with children that involve pretending.		

Scoring

If you answered 'Yes' to questions 2, 4, 5, 6, 7, 9, 12, 13, 16, 18, 19, 20, 21, 22, 23, 26, 33, 35, 39, 41, 42, 43, 45, 46 score 1 point.

If you answered 'No' to questions 1, 3, 8, 10, 11, 14, 15, 17, 24, 25, 27, 28, 29, 30, 31, 32, 34, 36, 37, 38, 40, 44, 47, 48, 49, 50 score 1 point.

Add the points together to get your score.

Aspergers' own websites or articles as featured in this chapter

Marc Segar www.autismandcomputing.org.uk/marc2.en.html

Kevin Phillips www.angelfire.com/amiga/aut

Jane Meyerding http://staff.washington.edu/mjane

Wendy Lawson www.mugsy.org/wendy

Joel www.geocities.com/growingjoel

Larry Arnold www.geocities.com/CapitolHill/7138

Kalen www.worldapart.org

George Handley www.angelfire.com/co4/asperger

Personal accounts by Aspergers

Gunilla Gerson, *A Real Person: Life on the Outside*, Souvenir Press, 1977

First-hand, moving account of a painful childhood in a dysfunctional family. Gunilla was diagnosed in her mid-twenties.

Temple Grandin and M.M. Scariano, *Emergence Labelled Autistic*, Warner Books, 1986

The ground-breaking personal account of high-functioning autism. Dr Temple Grandin, an American academic in the field of animal handling, was the subject of an essay by Oliver Sacks in *An Anthropologist on Mars*.

Wendy Lawson, *Life Behind Glass: A Personal Account of Autistic Spectrum Disorder*, Jessica Kingsley Publishers, 2000

This is the full story of Wendy's struggle to survive her early misdiagnosis of schizophrenia and her life after diagnosis, told in the warm, open style which characterizes all her writing.

Jerry Newport, Ron Bass (Foreword), *Your Life Is Not a Label: A Guide To Living Fully with Autism and Asperger's Syndrome*, Future Horizons, 2001

Jerry's account of his life as a high-functioning autistic in the USA has a foreword by the scriptwriter of Rainman, Ron Bass.

Marc Segar, *Coping: A Survival Guide for People with Asperger Syndrome*, obtainable from Early Years Diagnostic Centre, 272 Longdale Lane, Ravenshead, Notts, UK, NG15 9AH

This is the published version of Marc's story which can also be read on the website.

Stephen Shore, *Beyond the Wall: Personal Experiences with Autism and Asperger Syndrome*, Autism Asperger Publishing Co, 2001

Stephen is a thoughtful Asperger, having recently completed (as a mature student) his PhD at an American university.

Liane Holliday Willey, *Pretending To Be Normal. Living with Asperger Syndrome*, Jessica Kingsley Publishers, 1999

Liane is an American university lecturer whose diagnosis came in adulthood. She has an Asperger's Syndrome daughter, too.

Donna Williams, *Nobody Nowhere* and *Somebody Somewhere*, Transworld, 1992 and 1994

Donna's books are particularly influential. These two track the history of her high-functioning autism, and the changes she discovered when her diet was modified to exclude gluten and casein. Riveting reading.

Fictional characters who display characteristics of Asperger's Syndrome

Mr Spock (*Star Trek*) – the typical left-brained logician

Frank Spencer (*Some Mothers Do 'Ave 'Em*) – the innocent dyspraxic

Mr Bean (*Mr Bean*) – inappropriate gesture, facial expression, and obsessional behaviour

A.I. Artificial Intelligence – lack of innate understanding of social and emotional behaviour

Raymond Babbit (*Rainman*) – an exaggerated picture, but useful for understanding some of the routine behaviours

Cliff Clavin (*Cheers*) – a mine of factual information without real understanding

Professor Higgins (*My Fair Lady*) – a tendency to dismiss the human reality of others

Sherlock Holmes (Various) – the obsession with detail and how problems are constructed

Cary Grant in *Bringing Up Baby* – see Chapter 4

4 Bringing Up Baby

I chose this chapter heading carefully.

It's the title of a film that was always my favourite, a screwball comedy starring Cary Grant and Katherine Hepburn.

It could have starred Danny and me.

In the movie, Katherine Hepburn plays Susan, a woman with a mission to get her man. To help her, or hinder her, she has a leopard – the 'baby' of the title.

The man she's chasing, David, is building a dinosaur skeleton, and looking for one bone, an intercostal clavicle with which to complete it. The bone is stolen and buried by a small dog.

If you've seen the film, you're probably already laughing at the joke. If you haven't seen it, please do so immediately as I've never seen any representation of a relationship between an Asperger man and an NT woman so wonderfully, and painfully, close to the truth.

David is a typical Asperger man. He's rigid in his behaviour, totally artless and innocent, driven by compulsion to complete his rituals and his obsessions – building a dinosaur. He knows none of the rules of behaviour, so breaks all the social conventions without realizing it. He's clumsy, dogged and distracted, dependable yet clueless, a man who prioritizes objects over people. People merely confuse him. He uses words inappropriately, choosing idiomatic language which he doesn't really understand. At one point he says, 'I've gone gay, all of a sudden!' It's the first ever movie use of the word, but it's one I'd like you to bear in mind. David dresses badly, in a dress, in flip flops.

That's Danny.

Susan is a wild child, graceful and iconoclastic, someone who knows the rules yet defiantly breaks them. She's capable of anything – winning at golf, or rescuing David from his narrow obsession – and will go to any lengths to succeed at her appointed task. For Susan, emotions and other people define the world she lives in. She's clever, confident, will resort to subterfuge and is fearless in all social situations knowing that she has 'misstery' over them. She dresses well, except when she loses the back of her dress, is charming when she wants to be, and is the human equivalent of that leopard, just as David is the human equivalent of that little dog.

Susan is me.

So we two stars started out playing our relationship as a screwball comedy, fast-paced, farcical, in the topsy-turvy world that we created together, and it was fun from the beginning to the end of each madcap day.

I loved the fact that Danny would wake up each day with a smile on his face, saying 'Hellooooooo,' in a surprised but delighted way, while rubbing his eyes ferociously with the heels of his hands. I knew you weren't supposed to do that with contact lenses, but he rarely took them out, and never rinsed them with solution, and who was I to argue? I overlooked the fact that this was after midday when I brought him a cup of coffee to stir him from his deep sleep. Well, this was the early days. Surely you remember that stage in a relationship where taking someone coffee in bed wasn't a chore? It's brief, but wonderful, in a slavish way.

I loved the wild plans he had, that we would be very rich, live in a huge house, buy a Land Rover Discovery, Danny's dream car, and live happily ever after.

'But I can't have your babies,' I told him.

'Men want children to be the same as the woman they love. The woman I love can't have my babies, so why would I want babies that aren't like you?' he said.

That was good enough for me. Well, more than good enough, actually.

I loved his enthusiasm for retail therapy, which became one of his excited buzz words. 'Retail therapy!' he'd whoop as we set off for yet another spree. Shopping with and for him was a total pleasure. I'd so much missed the shopping trips I'd taken with my son, when he was younger. Danny had, as my son has, an affinity for conspicuous consumerism. Unlike my son, he had no inherent dress sense whatsoever. He yearned to be well-dressed as well as comfortable, and both of us, brought up in frugality, searched for designer bargains in sales and at a sales' shop, which became our haunt. I directed him to plain classic garments he'd never have chosen for himself. Black T-shirts and black jeans suited him so much better than the garish check shirts and rugby tops, the pleat-fronted trousers and the ripped jeans he'd favoured.

He would happily try on our bargain finds for hours afterwards, preening in front of the bedroom mirror, disappearing for ages, only to return in a different combination of the clothes I'd bought for him. It was part of his complex and confusing Asperger nature to want to look and sound what he referred to as 'cool'. For him this meant that he'd adjusted to a world in which previously he'd been treated as different and unacceptable in most situations.

Coolness meant that he had beaten the social stigmas, and that now he had become elevated even over his peers. He was a force to be reckoned with, he assumed.

And I imagine that my position and lifestyle helped in his mission to become the king of cool. He was sometimes almost in awe of the attention I could command, standing back yet beaming at me when I caught his eye if I talked to someone who had seen me on television. If I was important, and he was important to me, then, by syllogism, he was important.

'We're cool,' he'd say to me, proudly.

The word was dated and incongruous, what it implied wasn't worth having, yet it mattered to Danny, so I gritted my teeth and let cool wash over me.

After almost two years of deprivation, Danny now had his driver's licence back, and we had a car. It was my car. I'd bought it for my son the previous Christmas, but he'd found that living in London made car-ownership impracticable. When he'd been badly scared by a huge bill for car-parking fines, he decided to bring the car home, an occasion which neatly coincided with Danny's moving in. So the car-ownership was mine, and the driver was Danny.

This was as exciting for me as it was for him. I'd stopped driving fifteen years earlier, and had resolved never to start again. Driving had become something I feared, so I'd moved to within walking distance of the city centre shops and the railway station, resolving never to get behind a wheel, a decision no one could understand.

On the other hand, I yearned to be driven, to have that freedom of movement, to be liberated from checking timetables and routes to get me to where I sometimes wanted to go. Without a car, doing something on a whim is impossible, as we all know.

Now there was Danny, renewing his love affair with a world on wheels, whizzing me out of the city and round the countryside, to visit places I hadn't seen for years. It seemed symbolic of the way my life was opening up to new experience, and coping with it – more than coping, exulting in it. Getting to the studio for my radio show was easier with Danny driving than it had been when I had to rely on, and pay for, taxis. Shopping for food became so easy, although there were new etiquettes for me to learn about supermarket parking, trolley-loading and boot-filling. Yes, I know that sounds childish, and I should be ashamed of myself, but if you've never had a car, how do you know about these interesting things? The excitement this generated made me start to wonder, very tentatively, whether I could do it. With Danny at my side, could I start driving again? I almost didn't dare hope that his confidence, tenderness and calmness could help me overcome my one major hang-up. He was a very competent driver.

Almost as if Fate were conspiring to promote this crazy partnership, there was another donation to our happy fund. When I arrived for my radio show on the week Danny moved in, the programme controller was waiting with a bottle of champagne. My show had quadrupled the number of listeners on Sunday nights within the year we'd been running. It was the biggest audience gain ever, for the station, and my reward, apart from the champagne, was a pay rise and an extra night, Wednesdays.

'You're my lucky star!' I laughed, hugging Danny.

'And you're my guiding star,' he said, movingly.

It was all the best fun I'd had in years, as you can imagine. Writing is a reclusive job. Answering painful telephone calls on a radio show is a stressful job. And here I was, suddenly with a stress-busting package of new moves to make and a new cuddly toy to play with. And yes, he was cuddly. He was sweet and loveable with an entire battery of captivating little expressions, child expressions. He would bite his lip and raise his eyebrows, looking for all the world like a mischievous, seductive mouse. He would place one flat finger on his pursed lips and make an 'oooohh' sound when he'd made an innocent error. If you've seen the old British television comedy, *Some Mothers Do 'Ave 'Em* then you'll recognize this Frank Spencer move. I wondered if Danny modelled himself on Frank Spencer, or whether the Frank Spencer character, bumbling and innocent, was based on an Asperger.

At other times Danny was mentally acute, communicative and eager, asking for my opinion, asking for help, asking for logical explanations, providing even more information about the way his mind and his life worked. He was always switched on at these times, intelligent and articulate, groping for self-awareness, and often, seemingly, finding it. He liked me to read to him, especially poetry. He enjoyed our quiet meals when we sat outside until dark, talking, and listening to music. His tastes were identical to mine, and as eclectic as mine – Mozart and Radiohead, Elgar and Oasis, Boccherini and Blues. He was freed from his stress too. The move had lifted his mood, solved his financial problems, given him the lifestyle to which he aspired and the option of finding what he was looking for.

I thought that was probably a job in the wine trade.

Strangely enough, I read only recently a piece by the British expert on Asperger's Syndrome, Tony Attwood, in which he mentions working in the wine trade as being a perfect job for an Asperger. The Asperger love for information and the rote-memory skills take in the details of vintages and grape blends, while the fine palate, an example of sensory excitation common in AS, makes for a great wine-taster.

I asked around in the city I live in. I call my city a village, as, despite its two universities and its student population, it's compact enough for every settled resident to know everyone else, which can be disconcerting at times, but useful when you're in need. Finally, in a prestigious wine shop owned by a wonderfully eccentric rotund rugby fan, I had an offer. Danny could work for him as a commission-only salesman. It was the job of his dreams. He was determined to make it work. Eventually he would set up an import–export agency, and we'd buy a second home in France. Yes, I knew I was playing make-believe, and I was in the frame of mind to add that to the list of fun and games. I don't think Danny did ever separate his hopes from what was attainable. Magical thinking, the experts call it. But it was a magical time. That year, the lazy warm summer lingered into September, and we lingered with it, sharing good wine and the best company. Ourselves.

At the end of *Bringing Up Baby*, if you know the film, there's a hectic scene of the seduction of the innocent, where Susan finally plants a kiss on David's lips, and both fall on to the dinosaur skeleton which disintegrates magnificently, intercostal clavicle by intercostal clavicle. I just wish our romantic denouement had been so easy and so dramatic. But the realization that Danny's Asperger's Syndrome might be more difficult to adapt to than I'd imagined was a slow and creaking process, one which, at the time, I barely understood. It's only now, in reliving and retelling, that I can identify the first sign of structural weakness.

It was a Thursday night, the first after his triumphant return to his home town, with the car, to collect all his worldly possessions. Actually, he hadn't collected and returned with many of them, just what was essential to his daily living – his entire wine stock. This, then, had to be given a home, which he'd done with his usual neat hyper-focusing organization, clearing out my understairs cupboard and installing his wine racks, transferring his 'laying down' wines into my garage. He'd even checked the large storage room beyond my garage with its sagging plywood floor, and declared that he'd buy some two by four, replace the plywood with boards, and make this our cellar. The temperature, he decided, was perfect. This was where we'd keep our stocks for the import–export business. I was not, yet, at the stage of saying, 'Yeah, yeah, yeah, whatever…' to this fantasy plan, although I knew that he'd left his own home in a state of half-completed bungling. I was surprised that he even knew what two by four was. Needless to say, the refurbishment never happened.

He'd returned, too, with news of his mother's response.

She'd said, he announced to me, 'So, what're you going to do this time? Bleed her dry then dump her, I suppose?'

I laughed when he told me this, shocked at her predictable unkindness and bluntness.

'I knew you'd do that!' he said.

'What?'

'Laugh. I told mother, "I'm going to tell Barbara what you said, and she'll laugh."'

He was very pleased that I'd reacted as programmed. He thought he could read me perfectly. Oh dear.

So, on this Thursday night, we sat outside over the remains of our meal, in the dusk, with candles and wine on the table, talking about the first Wednesday radio show of the previous night, listening to a CD. He wasn't as attentive as usual. He was replying to me with more of his catch-all multi-meaning sounds rather than with words, and tugging at one of his curls, repetitively. I was tired. The previous two or three weeks had been an emotional storm for me, and the radio show always drained me for at least twenty-four hours.

'Are you all right?' I asked.

'It's Thursday,' he said.

'Yes? And?' I wondered if there was something he wanted to watch on television.

'I usually go out for a drink on Thursday,' he said.

'Oh?' We'd talked about his cutting down on his drinking, now that he was happy.

'It's…it's not the booze,' he tried to explain. 'It's the buzz. I miss the buzz.'

'You want to go out? Now?' I asked. It was almost ten.

He nodded, quickly. 'Yes, please.'

So we went out. I promised him a quick view of the city's bars. And that's exactly what happened. I showed him the student places, the upmarket places, the secret places, just a few of them, and we were home moments after midnight. He was as good as his word, drinking very little.

But that night disconcerted me, in ways which may be difficult to explain, so bear with me.

Asperger's is very subtle, and the behaviour that I'm about to describe here, you may well think is nothing that out of the ordinary. But, unless you know an Asperger, it's unlikely you have ever seen anything quite like this.

He was eager, desperate to get his coat and leave. Smiling as usual, there was a stiff tension in his body, despite his silly little antics which were designed to amuse me and put me at my ease so that I'd allow him what he genuinely needed. He made his little baby faces, his speech became animated, he did a funny walking step, a double march to keep his footsteps in time with mine. It was endearing, but oddly graceless.

He'd warned me. He said he needed space, but I thought that meant he didn't want to be crowded out by too much of my presence or demands, and I understood that completely. Both my son and I hate space invaders, yet had managed to live comfortably, cheek by spaced jowl, for twenty years. But the space Danny needed most of all was in his head, and one of the places he could get that, as he knew but I didn't, was in a crowded bar with music playing and people talking. The busier the better. That's something that nothing had prepared me for, not anything I'd read, nor anything I'd worked out from his previous behaviour.

He hung back, slightly behind me as we walked into each bar. Unlike a genuine alcoholic, who would march purposefully to the bar to shorten the distance between himself and his addiction, Danny was in no hurry. I was the one who bought the drinks. Even my question 'What will you have?' was met almost with blankness. As soon as we walked in, his face changed. It fell into a kind of smiling emptiness. If you'd seen it, you'd have asked, 'Are you still with us?' It was the kind of expression you usually wave your hand across, to try to gain attention when someone has gone off into a world of their own. You might have assumed he was high on something, seriously preoccupied, or in the middle of an important daydream.

It wasn't system overload. This was system shutdown. It was the message on your computer screen which says, 'Please wait while your computer closes down.' Can you imagine sitting watching that message for hours? I talked to him. He responded vaguely, just about recognizing that he was not alone. I knew this was happiness, but I had never seen happiness like it. This must be like a car engine feels when petrol is being fed into its tank.

I've read about sensory dissociation. I'd never seen it. But the odd thing about this particular dissociation was that it seemed recuperative. Around him, from bar to bar, things happened that might, you would have thought, cause sensory overload in a vulnerable Asperger – sounds, smells, happenings, textural changes. But he was using that chaos to help him switch the world, and me, off, and connect with some restorative inner mechanism. It was almost antagonistic in function, in its use of all those external sensory experiences to drown out internal sensory experience, like rubbing a painful muscle with some distracting heat or cold to numb it. It was hyposensitivity. Just as some Aspergers almost scream at the slightest sound, others need loud noise, and even welcome it, as Kalen said.

Sometimes he made 'Shuu shuu' whispering sounds with the loud recorded music, moving his head to one shoulder, then the other. If he was standing, he swayed very slightly, almost rhythmically. More disturbingly, he 'danced' his eyes, making the irises jump around like animated hamsters.

'Please don't do that,' I begged. It made me feel sick.

'Don't you like it?' he laughed.

'No,' I insisted.

It was as if he were using his own body parts like disconnected objects, manipulating them, much as you might do in puppetry. He'd done it with his funny walking step. This was a million times more incongruous and self-fragmenting.

'One of the girls I went out with liked it, so I've been doing it ever since,' he explained. It wasn't much of an explanation, nor was it one I accepted. It was dissociation of the most extreme kind.

But the evening ended happily. Danny's strange wiring system had been oiled, redirected and refuelled, enabling it to function efficiently. He slept easily, comfortably, with one arm flung over my sleepless body. I had never witnessed before anything like that plug-in to normalization that I had seen with Danny that evening.

So let's go over the Asperger features here. First, 'It's Thursday, therefore I must do…' This is repetitive, routine behaviour. We know all about that. Danny's routines. I'd underestimated their power.

Next, 'I'm getting overanxious with too much emotional bonding, therefore I must do…'

This is an overload, which I hadn't even realized. Until he started to self-stim, pulling at his hair, I'd thought that he was happy and settled.

Finally, 'I must get a fix from some buzz.'

And this was the one where my all-encompassing understanding had come to a cul de sac. The behaviours he'd shown just hadn't figured in my lexicon. I was beyond the limits of my knowledge, but my compassion was still in place. My logic, which Danny admired so much, told me that if one way to deal with overload is to separate and hibernate functions of mind, body, feeling, in order to revitalize and restructure the functions in turn, then I was not incapable of coping with the idea, was I?

What do you think?

And now, more cracks appeared in our skeletal relationship.

In a questionnaire I sent out to partners of people with Asperger's Syndrome (see page 143) I asked the question, 'Is your partner passive, passive aggressive, or controlling?' Every questionnaire had the same response to that question. The response was, 'All three.'

Let me show you what they, and I – who would have written exactly the same – mean by that.

We were at 'our' club. It was the gay club we'd been to before, one at which Danny felt very much at home. He had an affinity with transgression, loved the feeling that he was in the company of those who might be marginalized by the majority, just as he was, and loved the noise and excitement of the place. So did I. There was plenty to see. Troupes of brilliant amateur divas would crowd the podium to do their version of the Steps song, 'Tragedy', with all the actions. People knew me there. It was frequented by the media crowd, straight as well as gay, there was no prejudice, and I always had friends to chat to while Danny was spacing out in recuperation.

He had settled on a routine for Friday or Saturday nights. We would start with a visit to a bar, also gay-friendly, which sold double measures of spirits, with a mixer, at the cheapest rate in the city. Here, while I drank water, or a single brandy poured on a large glass of ice, he would order ten gin and tonics, one after the other. Sometimes, in an effort to speed up the process, he would order all ten at the same time, pour them into a pint glass, and drink slowly from this until he'd achieved the correct level of numbness.

He was a gentle drunk, a smiling, cuddly, nuzzling drunk, once his spacing ritual was complete. As a former rugby player, he'd been well trained in the drinking culture, so even though I, as you would be too, was disconcerted by the amount of alcohol he consumed, he usually handled it well, on the surface.

That night, after his gins, he ordered a pint at the club, installed himself as usual on a stool at the bar, and danced his little 'shuu shuu' head dance as he drank. Suddenly he turned to me and said, 'I don't like you smoking.'

This was an odd statement. I'd once given up for ten years, was a non-smoker when he met me, but, stressed by his absences from my life and his inexplicably bad behaviour, I'd started again, this time rolling my own cigarettes by hand, something he found fascinating and 'cool', as he'd pointed out several times.

Now it irritated him, in an instant.

'Why?' I asked.

'I don't like the smell,' he said.

This was fair comment, brooking little argument. However, he smoked too, at weekends while he drank. He smoked cigars. And every one of the women he'd partnered, except for Heather, had smoked. This appeared inconsistent.

'OK,' I said. 'I won't smoke.'

I actually didn't get much from the habit, and I hated the smell on myself, but could I manage to quit?

I put my tobacco, papers and lighter in an ashtray, and said, 'You'll help me through it then?'

'Yes,' he said.

He didn't. He never mentioned it again, never congratulated me on the effort, never commented on how much better everything was without my nasty habit. In fact, it seemed to impact on him hardly at all. For three months I kept it up, occasionally sneaking out to see my friend who lived across the road, to borrow a roll-up from her when things got bad. At weekends he'd allow me a small cigar.

It had become a means for him of asserting control.

Then the control spread to both time and place. He needed to re-establish the order in which he'd previously lived, his own timetable and his own spaces. Passive, a natural receiver rather than a transmitter, it was the only way he could stop the world giddying round his head. Space to be his secret self, space where he could decompress, wind down, assume a position of safety, was his first priority again, as it had always been.

He established his own parallel home in the back bedroom. The parallel play of the Asperger child, remember that? Aspergers as children play alongside rather than with others. This was a noisy room, as the one-bedroomed flat above was occupied by a dysfunctional family of three with a hyperactive child, a mother who had frequent tantrums, and a father who drank heavily. I preferred not to sleep there, as I was always disturbed by a late-night argument, the child's morning hysteria or the rollicking sounds of love-making.

Danny didn't mind any of these things. He slept through anything, as I've already pointed out. So when he collected his computer from home, he set it up in this bedroom, and would hide there all day, surfing the Internet, pretending to work, or perseverating on a task he hadn't been asked to do by the wine merchant. He took to sleeping there too.

The change was subtle, and very gradual. At first it was just, 'I'll work a little longer, you go to bed,' but he would rarely join me. If I woke and went to the bathroom, he'd be fast asleep, the computer still shedding grey light across the bed. He had taken over the room.

He also took control of the car. Yes, I know that this is natural, the driver usually assumes command. And most women know that the two things a man claims as his are the car keys and the television remote control. But Danny took control of the car as a coping mechanism, something that provided him with the means of escape in all senses of the word.

He'd told me that one of the activities which relaxed him totally was driving. I believe that when he was driving he assumed the 'auto-pilot' stage of consciousness which helped, just as the refuelling by noise and music did, to burn off the tensions which socializing always caused.

In one of the questionnaires I sent out to partners of AS men and women, a woman told me that when she met her Asperger husband he had some strange habits which he couldn't explain. One of these was driving sixty miles each day, for his lunch. The drive would take over an hour each way.

An Asperger from the US told me of a visit he had made to his home town to see relatives, after which he got straight into his car and drove the thousand miles back to where he lived without stopping. He said that he was exhausted, but throughout the drive felt his 'self' returning, coming back from behind the social mask he'd had to assume while behaving in accordance with his family's expectations of what was normal.

In Danny's case the obsessional need to get away and get behind the wheel of the car became more apparent the longer he lived with me. My hopes that the car would open up my world were dashed. Danny was always in the car, out with the car, returning later than expected, unable to take me to hospital appointments because he was 'working', unable to take me shopping very often as he'd be elsewhere. The only time he drove me was, as arranged, to my radio shows, and soon even that was slightly re-organized.

Every other week he made the long trip which he loved, three hundred miles each way back to his home town. There was always some reason for this journey. Sometimes he was picking up possessions, but, as he became established at the wine merchant's, he set up a delivery route of wines to his old friend who owned the hotel in his town.

He would leave early on Thursdays, returning on Sundays in time to take me to the radio station. Then he re-arranged this timetable. I would get the train or a taxi to Birmingham for the show; he would meet me to bring me, and himself, home.

He was always happy and relaxed when he returned. He'd been able to indulge in three nights' drinking, on the pretext of wine-tasting and hospitality. He'd been 'buzzed', and he'd had that long drive to restore his basic functioning. There would have to be 'chippy chippy chip chips' on the way back, and in his own time there'd be excited stories about how he'd made the breakthrough on wine distribution down there, boasting that soon he'd be supplying all the hotels on the coast, that he'd hire a van to take down the orders he expected to get. It was Danny at his grandiose best.

The other routine he had to re-assert was 'training'. I was never quite sure what this training was for, on a practical level. Occasionally, he'd talk about joining a rugby club, but he didn't even go so far as to accept the offer of the wine merchant, to join the club which he belonged to. That would have meant playing on Sundays, and Danny's Sundays were already allotted a slot in the rituals calendar. Sundays were for sleeping and teetotalism, after the Saturday night binge, and then for another drive to the radio station, with the radio playing on both outward and return journeys.

Funded by me, he joined my gym, set himself a punishing regime, and, when life became too much for him, he'd drive to the gym, exercise until he'd exorcised every demonic human contact, then return back, starving hungry, often much later than he said he'd be. But still, entranced by his tricks and giggles, I'd cook for us, rejoicing in his 'this is scrummy!' enthusiasm for a feeding frenzy.

So, you're probably saying to yourself, this is no different from most people's relationships. Couples do tend to lead lives in parallel, busy with their own careers, their own priorities. Yes, they do. But on the other hand, there remains a feeling of contact, team work, a sense that each is in it in order to satisfy the third party – not just 'me', not just 'you', but the separate and conjoined article we call 'us'. That feeling of contact wasn't quite there. There wasn't really an 'us'.

Of course we still had our Saturday nights, our chance to socialize. This was what initially I'd enjoyed so much, being freed from my reclusive life at the computer, on the telephone, on the air. I'd been able, in Danny's company, to rediscover the music that had always been a part of my young life, and the laughter, too, and the slightly voyeuristic mischief.

On the fortnightly Saturdays when he was around I would stand or sit at his side, watching him decompress, watching the initial inhibition which would then slip into giggles and nuzzles. But, as I told him, 'Drinking isn't a spectator sport.' The Saturday night ritual would then reach a plateau of cuddliness. Finally, without warning, he'd enter the next phase, one which most of us would describe as malevolent. During that phase, which could last up to an hour, anything could happen.

Sometimes it was relatively harmless. One night, during this phase, he suddenly reached across the bar with his cupped hand, neatly slopping half a pint of spilt beer into my lap.

'Look at my skirt!' I shrieked.

'I never liked that one,' he said.

On another Saturday he slipped from his chair to stand behind me. I talked to others who were around, but worried about why he was standing there, and what he could be doing.

Then I saw three girls in the corner, grinning at some point beyond my left shoulder. When I turned, there he was, making his little mouse faces at them, flashing his sweet innocent seductive glances at them, flirting. This was what he'd described to me as The Game, something he played every Saturday night, and which he had once played, on a holiday in Spain, with me. The object of the game was to entice, to provoke reaction, to bed. He said it was meaningless, just something he liked to do, to prove that he could.

'I think we should go,' I said, icy with fury and sobriety.

We did. He was unhappy, stamping angrily at my side.

'Why did you do that, Danny?' I begged. 'We were with friends. What on earth must they have thought? Flirting with those girls while you were out with me, it's just not on!'

'You don't know, do you? You don't understand anything!' he spat.

'Understand what?'

'Oh, leave it. Forget it. You don't know what I just did for you.'

'What?' I persisted. 'What did you do *for* me?'

'Well, all right. I'll tell you! Those girls just wanted me to go with them. They asked me to dance and then go back home with them. And you know what I said? I said, I can't because I love Barbara!' he squeaked.

So, where would I start? I was speechless. He'd just displayed one socially inept and inane move after another. First, the flirtation, which must have been going on for some time. There must have been some direct contact, some chat between him and the girls, perhaps while I was in the Ladies', for this invitation to have been made. His flirtation had announced his availability. Then came his refusal, in all its wrongly worded and accidentally hurtful innocence, belying the body language he'd been giving out. I almost felt sorry for the girls. They must have found the retort as strange as I did. But at least I understood that it came from social dysfunctionality that was part of a syndrome, which was sometimes beyond my capacity to deal with. This was one of those times.

How on earth could he have thought that the silly form of words he'd just used could wipe out the hurt he'd inflicted? When had 'I love' ever been made to sound so hollow?

'Oh hell, Danny,' I sighed. 'This thing really screws you up at times.'

It was October, only six weeks since he'd moved in, and while the joys still exceeded the pain, the rituals and the impairments were becoming very noticeable.

There was an autism conference on the Internet, which I decided to join. Each day there were presentations about different aspects of the spectrum. Many of them were illuminating, and some of the comments I'd relay to

Danny, if he was lounging about at home, or when he came back home after a busy day at work with his Big Red Diary containing the lists of things to do that day tucked under his arm. He never let that diary out of his sight. He'd insisted I bought it for him to keep his life together. It wasn't doing a great job so far. 'Take Barbara shopping' was dutifully written down in there week after week. It didn't happen.

At the autism conference there were message boards. I posted a message, giving an outline of my relationship, asking for any help from Aspergers, or partners of Aspergers, which might ease the way through for Danny and me.

There, online, I met an Asperger man who was willing to advise me. Creative and articulate, he was an academic, studying for a PhD in psychology at a US university where he also taught. I've told you that so that you can see how finely Aspergers can adapt to defy some of the notions which even experts hold about them. Aspergers as psychologists? Yes, it's possible. This psychologist's post to me, after I'd sent him some of the material I'd written about Danny, was empathetic, thoughtful, but very blunt, in that unmistakable Asperger way.

As far as sex and love are concerned, they are not necessarily connected, but the rest of the relationship is troubling to me. It sounds more co-dependent than egalitarian. Autistics are often childlike; Asperger even confessed he found an irresistible elfin beauty in them. That is how people often find me, but I am not Danny. My life has been surreal, and difficult. Things that most people only read about in novels, I have done. I learned to love, to feel, to be human. I think, from your description, that Danny doesn't possess this capacity. You would know better than I, however.

I can tell you one thing that is too true, and I'm sure you're aware of it as well. I only say it as a reminder. You can't save Danny. You can't really change Danny. Danny has to do that himself, and maybe he needs to be left to his own devices in order to learn. As long as he has someone that he doesn't have to be too close to, someone who he knows will insulate him from the world, he won't grow because he won't have the incentive to grow. It seems harsh and cruel, but then sometimes harshness and cruelty are what it takes to teach us about life. Danny seems to have a long pattern of relationships wherein he was looking for a caretaker, and not really interested in love.

In my humble opinion, and realizing what opinions are worth, I would say that he needs to be touched with fire – to be inspired. Unfortunately, this will probably require that you sit him down and explain in plain terms why you have to set him free. He won't like it, and he'll feel hurt, which will be hard on you. However, the alternative is to become the lifelong babysitter for him. I don't think that's fair to you or to Danny.

It all comes down to what you believe. Do you believe you would be happy being the nanny for a man with arrested development, who may never truly return your love? Are you willing to risk that? Or do you believe that he can overcome the obstacles in his life, if he knows he has a friend he can come to when things are very hard? What do you want? You can't help what Danny wants.

What do you want for yourself?

Oh dear. There were too many things in that email which I knew to be true.

There were also things which were too personal to share with this internet stranger. I'd told him the relationship was sexless, as that seemed to be the easiest way to describe it. The truth was far more complex, difficult for either of us to understand. There was an almost incandescent physical and sexual intimacy between us, something I've rarely experienced with anyone else. Together we glowed and fizzled and sparked, so powerfully that other people constantly remarked on it. Whatever he knew about himself, he'd share without limitation, and his painful eventual confession that sex meant nothing to him at all, and did nothing for him at all, was part of that total trust.

That it meant something to me was irrelevant to him. If I wanted him to go through the motions, he said he would, for my sake, but I would have to initiate it, because, unless he was playing The Game, he was completely sexually passive, a sexual object, and always had been. It explained why 'Have Sex' was on Heather's list for him of Things To Do. Where he truly loved and trusted, he couldn't perform unless compelled to, and compulsion isn't part of my armoury.

Once or twice, much later, he threw that at me.

'You could have had sex with me any time you wanted to!' he said. 'You just didn't know how!'

But I did know how. Meaninglessly. Robotically. It's not my style.

And what, that psychologist asked, did I want? I wanted Danny to be happy, whatever it took.

Sometimes, it almost seemed that he was. Excitedly, one day, he called me in the morning. It was one of those rare mornings when he'd got to the wine shop early, and he was now ringing to tell me that he was coming home because he needed to change his clothes.

'I'm going on television!' he squealed. He was like a small child, fussing over every detail of how he looked as he changed into the very expensive black suit I'd bought for him, and a lilac shirt.

'Which tie? Which tie?' he demanded, waving a selection in front of me. I chose. He agreed, and soon, with a little wriggle of his fingers in goodbye, he was on his way back to the shop for his fifteen minutes of fame.

The local television station was doing an item on fake champagne and had sought the expertise of the wine merchant, who had refused to appear in front of the camera. So it was Danny who had been chosen to comment on the contents of various bottles of cheap pomagne which had been dressed up to look like vintage bubbly, and to rate them against the real thing.

We both giggled over the transmission that night. He was authoritative, looked like a film star, and had learnt well from his six weeks' training as a wine salesman.

'Look at this,' he said in the news item, holding up the glass of fake champagne to the light. 'The colour's too pale, the bubbles settle when they come into contact with the air, and when I taste it' – which he then did, pulling a face – 'there's no body, no richness… Whereas this' – he poured a glass of Taittinger – 'Stunning! I could drink this all day!'

Too true.

We videoed the clip and rewound and replayed the tape, revelling in his debut. He had been…stunning.

The job seemed to be going quite well. He hadn't yet received any commission, but, as he said, it was early days, and although he'd managed to extract an order from the two leads supplied by his boss, the wine hadn't been paid for, yet. Nor had the wine which he'd been ferrying southwards. But when it was, he assured me, he'd be in the money.

'It's going well?'

'Fine!' he boasted. 'Just fine!' It was one of his expressions. As was the lisped, 'Ooooh, busy, busy, busy, busy', which was the mood he liked best.

He certainly seemed to enjoy himself with the wine merchant and the rather louche assistant who worked in the shop while Danny drove around touting for customers and planning various Christmas promotions. So I tried to forget that he gossiped with the two middle-aged dilettantes about some of the ups and downs we went through at home.

'I told them you weren't very pleased with me when they'd got me drunk last Saturday afternoon,' he'd giggle. He loved the Saturday afternoon 'wine-tasting' sessions in the shop, when the three of them, and various customers at random, would get falling-down drunk on ridiculously expensive wines… 'Stunning!' was just about all Danny could articulate after one of these sessions. One evening after a Saturday afternoon binge on Bollinger, he announced to me, 'I told them we had a pillow fight last night and I won!'

I really didn't want my private life to be the subject of knowing winks. Shouting at him would be acceptable behaviour in a responsible and respectable grown woman – but pillow fights? Hardly. But then Danny couldn't help himself. He never knew what information it was OK to share, with whom, and why, or why not. He didn't know the subtleties of friendship. For him the two men he worked with were his friends. Just as I was his friend. There were no degrees or gradations of friendship as there would be in most people. We, you and I, would describe our relationships with others around us in a range of words including acquaintance, boss, colleague, mate, and that slimy person you wouldn't want to pass the time of day with. But everyone was Danny's 'friend'. It's a trait he shared with other Aspergers. Here's what one Asperger's partner said about her husband – 'His friends come and go and are all the same to him. His best buddy could be the guy who tried to sell him something today.'

One day I found a pile of printed sheets in his printer, faces of beautiful girls with all the details of their backgrounds.

'What's this?' I asked.

'I printed them off last night from an internet site,' he grinned. 'They're Russian girls looking for a husband. I'm taking them for Simon today, because he's lonely. He needs to get laid.'

Simon was the louche assistant I didn't quite trust, an ex-public school man with aspirations beyond his current bankruptcy. He wore a knotted bandanna around his neck, had a sneering manner, and, from what I could judge, was deeply suspicious of Danny. I didn't think a Russian bride could solve that problem. But Danny had no idea that Simon didn't like him. He couldn't sense the sneers, work out the condescension in his drawling asides, feel the body language of disdain. So Simon exploited him, and got him to design internet advertisements for his sideline as a private pilot. Later on he went to Danny's boss and accused Danny of drinking more wine than he sold. I could have seen it coming. Danny was stunned. He never could work that one out.

But he did, very slowly, arrive at the conclusion that the sales job was not working out as he'd hoped.

When I say he arrived at this conclusion, this is misleading. It suggests that he consciously decided it was going nowhere. This isn't what happened in Danny's jigsaw mind. Unable to differentiate clearly between causes and effects, senses and sense, he slept on it, or rather, he didn't – not at night, anyway. I discovered him prowling in the early hours, raiding the fridge while talking out loud to himself, 'Now what shall I have?', crouching pre-pounce at the open fridge door at four in the morning. Or he'd be lying full length on the living-room sofa, watching Dutch soft-porn movies on satellite television at five, the sound turned to whispering level so as not to wake me. He'd sleep the next day until afternoon, as I became more and more angry with his withdrawal and his inertia. Inertia, although I didn't know it then, is a major problem for Aspergers. There's even a name for it: 'Autistic inertia'. Coffee I took him would be left untouched. My patience wore very thin. There was still no commission paid on the sales he'd made. I didn't realize that he hadn't claimed any.

Then suddenly he cracked. Two wild incidents within a fortnight convinced me that something was desperately wrong, and that, yet again, he was at the end of his tether.

The first was in the club on a Friday night. He had reached the malevolent drunk stage, the hour when anything could happen. He suddenly turned on me, slammed his glass down, and disappeared.

'Now what's up?' sighed one of my gay friends.

'Do you really have to put up with him?' another asked me, gently. 'He puts you through hell. We've all been talking about the way he treats you.'

That brought tears to my eyes. Oh, it wasn't just that I was touched by someone being concerned about my feelings for a change, it was the more complex reason that I, who had been the subject of respect, had now become the object of pity. And there was more. I couldn't explain this apparent bad behaviour to anyone.

'He's got a problem...' I started to say, wondering if in the next ten seconds I could explain Asperger's Syndrome.

'Just the one? Tell us about it!' another friend cooed, disparagingly.

'I'd better look for him,' I said, hurriedly, before anyone could see the tears.

Just as I reached the door, he was leaving. I saw his back. He hadn't collected his coat, so I did that, reclaiming both mine and his, holding his in my arms as I followed him. He was walking away purposefully, bouncing in that odd way of his, dressed only, on this November night, in his black sleeveless T-shirt and jeans.

Then he turned, glared viciously when he saw me following, and stood for a moment as if frozen. Then he ran.

Danny running was usually a thing of beauty. I have him captured in a snapshot which I took on a visit to his coastal town on a strange December day, his birthday, when snow fell on the beach. That photograph shows him in mid-stride, leaping through sand and snow, backed by surf. The image is silver and gold, shot through by sunshine and he is centred, gloriously alive, floating through and on light.

But this was different. The running was aggressive, fearful. He ran first in one direction, then in another, away from, parallel to, skimming through side streets. It reminded me of the rapid scurrying of a wolf spider, rearing up on its eight legs, tacking across the carpet towards some shadow, any shadow.

So I stood there, hugging his coat, only wanting to tell him that he could run if he wanted to but that he might be warmer if he would stop to put it on. Then I walked home. He arrived an hour later. I'd left the door unlocked for him.

Very recently I found a piece written by Jane Meyerding. You remember Jane, from the last chapter? Someone had written a note on an internet message board, asking if she ever ran away, and she said that yes, she ran often. Once she had to get out of a friend's car, three thousand miles away from her home. She just opened the door and ran without any idea of where she might be running to or why. It was the urge to get away that counted, and no other consideration entered into her overloaded brain at the time. This is the kind of behaviour that stuns those who tell you that your Asperger friend or partner isn't any different from the rest of us. Simply, it could be explained that if there isn't enough space an Asperger has to create it, by whatever means possible. Space, enough space, could be created by blank silence, by stimming, by the numbing effect of alcohol, by hiding, by living in the night rather than the distracting day, by driving alone, or, as in this case, by running.

The next afternoon, when Danny woke, he was abject with remorse. Usually, after his binges, he could remember nothing. This time, he did remember running away from me.

'I only wanted you to put your coat on,' I said. His unhappiness made me desperately sad. I held him close, because this time he wanted to be hugged.

'I'm sorry,' he kept crying.

'Let's just lay off the booze tonight?' I suggested.

So we went out for a meal instead. He was subdued. All he managed to tell me was that he knew that the wine job wasn't going to earn him enough to live on, and that perhaps he should think of something else that might work out.

'I could go back to selling windows,' he said, hopelessly.

'Could you? Really?' I smiled.

'No, I couldn't,' he smiled back.

'Do you think it might be better if you moved out and got a flat on your own?' I asked gently. 'I'd help you find one, and we could still be best friends, and I'll help you, like I do now, but you could have your own space.'

He looked stunned. He stared at me, his eyes filling with tears.

'No!' he cried. 'You wouldn't do that to me, would you?'

'I just thought you might be happier,' I tried to explain.

'No!' he insisted again. 'That isn't what I want!'

Within a day or two he was sullen and uncommunicative again, deep in thought, as I realize now. But although logically I knew that this wasn't anger directed specifically at me, that he wasn't trying to upset me by neglecting to eat, or refusing to talk, this is what it felt like. Part of me understood, but part of me yearned for him to react as I knew he couldn't and just try to make me feel better about whatever it was he was worrying about. Mission Impossible.

Then I finally reached breaking point.

It was late one night. We were watching television together, more or less apart.

'Coming to bed?' I asked.

'Huh?' he responded, playing with the remote control flicking through channels. 'No, I think I'll watch this. Not tired yet,' he said.

'This' was a Laurel and Hardy film. Now, call me humourless if you like, but I truly can't stand Laurel and Hardy. The inevitability of chaos and pain is something I just can't laugh at.

'I'm going then,' I snapped, pecking his cheek. 'I'll be with you soon,' he said.

I already knew about Danny's 'soon'. We had, besides 'Danny's Rules', something called 'Danny Time' which was incompatible with Greenwich Mean Time, the mean twenty-four-hour clock, and everyone's patience. I have this happy knack of being able to tell what time it is at any time of the day, but to him, time was a melting Dali watch. He could sit staring into the space behind his eyelids for an entire day and imagine that only five minutes had passed, a trait he shared with many other Aspergers.

At one, I woke up. Total silence. I checked to see whether he'd crept into his bolt-hole, but that bed was empty. He had disappeared.

At two, I collected some bin-liners from a cupboard in the kitchen. Sobbing with anger, I began filling them with the detritus of Danny's chosen living-space. I locked the clothes I had bought for him in the wardrobes, packed the rainbow warrior clothes he had brought from his home into the bags, along with his wine catalogues, his piles of printouts for wine-tastings that never happened, the elegant business cards I'd had printed for him, the files relating to his previous business and the solicitors' letters about that, the piles of unanswered mail from the VAT office and the Inland Revenue… It all went into the bags in less than half an hour, even his 'training' bag containing that night's gym clothes and his smelly trainers.

By three I was Hurricane Barbara, a force to be reckoned with, and one which had destroyed his base camp.

By half past three, when he returned, and I'd found some tobacco and papers I'd secreted away, I had chain-smoked for over an hour, in 'his' room, now reclaimed. I'd left a key in the lock so that his wouldn't work from the outside.

I could hear him fumbling, making lots of 'hmmmm' and 'ooohhh' sounds to himself as he struggled, before I finally opened the door from the inside.

He was cuddly drunk, a small furry animal, blurry-eyed and lost.

'I just thought I'd go to the club,' he said. 'You were asleep.'

'No, Danny, you waited until I was asleep!' I spat, and he giggled and nodded.

'Whoops!' he grinned.

'You can sleep outside tonight. You leave in the morning!' I said.

Within twenty minutes I'd softened. It was that old maxim about the sun going down on your wrath, although by this time the sun was almost coming up, and Danny was curled on a patio chair, his head cradled on his arms which he'd spread on the table. He was smiling, the way small children and large drunks do, in his sleep.

'You can come in and sleep, but you still leave tomorrow,' I told him, leading him to bed and helping him get undressed.

'Ooooooh!' he complained, stumbling over the bags, 'there's bin-liners here!'

'Don't worry, they'll be gone tomorrow,' I said.

Of course, I hardly slept, but Danny slept and slept, and then pretended to sleep some more, all the next day. I wasn't idle, in my angry and sleepless mood. I walked to the shops, bought a local paper, and spent the afternoon circling suitable flats for Danny before taking him his coffee at teatime. I'd also bought some more tobacco, and talked to my friend who said, 'About time you came to your senses. Kick him out. He's a waste of space!'

This time his waking mood was different. He was usually terrified of my anger, crying, reverting to infantilism. Now he listened to my controlled and reasonable explanation of how I could no longer see a future in living together as it was draining both of us, and considered my plan of moving him into a nearby flat.

'It wouldn't work,' he said. I was talking to an adult, albeit a shame-faced one. 'You know what I'm like. It's always all or nothing with me. And this, with you, it's all or nothing. Can't you see that if I left I couldn't see you ever again? I'd think that was the end of the trust between us. I trust you. I don't want never to see you again, but I know that's what I'd do if you betrayed my trust by making me leave you.'

'You'd be happier,' I said, as firmly as I could. 'You need the freedom of your own place. You need to get on with life in your own way.'

'It doesn't work though. I always mess up. I want us to be together.'

'But I can't cope with you, Danny!' I cried. 'You're a law unto yourself. I mean, whatever made you go out last night behind my back – and to a gay club? Can't you see how stupid that was?'

Silly question. He puckered his brow as he tried to think of why he shouldn't go on his own to a gay club, but the question was too baffling. Social rules hadn't been fully transcribed from AS into NT in the Danny rule-book.

'I love you. You're the only person who ever understood me,' he murmured. 'Please don't make me go and leave you. I want to help you, like you help me.'

We talked for most of that night. He told me afterwards that he'd been locked into his own world, and that it was only when he opened his eyes, around midday, saw that I'd packed all his things, and understood that I was serious this time, that he'd been jolted into the real life he shared with me. He'd been lying in bed since, with his eyes closed, wondering what he really wanted to do. He wanted to explain why he'd been unhappy and why the Asperger hiding and running away had got the better of him again.

That's what he did. He told me how impossible it was going to be to continue to do the wine job, as he wasn't earning any money. The wine merchant had told him that he wasn't due any commission as the samples he'd taken out to his clients had wiped out any profit there might have been for him – and he'd refused to reimburse Danny for the petrol he'd used, the petrol I'd paid for. He had to get another job. Being dependent on me was something he hated, as he'd never been dependent on anyone in his life and it had destroyed his self-respect. I could understand that. What he wanted was to get another job, earn some real money, pay me back for what I'd spent on him, make some contribution to our home together, and try to make me proud of him. I cried. He hugged me until I fell asleep in his arms. We woke, warm and loving, the next day, surrounded by bin-liners, keen to try again, more honestly. Call me a fool if you like. My friend across the road did just that. But perhaps you've seen more of the picture than she did, and I'm hoping you're still on the side of the Danny and Barbara experiment in alternative living and loving.

At this point in the story, please welcome Ali. I did, initially. In fact, the job I saw advertised in the local newspaper appeared to be the answer to Danny's desperate need for help. It was a job as a sales representative for a company supplying fruit and vegetables to the restaurant trade.

Danny had started out in the wholesale fruit and vegetable business. In fact, he'd left school in the sixth form on the invitation of a father of a rugby-playing friend of his, who saw Danny's future as an accountant in the business. But Danny's mental arithmetic skills were better suited to telephone trade sales so this is what he'd moved on to.

This background gave us another major shared interest. As a lesser gourmet, once married to a chef, nothing gives me greater pleasure than talking to a man who knows his lollo rosso from his frisée. Danny had the same total knowledge of fruit and vegetables as he did of wine – he knew which varieties of vegetables were best in which season, could refer to countries of origin, and was a pleasure to shop with. It also gave him the opportunity to demonstrate his superior knowledge, something Aspergers love to do. It's the Little Professor/Little Dictator aspect of their character. He'd say, 'No, don't go for the Spanish tomatoes, these are better and this variety will be sweeter in November,' or 'I bought us these Estima potatoes.' He was a compendium of useful practical knowledge.

'Mmmmmm,' he said, when I showed him the advertisement for the job, 'that's me, isn't it?' as, of course, it was. Ali, who owned the business, was stunned by Danny's mastery of the trade. No other candidate was inter- viewed. The job was his. No contest.

But, as always with Danny, there was a but. He refused to take the job as advertised, Monday to Friday, nine to five, at a regular pittance of an annual salary, but one which would have given him independence and stability. Instead he decided that he'd work on commission only, and at times to suit himself. My heart sank when he boasted that this was what he'd done.

'Why?' I asked, trying to sound neutral, and was immediately whisked into Danny's La La Land, on the magic carpet of his Asperger aspiration and bombast.

'What I'm going to do,' he confided in me, 'is to continue with the wine business too. I'm going to contact the companies who supply the wine shop, deal with them direct, and, while I'm selling the fruit and veg to the restaurants, I'll see if I can sell some wine at the same time! Great idea, isn't it?'

I had to agree, be positive. Danny needed all the encouragement I could muster if this relationship was to continue in any useful way. One of the major problems for any Asperger is motivation, getting geared up to actually doing something, shaking off the natural passivity which can draw them into depression. I'd seen how Danny operated when there was no working day or routine. He seemed unable to impose a structure on himself that was rational, edited, time-managed and prioritized. Do you remember that Asperger problem of weak central coherence? This had always been Danny's stumbling block.

However, I thought, there were certain bonuses in this job. Ali would not recognize Danny's idiosyncrasies easily. He would just imagine that it was cultural differences which made him behave in the eccentric way he did. And Danny would work very hard at first. I had no doubt at all about that. Once motivated, Aspergers go on stoically for ever, enduring the rigours of hard work much more ably than most. Unfortunately, this action would have an equal and opposite reaction. He would be even less communicative and malleable at home.

To give him his due, he did warn me, very pompously.

'Once I start this job, it's going to be hard, you know. I'm going to have to get up very early sometimes to go to the markets, and I'll have to work late at nights too. Ali knows next to nothing about the job, and he's been taken for a ride by his previous salesman, so I'll have to put the business on its feet. I've got plans, big plans. I'll get tired, and you know how difficult I can be when I'm tired!'

I remembered how he told me that Heather used to get very angry with his blank moments, when, exhausted after a day's work, he'd just sit in front of the television and stare at it without moving. She used to throw things at him to try to make him take notice of her.

'In that case,' I grinned, 'I'm going to have to throw things at you.'

'Ooooohhhh!' he said, his pomposity punctured instantly by a Frank Spencer moment, 'I hope I'm not too tired to duck!'

Danny's literal unpredictable humour made the love and laughter spark like rockets. The reasons why I loved him almost outshone the reasons why I was considering getting some counselling help for myself. I had almost forgotten that this was supposed to be fun. That moment of humour reminded me, cruelly.

It was November. This screwball comedy had been running for only three months, but it felt much longer. Half of my head was always murky with the fog of the Danny problem. Capable, logical and organized, I'd become the very thing Danny would rebel against – authority. It was a dilemma beyond solution. The more Danny needed me to direct him, to make him safe, to be the hand that stopped him falling, the more, in his mind, I would become the hand that closed his escape hatch. Although he showed little evidence of understanding how he was limiting my role to that of his super ego, that role is exactly what he designated for me. And what was left of the lost mad child inside me, the mad child who had, she thought, found a wicked little playmate at long last? I couldn't be irresponsible in my spare time, as I had someone always there who demanded I put his confusing world to rights. And, because he knew there was someone to keep him in line, he would play on the drawn boundary for the sheer hell of it.

Let me give you the most outrageous example of that.

Danny had been working for Ali in 'busy busy busy' mode for a fortnight, and my reservations had deepened rather than lessened. He'd already chased several wild geese, and had started to regard Ali, a newly divorced thirty-something, as his new 'best friend'. I could see tears before bedtime.

However, Ali wasn't the problem this particular weekend. Danny's rugby team, the one he'd played for, was coming to a nearby city, and Danny, excitedly, was going to meet up with his old team-mates and watch the game, then go for a night on the tiles with them. Fine. He needed recuperation. I was just thankful that it would be within some other city walls. Danny with team-mates, playing games on my doorstep, was a thought too frightening to contemplate.

I waved him off, in his little navy overcoat and his red scarf, like a fond mum waving to her firstborn as he left for his first school trip. The day was Dannyless and all my own, and after the fortnight of excited babbling punctuated by irritable snapping and blank immobility, and nights when he didn't sleep at all but sat at the computer, I was rather glad to see the back of him. I relaxed totally. I just left him with the one instruction I saw fit to offer, 'Stay the night if you're drunk. Come back here tomorrow. But whatever you do, don't do anything bad here. I have to live here, remember?'

He'd nodded agreement. We'd had all this out. I didn't mind him acting too crazily elsewhere, but I didn't want a repetition of his performances at the club, because this would impact on my own reputation. He understood. He was going to misbehave privately in future.

It was after five when I heard him trying to open the back door, eventually managing it, and staggering into the back bedroom, thankfully alone. I slept on. There was no point in checking up on him. If there was anything untoward, I didn't want to find it in the early hours of the morning. I had to be at my sparkling best on Sundays for my radio show.

So it was after eleven the next morning when I put my head round the door. He was dead to the world, his head back, snoring like a puppy. I picked up his clothes from the floor and got on with what I had to do, and it must have been two or three hours later when it occurred to me that all his clothes hadn't been there.

I went back to check. I'd been right. His coat and his red woolly scarf were missing. The coat had been a very expensive gift from me to him, part of a package I bought him at Harrods in an indulgent day of retail therapy which had included a designer suit, a pair of the shoes he'd always wanted, several pairs of trousers, shirts and knitwear. The cost was astronomical.

'Danny!' I shook him into consciousness.

The stench in the bedroom was almost intolerable. His alcohol breath and sweat had soaked into the bedlinen, the curtains, everything.

He woke fuzzily. 'What?' he demanded, before putting his morning smile in place, rubbing his red eyes, making a chorus of little stimming noises.

'Where's your coat?'

He looked round. Shrugged. 'Don't know.'

'Where did you go?'

'Can't remember.'

I shook his trousers, and a cloakroom token dropped from the pocket. It was a very familiar token. It was from the club.

'You went to the club?!' I shrieked. 'With the lads?'

This was beyond belief. Surely Danny's Asperger social ineptitude in his uninhibited drunken state hadn't led him to take a gang of rugby players into a gay club? For a moment, my heart stopped.

'No...' and it started beating again.

'But you promised me you'd stay away!' I cried.

'I just wanted to show them the town, so we got the bus driver to bring us in after the match,' he said, struggling to remember. 'It's all a bit hazy...'

I fed him coffee after coffee, perched on the side of the bed while he tried to access reality. Slowly the picture emerged, what was left of it. He remembered the drinks. I counted. Forty-eight units of alcohol. The units included two bottles of port, eight pints of Guinness, at least ten double gin and tonics, along with various cans.

And the itinerary? It had not included the club. He'd wandered there alone after he lost everyone. The reason he lost everyone became blindingly clear. The few who had remained resolutely with him as he self-destructed, he'd taken into 'our' bar, the one with the cheap drinks, the one frequented by drag queens, same-sex couples, men with make-up. Perfect.

'I don't think they liked the bar very much,' he said. 'They couldn't take it.'

I would have guessed that. The thought hadn't entered his mind that they might question why he went there, so I didn't suggest it. I just sat in dumb horror, feeling more and more uncomfortable, thankful there hadn't been a fight, but aware that now he had burned his boats with his former rugby team-mates. They didn't know he was Asperger. They would now believe that, like Cary Grant's David, he'd gone gay, all of a sudden.

'So you left your coat at the club?'

'Must have done.'

'And your mobile phone was in the pocket?'

At last, something penetrated.

'Sheeeeeesh!' he said.

'So you won't get those deals you were expecting to set up this week? They were going to phone you, weren't they?' I asked. 'The club doesn't open again until Wednesday night.'

'Ohhhh,' he said, then flapped his hands. 'Pssssssssshhh-hhhhtttttttt!' That was his sound for all seasons, the sound that could mean anything he couldn't put into words, but we both knew what the words were.

'And you do realize that it takes an hour to metabolize a unit of alcohol, and that in no way can I have you drive me to work tonight?' He burrowed down under the duvet, as I began to rise, hating myself for being the voice of reason, yet again, the voice of hated authority.

But I felt uncomfortable in that stinking fetid atmosphere, and…I was damp. I checked the rear of my jeans, then looked down at the bed. There was a brown stain just behind the pillows.

Furiously, I whipped the duvet off his curled hot body. I'd been right. He'd wet the bed. Hours ago, by the look of things.

'Get out! Get out!' I screamed, losing all control. 'Look what you did! Just look! Is this what you've turned into? Some filthy drunk, lying in his own urine?'

Crying with rage and hopelessness, I flew into the kitchen, poured blisteringly hot water and bleach into a bowl, found a scrubbing brush, and hurled back into the bedroom where he was cowering, shaking in a corner.

'Clean that and yourself up!' I demanded. 'I've had as much of you as I can stand!'

As I stormed round the apartment in the next few hours before I left, tight-lipped and distraught, I'd catch sight of him occasionally. He was abject with humiliation. For over an hour he scrubbed the mattress, then washed the sheets and pillow cases, numb with exhaustion, hangover, and a new fear that he had slipped down the evolutionary ladder. I knew, of course, that the Asperger's was at the root of his drinking problem, but what I couldn't quite get my head round was that he was perfectly capable of functioning without drinking at all. He never, for instance, drank if he was driving, no matter what the temptation. The eighteen months in which he'd been deprived of one of his recuperative processes, driving, had shown him how essential that was to his well-being, and he wouldn't risk it. On the other hand, if I pointed this out to him, and asked him to stop drinking, that would label me even more graphically as the authority figure he was learning to fight against. Unless he decided otherwise, if I wanted to help him to be happy, I had to grit my teeth and understand. It was becoming all too much. As it would be for you. As it would be for anyone.

I think that was my real breaking point, that incontinence. Now, with time to consider, I wonder if he'd had another seizure in his sleep that night, and had wet himself in the process? It happens.

I ask myself that because he did the same thing the following weekend, when he'd limited his alcohol intake. We had a good night together, and great fun on the way back, when he insisted on giving me a running piggy back through the night streets. He wasn't blind drunk. He was trying hard to win me round, and partially succeeded, although something had died in me. But that night, apparently, he wet the bed again, after I'd moved into the front bedroom as his hot body was distracting me from sleep. He successfully concealed this from me until the day he left, when I changed the bed and found another stain.

So was it seizures? Neither of us will ever know.

Christmas was approaching, Danny was spending more and more time with Ali, and at work, and I had decided we were coming to the end of our live-in relationship. Although I felt it best not to discuss this with Danny. We had had too many discussions. Each time, I felt myself blurring further from the vision I had of myself, free and feline, a leopard lady with a disregard for convention, and a love of anything just beyond my grasp. I thought Danny would be happier spending his life in dinosaur construction.

Meanwhile, as long as it lasted, I would make it as happy for myself as I could. So I planned with Danny a happy Christmas, preceded by his happy birthday, and followed by the happiest New Year of all, a new millennium to celebrate.

Before that I had to go away to teach at a weekend conference, leaving Danny to his own devices. He had a job to do, one he'd arranged when he was working at the wine shop. It was to be a Sunday presentation, in an exclusive fashion store, of champagne. Danny had decided he would sell at least twenty bottles, bringing us in a handsome profit. I say 'us' as the owner of the wine shop at the last minute refused to sponsor it, almost provoking one of Danny's meltdowns. He managed to tear out of the shop and reach home before his temper exploded. It took me hours to calm him. By the end of those hours I found myself again offering solutions – I would buy the champagne myself, and he would sell it. And, yes, we all know already, don't we, that this was just another of Danny's pipe dreams.

He sold nothing. But it was hardly surprising. He'd spent the weekend carousing with Ali, had gate-crashed a Christmas party, had tried to find a woman for Ali by playing The Game, had been up until dawn, and when I arrived home and went to pick him up, he was swaying, blank, standing in front of his champagne display with nothing to show for it except twenty empty bottles which he'd given away by the glassful as inducement to buy.

I wouldn't have bought anything from that stiff, odd, expressionless person either. He was exhausted by the good times he'd tried to have with Ali, too tired even to drive me to work. I had to dispatch him to bed and find a taxi.

Have you noticed how morose I sound? Do you blame me? Inside that automaton on Mogadon was the man I loved, a man whose exultation could lift me to its heights if he chose, a man whose intelligence could sear through any logical problem, a man whose feelings were innocently tender, whose sensibilities were sophisticatedly refined, whose knowledge and humour lit up my life, but who couldn't stop himself self-harming, and who dragged me in to get hurt too. It was this paradoxical inconsistency I couldn't bear. I knew how wonderful he was but he couldn't be wonderful except in bits, and the bits that were missing led me on emotional hunting expeditions over and over again, always ending with a heart-felt plea to someone who had, because it was Tuesday and these things happen on Tuesdays, left his heart somewhere but couldn't remember where. The reasons appeared as random as that. Scatter skills and scatter deficits is what Asperger's is all about.

Christmas was a pudding, a spicy mixture of all that was good and all that was insupportable to the average digestive system.

I'll quickly run through the list of the insupportable, as this is getting all too much for me to take. You must be feeling the same.

The weekend after his birthday, the one immediately preceding Christmas, Danny decided he had to make the journey to his home town, despite the fact that we were going there for New Year. He had to sell some wine, he said, and to do a job for Ali. What could I say? What, me? Come between an Asperger and his routines? You must be joking.

On 23 December my son came home for Christmas. We went out for a wonderful meal at the best restaurant in town. Then Danny made a scene because he was asked to leave the table and go to the bar to smoke his cigar. He'd seen me standing up for my rights in restaurants. I did it quietly and with dignity. But this wasn't a rights issue, it was common sense. Danny, petulant and childish, insisted that his entire evening had been spoilt by the head waiter. No, Danny, our evening was spoilt by that social blunder, and the ham-fisted job you made of pretending to be me.

Then on Christmas Eve, when food had to be bought and family celebrations entered into in good spirits, Danny announced that he was going for a lunchtime drink with Ali. He'd arranged this ages ago, hadn't he told me? Ali was his boss, and he couldn't refuse, could he? he explained.

'Hmmmmm, but this wasn't Ali's idea, was it?' I asked. It smacked far too much of the Danny routines, and my suspicions were confirmed when he changed into his dinner jacket and bow tie.

'So what's this in aid of?' I asked.

'I always do this when I go out boozing on Christmas Eve!' he explained, spreading his stubby hands as if to say, 'Why are you asking a silly question?'

'When will you be back?'

'Oh, later this afternoon,' he said airily, pecking my cheek and disappearing.

'Don't be later than six,' I shouted after him.

'I won't!'

We were to eat a special meal that night, lobster and champagne. I'd wanted it to be an excited foraging round the shops as we three shared the chores and the thrill of the day before Christmas. But there was only my son and myself to collect the lobsters, champagne, the duckling, the fruit and vegetables (Danny had promised to bring these from work but brought only carrots and some tired parsnips) and the last-minute treats, and to share lunch in a good restaurant. Just the two of us. As per usual.

'Don't worry, Mum,' my son kept saying. He's always been tuned in to me. He always was my best friend in the world.

After repeated mobile calls, Danny finally showed up at half past seven, much the worse for wear, until the lobster hit his bloodstream.

And now the good.

First, his birthday, a week before Christmas. That was a wonderful day. As a surprise I'd bought him a flying lesson for late morning. I knew he'd love it and he did. The feeling of freedom, the views from the skies, buzzed him more than anything in his life to date. Afterwards, we had lunch in a smart restaurant, and he talked non-stop about the pleasure of the flight. Naturally, he decided that when he'd really earned big money from his fruit and vegetable job, as he would any day now, he would take his private pilot's licence and buy a small aircraft. Ah well.

Then, surprisingly, there was Christmas Eve night, when after his day on the loose with Ali, he was more than willing to spend the night dancing with me at the club.

'We're cool!' he kept saying. Praise indeed.

And on Christmas Day, despite a late start which had my son hanging around impatiently, ready to open presents, he'd bought me the perfect gift, a day of pampering at a local health spa.

So, it was the millennium celebrations and their aftermath, rather than his Christmas foibles, which were to signal the end of the road.

We travelled to his home town in the car, staying at the hotel where he had acquaintances he could trust. He had no idea that his behaviour had alienated some of them so deeply that their willingness to share a table with us on New Year's Eve was because I was coming.

'You're the only person who can handle him,' the wife of his former business partner said. 'When he's with you he's totally different, like an adult.' I don't think she realized what an effort acting the role of adult was for him. While he could rein himself in to behave fairly responsibly at work, his leisure time, preferably, needed to be devoted to rediscovering the strength to go on pretending.

I talked very seriously to him before the celebrations he'd planned – a drink at his favourite pub, followed by the gourmet dinner and dance at the hotel, then finally a wine-tasting of a very special Chablis he'd bought – got under way.

'I want you to try to remember that these are your friends, and that I don't really know them,' I told him. 'So it would be really good if you could bear that in mind. I need you to look after me.'

That was always a useful button to press. Danny liked to imagine himself as an heroic figure, someone respected and needed, someone who could take charge. Perhaps it was wrong of me to call upon this facet of his Asperger personality for this night of hedonism, but I was deadly serious. The last thing I wanted was to be marooned in a place I hardly knew, with people I hardly knew.

'Don't worry,' he said, proudly. 'I'll take care of you.'

'Promise?' I asked.

'Promise.'

'And if you want to wander off, can you take me to wherever you're wandering off to? You don't need to talk to me, but I'd like to feel that you weren't abandoning me.'

'I won't wander off without you,' he said solemnly, and meant it.

He lied. It was, as he would have said 'completely involuntary', just as I'd come to realize. He had to go off on his own. The effort of sitting at a table, making small talk which he consciously thought he enjoyed, but subconsciously hated, became too much for him. I could now predict his behaviour, but it was always disappointing when my predictions came true. What could I do, though? Reminding him would be an intolerable system overload, and would result in yet more disappearing acts.

After the third unexplained absence, feeling the eyes on me, feeling that pity that I didn't welcome flood over me again, from all the other neurotypicals at the table, I glanced at my watch. It was quarter to midnight.

'Can you go and find him?' I asked his former partner, quietly. 'It would be nice to have him here by midnight.'

There's a photograph taken five minutes later after he'd been returned to me, glowering, dragging his feet. He hadn't wanted to come back from wherever he'd been hiding. In the photograph I'm assuming a position I'd taken all too often. My chair is drawn up to face his chair, alongside the table strewn with the debris of empty celebration in which we'd played no part – streamers, silly hats, balloons, empty bottles. I'm holding both his hands as he's allowing me to, and I'm leaning forward towards him while he glares into his lap at our joined hands.

I can hardly bear to look at that photograph now. It's the clear image of despair, mine and his. I can almost feel again my eyes stinging and hear myself whispering plaintively to him, 'Please don't. Please don't leave me at midnight. It isn't fair.'

'It isn't fair' was my last resort. It was such clear emotional blackmail, using the one plea which would always make him respond, because this was his mantra, his call to the common humanity we shared, his own childlike appeal for justice to be done.

The room had fallen silent to listen to the countdown to midnight. We made it to our feet just after the announcement that we were now in the year 2000, and although he was still avoiding eye contact, he allowed himself to be hugged as he came back from what was in his head to what was in the room.

And, for the rest of the five hours we remained awake, he stayed at my side, at times even affectionately. Once we danced for a while. I enjoyed that. I'd asked him, before I knew, 'Are you a good dancer?' and he'd said, 'I'm an enthusiastic dancer. Someone once told me I shake my bum. Is that good?' But he was a very good dancer, and we were a good couple, responding easily and laughingly to each other's moves. Yes, I enjoyed that. And I enjoyed the nuzzled night's sleep we had, curled together in one single bed like a happy asymmetric smile.

It was the last night we were to sleep together – one lucky shooting star and its attendant guiding star sliding down into the darkness.

The next night I was anxious and tired. Danny insisted on taking me to a restaurant rank with the stench of over-used chip fat. My stomach heaved. I picked at pieces of coarsely crumbed fish, while he fought his way through some pallid chicken. He drank sickly mead. I drank orange juice. I had to work the next night. I hoped I'd recover in time from the late night and the celebration that wasn't.

'We'll have a drink in the hotel pub,' he announced.

'I'm not really up to it,' I protested.

'It's OK, I won't have much,' he reassured me. 'I know I have to drive back tomorrow.'

By eleven I'd had enough orange juice, and enough standing at the bar, talking to the new fiancée of Leon, one of Danny's ex-team-mates. She didn't have much to say, and I was too tired to tease out of her any more than a few odd comments about make-up, engagement rings, and wedding preparations.

'Let's go, shall we?' I whispered to Danny.

'You go up. You look all in. I'll just finish this and be with you in less than half an hour,' he said softly, kissing me.

I was asleep moments after I reached our room.

I awoke at two. The other bed was empty.

I crept out of bed, put on my jeans and sweater, and went to search through the deserted hotel. Everything was quiet. The lights were out in the bars.

At the door was a porter.

'You looking for something?' he asked.

'Danny Wheeler,' I said.

He laughed. It felt as if he was laughing at me. I'd protected Danny's vulnerability and it had opened mine like a raw suppurating blister.

'Him?' he chuckled again. 'Disappeared has he? Again? He's famous for it round here!'

He was telling me I wasn't one of 'them', one of the townspeople, and should have been more careful who I was getting involved with. His laughter was a dismissal of any claim I might have on the man I loved. He sneered, as he might have done at any of the other silly women Danny must have bedded in this very hotel.

'Have you seen him?' I dared to ask.

'No. He'll come back when he's done whatever it is he's doing!' It was evident what he thought that might be, and naturally the thought had occurred to me too. Danny may have disappeared into the night with someone else. The Game again.

I found my way back to the room, and flopped on to the bed. I couldn't sleep for hours. I cried, and listened, listened and cried.

And I realized that I felt something I'd never felt in my adult life before, a feeling which had fleetingly surfaced over the last month or two. Unlike Danny, I'd never had any problem identifying feelings, but this one was mysterious, somehow, a vague childhood memory of something that hurt, that really hurt. And at about four o'clock in the morning, just before I fell into a restless doze, I remembered the name of the feeling.

Loneliness.

I was lonely.

It had been more than thirty years since that cold alienated emotion had fallen out of my consciousness. Married, divorced, single-handedly bringing up my son, choosing celibacy, not once had I ever felt this total desolation of being abandoned, neglected and needy.

By half past eight, as I dozed and watched the clock, I allowed myself to start making phone calls, first to the hotel owner. He hadn't seen Danny. Then to his old business partner. He hadn't seen him either.

'Where was he when you last saw him?' both of them asked me.

'With Leon,' I said, both times. But neither of them knew Leon's surname.

At ten, the hotel owner sent me up some breakfast. I'd hardly eaten the night before, and I needed it. I was so grateful for his kindness. In 12 hours' time I was due to go on air, sweeping away the problems from other people's lives. How could I do that?

I checked the train times to find one train, at lunchtime, that would get me to the studio in time for my show. I could have the car driven down to me. I had to work fast, yet I was trembling from head to foot with exhaustion. Would I make it?

At eleven, after another frantic round of phone calls, there was a knock on the door. And there was Danny, smiling broadly.

'Where the hell have you been?' I screamed.

He thought for a moment, spreading his hands, shrugging.

'Bacon sandwich,' he said.

I was lost. So this was an explanation for the 12-hour disappearance?

He marched in unperturbed.

'Leon and I went to the kebab shop,' he grinned, 'but it was closed. So he invited me back for a bacon sandwich, so that's where I've been. I slept in a chair.'

'And you didn't ring to tell me where you were going?' I screeched. 'You said half an hour! Is this half an hour?'

'I didn't want to wake you up,' he explained.

It was at that moment that I realized we'd never be able to bridge the gap between his Asperger's and my innate panic and concern for the welfare of those I love. He didn't consider for a moment that I might have been going out of my mind with worry. Why should he? He had come to a logical conclusion, that if he phoned it would disturb me, and he shouldn't do that. Our worlds were too far apart for lessons to be spelt out, by me, to him, for the rest of my life.

'It's over, Danny,' I said. 'That's the last straw. Now would you like to stay down here, as there's a train I can catch, or do you want to come back, drive me back, but find your own place by the end of the week? I can't go through any more of this.'

Finally, the seriousness of what he'd done caught up with him. He fell on to the one pristine bed, curled like a fossil, still, brittle.

'We'll leave in three hours. I'll catch up on some sleep,' I said coldly.

Cold was all I felt. But this time I slept, and when I woke, I had to wake him.

We hardly spoke on the four-hour drive. He was impassive, I was dead. There was nothing left in my head or my heart. We arrived in Birmingham, had a silent meal, and then I had to go in for the show.

'I'm going for a walk,' he said. It was the first time he had ever missed a show. Afterwards, when I came out, he was bouncing.

'I got picked up by this girl!' he boasted. And that's all it was. Just a way to grab my attention.

'Good,' I said.

Danny had never seen me emptied. I was always the resourceful one with so much to say and do, no matter how unpalatable. He had emptied me. At other times, my compassion would have slithered in to fill the gaps, but I hardly knew where that was any more.

'Ali can find you a flat. He's your new best friend. I'm sure you can count on him. Just get out of here by Saturday, will you?' I asked as we pulled up outside my flat. I let myself in, left the door open for him, and didn't speak to him for the rest of the week. There wasn't anything to speak to. There was just a shape in the bed for three days while he slept on it. Once, my heart would have been lying there, too, beating to drown out his inadequacies, stirring him to action.

I just left him to his hiding.

This is not like me. I tell you, this is not like me. I'm larger than life, alive, alert, aggrieved, aggressive or amorous, but now there was just a gap between the self that walked and talked and cooked and ate, and the self that felt any of those actions being self-preservative.

On Friday he told me he had found a room, and asked if he could stay until he could move in, after the weekend.

'As long as you don't bother me,' I said.

But of course, I relented, allowed him to have use of the car after he'd moved on the proviso that he'd take me to Birmingham twice each week, and I said I'd cook us a meal for our last night together.

He didn't manage to get back for the meal. He was busy with Ali. So I scraped the lovingly cooked food into the waste disposal and cried myself to sleep, thankful that some emotion was finally returning. In the morning I found a note from him apologizing for upsetting me, but saying that his future lay in making a sound financial basis for himself. He hoped I understood that now that he was independent he would have to pay his own way, so this was his first priority.

He had gone, taking his wine and his clothes – all those clothes I had bought for him.

The tears wiped any response.

I was just glad to be alone. Loneliness might be something I could get used to, in time. Aspergers live with it, don't they? So I'd just gnaw on an intercostal clavicle, and shoot the leopard.

Asperger questionnaire

This was the questionnaire I produced for partners of Aspergers. It was circulated to women and men I met on the Internet, and to couples in the UK. Quotations from this questionnaire are in Chapters 6 and 7, but this is a summary of the results.

How did you meet?

I was surprised by the number of couples who met at university or college. It led me to suspect that this might be a time when eccentricity is accepted and even approved, and when the pronounced intellectual gifts of some Aspergers might balance any negative effects of poor social skills.

Is there an age, nationality or culture gap between you and your partner?

I expected to find many more relationships with an age or culture gap than I did. But in about 10 per cent of couples there was either a socially unusual age difference (woman older than man) or they had married someone of a different nationality. However, I also had an unexpected finding – that many couples had, after marriage, emigrated to another country.

How did you find out about AS?

Over a third of the partners had discovered Asperger's Syndrome when one of their children had been diagnosed with the condition. It was after the child's diagnosis that the NT parent had recognized the same traits in the partner. A surprising 42 per cent of respondents had discovered Asperger's Syndrome through media resources – a television programme, a radio show, a magazine or newspaper feature, or a book. The remainder had been advised of the possibility of Asperger's Syndrome by a friend or, less likely, a professional counsellor or medical expert. Most of the information they had since garnered had come from the Internet. This is hardly surprising given the high proportion (76 per cent) of respondents discovered through internet message-boards and support groups.

Has your partner got a diagnosis? If so, where and when?

More than half were officially diagnosed, with UK respondents more likely to have a diagnosis than those in other parts of the world. Of those who hadn't been diagnosed, the reason most often given was the partner's refusal to accept that there was anything wrong. The next most common reason was difficulty in finding a diagnostic expert.

Has diagnosis improved or hurt the relationship?

For diagnosed AS partners the positive and negative replies were evenly balanced. Denial was evident, but so was the acceptance and relief in others. However, all NT partners of Aspergers reported that they themselves felt happier after the diagnosis.

What attracted you to your partner?

A high proportion (47 per cent) mentioned the good looks! The majority of the remainder claimed that they were attracted by intellect, but a sizeable minority were impressed by the apparent kindness and passivity of the Asperger.

Describe your partner's face and facial expressions

By far the most common reply to this was 'blank'. Some said 'sulky'. One said 'smiling'.

Does your partner have a sense of humour?

The majority of those who answered this question (52 per cent) said that there was a sense of humour but many complained that it was childish, silly or incomprehensible. Some said that their partner's humour was in puns and word-play, which might be surprising to many experts.

When and how did you notice something 'odd'?

All respondents had noticed strange behaviour before the marriage. They had passed this off as awkwardness, shyness, or having a dysfunctional family background. A high proportion of respondents (36 per cent) mentioned that one or other of the partner's parents had appeared 'odd' or 'unloving' – a factor they had eventually realized was AS or AC traits.

Do you know anything about your partner's childhood and schooling which points to AS?

Of the few who answered this question positively – many knew little of their partner's family or childhood – there was a history of strange or unusual behaviour, which had, in a few cases, been the subject of psychiatric intervention in childhood.

What's your partner's eye contact like?

Sixty-eight per cent of respondents mentioned problems with eye contact, including the 'hard stare'.

Can you describe your partner's language differences?

A little over half of respondents said that their partner had some problems understanding words in common usage, or understanding nuances of word use. Some said that this was the principal reason for the relationship problems. Some AS partners had their own unusual use of words. A small proportion said that the AS partner was particularly skilled, verbally, but this was in an academic context. One AS partner was a dictionary compiler, another a linguistics professor.

Does your partner copy what you do? Copy other people? Use phrases and intonations heard from others?

This question had one of the highest rate of positive response, 82 per cent. Words and phrases seemed to be taken from television, reading, or from friends. Some behaviours also seemed to be copied. Most NT partners said that they themselves were copied, with words and phrases they had used in argument later used in argument against them, without any irony or recognition of the source.

Does your partner refer to him/herself in the third person, or by name?

No one responded positively to this question. It's rare in Asperger's, more common in classic autism, and is something that experts say disappears with maturity. Danny called himself 'he' several times in context where an NT would have used 'I', and once referred to himself by name: 'Danny Wheeler doesn't do that'. Perhaps I noticed this because word usage is my profession, but it did sound odd to me.

Does your partner stim? If so, how?

Some respondents didn't understand the word 'stim'. I should have explained it – my error. Of those who did, over 75 per cent reported stimming behaviour, usually quite subtle. One man referred to his AS partner having to wriggle her feet to get herself to sleep. Hand-rubbing was the most common stim mentioned, but hair-pulling or stroking was also referred to. A few had complex stimming routines.

Does your partner have any unusual sensory hang-ups – sound? touch? watching things? highly developed taste buds?

The sensory issue which was most frequently referred to was taste. Most AS partners seemed to have hypo- or hyper-sensitivities to certain foods.

Does your partner have special interests and/or special abilities? What? Does your partner collect and display things?

As expected, this question was the most frequently answered and drew the highest positive results. Ninety-two per cent mentioned special interests ranging from collecting sports statistics to collecting various types of memorabilia. Hoarding and displaying items was evident in over 60 per cent of replies about Aspergers.

What is your partner's intellectual ability and is this reflected in the job s/he does?

Although many of the respondents had partners with postgraduate qualifications, 40 per cent of the partners with these qualifications had never used them. There was a high proportion (28 per cent) whose highly qualified partners had university or college teaching jobs.

Does your partner have any unusual hand movements?

There was a curious response to this question, in that almost all those who answered that their partner had unusual hand movements selected the same idiosyncrasy – that their Asperger partner pointed with his middle finger, instead of the more-expected index finger.

Is s/he clumsy? Does s/he have a strange way of walking? What about sporting prowess? Any good around the house?

Most of the responses confirmed clumsiness in various degrees, but especially in attempts to do DIY tasks. Strangely, 20 per cent of the respondents reported that their AS partner had some sporting success, although this flies in the face of much of the accepted wisdom. The sports mentioned were baseball, rugby and hockey, in particular. One woman Asperger was captain of her school teams, and was also meticulous and skilled with her hands, although gawky in other respects. No one mentioned the autistic stance, but 42 per cent identified a strange gait.

Fanatically tidy or untidy?

The answers to this question were as contradictory as AS itself. Most AS partners were fanatically tidy in arranging their own collections, even arranging books and CDs, in some cases, alphabetically. But in general domestic duties most were hopelessly untidy.

Describe your partner's unshakeable routines

Many of these are intriguing – see Chapter 7 for the trash-can story!

Is your partner hard-working?

Seventy-six per cent replied that their partners were hard-working, although preferred to work at their own pace and in their own time. Many had problems with authority figures at work. Some reported that their partners had difficulty working with others, and 24 per cent were self-employed.

Is your partner anxious? Depressed? On medication?

Those with a history of undiagnosed Asperger's but who had been seen regularly by doctors and psychiatrists were most likely to have been treated for depression, although a small percentage (15 per cent) had been treated for schizophrenia. Most NT respondents reported that their AS partners were anxious and withdrawn.

Does your partner have allergies, eczema, asthma, etc.?

A sizeable minority, 31 per cent, replied positively to this question.

Does your partner have tantrums?

Although some partners, 22 per cent, agreed that there were occasional 'melt-downs', the majority said that silence and depressive episodes were more frequent, especially in older Aspergers.

Does your partner drink or use drugs for 'normalization'?

A few, 18 per cent, reported alcoholism but this seemed to be part of a family dysfunction where parents, too, were heavy drinkers.

Does your partner need space? Escape into silence?

Some of the highest scores recorded were in answer to this question. Only three respondents either did not answer this question or said that this was not a noticeable trait.

What are your partner's sleeping habits like?

Eighty-two per cent mentioned sleep disturbances, staying up all night, rising early, or sleeping for long periods. One idiosyncrasy mentioned very frequently was that the Asperger partner, despite tossing and turning once asleep, seemed to fall asleep almost instantly.

Is your partner naïve and gullible?

There was a mixed response to this question. While most NT partners recognized what they often called 'childishness', many also reported that their partner was not so naïve that they could not be manipulative. I think that the response may be an NT misunderstanding of AS egocentricity, rather than deliberate manipulation on the part of the AS partner.

Is your partner controlling? Passive? Passive aggressive?

I've already mentioned that the surprise answer to this question was always – all three.

Does your partner handle finances or do you?

One factor which recurred was that many Aspergers have intensely frugal habits as regards household expenditure, although they can be extravagant as far as their own needs are concerned. Again and again NT partners reported that it was exceptionally difficult to separate their Asperger from his money, even when that involved providing for the children's lunch money or living expenses. One respondent, married to an academic specializing in finance, found her life totally dominated by her partner's frugal ways.

Do you teach your partner how to behave or was/is there another mentor?

Several respondents mentioned a mentor figure; in one case this was a former girlfriend who remained her husband's best friend.

(Big question) How do you communicate?

By far the most common response to this question was 'we don't'. Some partners found it easier to communicate in writing than by speaking when something important had to be conveyed.

Has your partner ever been unintentionally cruel?

Most chose to ignore that question. There were a few answers which showed the gulf of misunderstanding that could arise, and which at the time appeared to be callous and unfeeling. Examples of this are in Chapter 7.

Can your partner understand when s/he has hurt you?

Although 60 per cent of partners reported that there was a complete lack of understanding, some couples had developed a rapport which did seem to draw out empathetic responses from their partner.

Is your partner affectionate? Is your sex life OK? Do you sleep together?

Again, there were mixed responses. Those in the younger age group were more likely to report affection and sexual satisfaction. One reported an excessive interest in sex in her partner, but 45 per cent said that there was no longer sexual activity in the relationship and that when there had been, it was repetitive and mechanical. Most often, this was because the relationship had broken down. In one case a newly wed partner said that her husband was unable to consummate their marriage as he had a genital problem which their doctor believed was psychological in origin. This was not necessarily linked to Asperger's Syndrome.

Do you mother your partner?

The most common reply was 'He'd like me to, but I try to resist.' One woman partner wrote, 'I father him.' This more masculine role in the relationship was adopted by many of the respondents, who had taken over executive functioning within the marriage or relationship.

Is your partner sociable? Is your partner's behaviour in public different from her/his behaviour with you? How does your partner behave at social functions? How does he behave at home-based functions?

Almost all who answered this question pointed to the paradox in the Asperger personality that although there was a belief among friends and colleagues that the partner was a friendly person, this was because there was a real effort by the AS partner to behave well in social settings to which they had been invited. However, this often contrasted sharply with behaviour at home. Many partners reported that sullenness and silence set in as soon as the couple left the function to drive home. There was a reluctance to join in with home-based social occasions and family occasions.

Does your partner love you? Do you love him/her?

Over 50 per cent of partners replied 'yes' or 'I used to' to the second part of this question. The answer to the first part was most usually 'I don't know'.

Have you had counselling?

Thirty-five per cent of NT partners had sought counselling with very varied degrees of success.

Do you get support? Does anyone believe you when you tell them that your partner is AS?

This was the saddest set of responses. The picture emerged of little support, and a refusal both in friends or in medical practitioners to believe the NT partner, or to try to understand Asperger's Syndrome. It seems that society in general is still playing the Freudian game of fault and blame, attributing any problems to a failure of the NT partner to just 'get on with it'. Asperger's Syndrome is not easy to understand, and many people refuse to accept it as a reason for relationship problems.

5 A Working Model

Danny was right, and my tears over his discourteous exit were wasted. He had to make himself financially independent. It was the most important issue that faced him. Since it's always best for Aspergers to do just one thing at a time, perhaps I should never have expected him to sustain a relationship and find a settled and acceptable working environment simultaneously. His logic was, as ever, impeccable, although his methods were flawed.

What he imagined was that he could now devote his time to making a fortune, which he had announced was about to arrive with every rainstorm and every rainbow. He drove me to work twice weekly, sullen, angry that he was taking time out of his busy schedule to do, as he thought, me a favour. He blanked out the idea that his continual use of the car was dependent on his driving me to work. I was intruding. It was his car, his office, his workplace. He had things to do. To demonstrate this, he took calls on his mobile from Ali as he drove me home, and refused to discuss what these were about. His responses were sufficiently neutral to deprive me of any clues.

It wasn't easy, that drive to and from work. I was preoccupied by his blankness.

'You didn't talk to me,' I complained after one of the journeys home.

'You could have talked to me!' he said, crossly. More Asperger logic.

One night it was all too much for me. We'd driven home to the sound of his mobile constantly ringing. He was going to come in for a cup of tea, but as the mobile sounded again, he suddenly announced that he was leaving. Then my house phone went, just as he'd left.

It was Ali.

'Is Danny with you?' he asked.

'He was,' I snapped. 'Sunday nights and Wednesday nights, as you know, he works for me.'

I can get very arrogant when I'm angry, and I was angry. This was my home phone, and there was no excuse for disturbing me, as well as chasing Danny.

'What's all this about?' I asked.

'He's supposed to be picking me up,' Ali explained, weakly.

'What? After midnight on a Sunday, and he's picking you up?' I queried.

'I've been borrowing his flat. I have to give the keys back,' he said.

It was a mystery. I knew where Danny's new flat was, although I'd never been there. Ali had advanced him the money for the rent, which he would have to pay back from his commission, which should have been very good. Danny had recently secured a deal with a chain of sandwich shops, which was very lucrative indeed. Or so he told me.

On a whim, I called a cab, and went round to see Danny. He had arrived home. The car was parked on the street outside. He'd promised me that the flat had car parking. Another lie. So there was my new car, parked in the gutter.

I rang the bell for ages before Danny emerged.

'What's going on?' I asked.

He invited me into his new home. It was a recently refurbished and redecorated room with a large en-suite bathroom, but it was miles away from anywhere, and the house, a 1960s box, had a ghostly, empty-building feeling.

Danny looked embarrassed.

'I didn't want to tell you,' he mumbled. 'Ali's seeing someone, so they use this room while I'm out driving you.'

'Ah,' I grinned. 'So that was the big secret? So that's what all the phoning's about? You know, you ought to get another set of keys cut, then I won't have to take calls at home.'

'He phoned you? After I left?' Danny asked. He seemed angry too.

'Just tell him not to do it in future, will you?'

I left it at that. But it was weeks later when I found out the full extent of Danny's problems. I'd decided to sell the car. The journey with sulky Danny was more than I could take. I just needed to cut the apron strings and stop worrying about him all the time. The journey to work, with its attendant worries – would Danny make it on time this week? would he take my calls if he was running late? would he at least be communicative? – was not helping the pain of the failed relationship to ease.

So, on his assurance that he could use Ali's company vehicles any time he wanted to, I took back the car, sold it, and expected that I would never see Danny again. We parted as amicably as we could, given the fact that I was letting him down, as he saw it.

But he was back before the week was out, looking more hang-dog than ever.

'I need to collect some papers,' he explained.

'Please just bring one of the vans from work and take the rest of your stuff,' I sighed. I really didn't want this constant back and forth which he seemed determined to stick with. He'd left his computer, some of his clothes, all his old papers. It was almost as if, having established his territory, he wanted to leave his flag planted there, just in case anyone should dispute it.

'OK, OK,' he grunted.

He was not at all happy, and I knew what I'd do, even before I invited him to share a pot of coffee and tell me all about it. I'd get myself involved all over again.

'It's Ali,' he said, finally. 'He says he's only paying me two hundred this month instead of the six hundred I've earned because all my commission has to be paid back to him for the rent and the deposit on the flat. It was good of him to loan it to me, but once I've paid this month's rent, I'll have nothing left. So I'm going to look for another job. I came to collect my CV.'

Here was a man who could put together in an instant a deal to sell lettuces, could work out cost price, price of labour, add tax and profit, and quote by the box-load. He could persuade a customer to have something he didn't want, yet in a real-life situation he was totally incapable of negotiating with Ali. Again, he was being stitched up. It's the Asperger gullibility. In all the time he worked for the wine merchant, he left without any pay, didn't he? It was happening again.

I pointed out that Ali would get the deposit back once he moved on, as he intended to. This room was only temporary. I suggested that he ask Ali to take out the deposit in four equal amounts over the next four months, adding a little interest if he wished. That would mean that he'd have enough to live on, and enough to pay the ongoing rent.

'I didn't think of that,' he said. But he wouldn't have done. His way was to take whatever anyone said to him, become very angry about it, but not dare to challenge it with a viable alternative.

I wonder if negotiating is a particularly neuro-typical quality because it involves thinking so carefully about what someone else might accept as a compromise? And to do that you have to have an idea of how someone else's mind works? Theory of Mind again.

So, it occurs to me that while in a general way, Aspergers may be able to make rules about social behaviour, it must be extremely difficult to invent a rule which complies with an individual mind-set, personality and situation. Perhaps that involves just too much theorizing about mind. It also involves making subtle changes from what's known about the general, and tweaking it to fit the particular. So while Danny could easily make a deal involving lettuces, knowing about what the market itself might stand, knowing what in general someone else would think was a good price, how could he, with his impairments, deal with another complex human being on an issue which affected his own welfare?

The other problem, too, is motivating yourself to do this, while your natural inclination is to be passive and accepting or inert. Considering yourself to be object rather than subject is to feel continually at the mercy of whatever unscrupulous scheme someone tries to fob you off with. Ali, cleverly, had worked out that Danny was at his mercy, and was now trying to turn the screws even though he had originally stepped in to save Danny – and of course, his own business.

The fundamental social interaction and social understanding which drive romance and friendship, and which can be bewildering to an Asperger, are intensified, often, in workplace conditions. The simple Asperger formula of 'I work hard, I take home my wage,' is only a part of the story of getting and keeping a job.

Danny's experience in this perhaps trivial matter with Ali arose from a series of blunders which he'd made since he'd started working for Ali. Each of them was small, but each, in time, added up to a total package of a kind of exploitation to which he was prey, but to which he was a party as well.

'You did tell him that he owes you something for using your room?' I had to ask.

Danny shrugged that off with a wave of his little hands. 'We sorted that out at the beginning,' he said. 'I wanted the small room in the house, Ali wanted the room with the double bed. It was only a few pounds a week extra, so he said he'd pay the difference.'

'As long as he was using the room,' I reminded him. 'So now that you're not out on Wednesday and Saturday, you have to pay the extra?'

'Yes,' he said.

He hadn't been able to foresee the possibility of change in the longer term. It was another example of Danny only living in the present.

Seen by cynical NT eyes, the generosity shown by Ali in advancing Danny the cash for the deposit and rent had been self-serving. It had made Danny dependent, grateful, and all the more easily manipulated. I knew about some of Ali's manipulation. One of the promises I'd extracted from Danny when I'd lent him the car was that he'd not become a chauffeur for Ali, who had his own car, or act as delivery service for Ali's son, who was passed like a parcel between father and mother every night after school. Ali looked after him, incompetently, as I'd seen when he twice brought the child round to my flat to kill the three-hour babysitting he did until his ex-wife returned from work. The child was hyperactive, upset by the break-up of the marriage, and couldn't get his father's full attention.

When I got my car back, there were tiny sticky fingerprints all over the back windows. Danny had been driving the child, in my car, without a car seat, obviously on Ali's instruction. Not a good idea.

But Danny had played the whole employer/employee role badly from the beginning. He'd assumed that Ali was his friend, and hadn't taken account of the distance Ali would create when the time was right. True, as a recently divorced man on the loose, his new employer was particularly interested in having someone to go out to clubs with, someone who could so easily attract any passing girls. But he was never Danny's best buddy, just as the men at the wine shop had never been what Danny assumed they were, his loyal friends.

You remember I told you about the night Danny and Ali went out on the town, while I was teaching at a conference just before Christmas? You remember I said that they'd gate-crashed a Christmas party?

The full story was far more complex and can point to how Danny got this relationship completely wrong. It's a series of examples of social impairment.

The first night I was away, my friend from across the road promised that she'd keep an eye on him, and take him for a drink. She was a mature student, who worked at weekends in an upmarket furnishing store. She happened to mention that the next night, Saturday, was the staff Christmas get-together at a restaurant and bar in town.

'Say hi if you're passing,' she'd told him, in exactly the polite meaningless way people say, 'We must do lunch.'

So he did say hi, as invited, turning up with Ali when the staff were in the middle of a meal. He'd said hello, and left. So far, so good. The rules at this point were well understood. You don't disturb other people when they're eating. My friend assumed that they had now moved on.

She was wrong. Danny took Ali to the restaurant next door for a meal, and after they'd eaten, they went back to the staff party, now on their coffee and drinks. Danny had bought several bottles of wine, and placed them on the table in front of the prettiest girls, inviting Ali to come and sit with them.

The girls, out with their colleagues, were embarrassed and annoyed, particularly as Danny made it clear to them that they should take a romantic interest in Ali and himself.

They felt that their evening had been invaded. We would all feel the same, wouldn't we?

Danny, unaware of their rejecting body language, had persisted. And, on a personal note, remember he was carrying on this flirtation in front of my friend, who knew him as my partner. No wonder she thought him a waste of space.

But there was another problem, too, which my friend explained to me later.

'I had to take Ali to one side and tell him that his behaviour with his employee was totally inappropriate. I said to him, how can you act as this man's boss when you're allowing him to pimp for you? And it should be clear to you that he's upsetting the girls. You're his boss. Do something.'

It was a point. She was quite right that Danny never could adopt a position which might be called 'employee' very easily. This in turn put pressure on whoever was employing him. On the other hand, Danny never considered himself to be anything less than Ali's business partner. It was so difficult for him to see the strict dividing lines which determine the role of a freelance self-employed contractor.

From the beginning, the relationship with Ali was all wrong. For a while Danny believed, and Ali encouraged him to think, that the company would become a limited company, and that Danny would be made a company director. He was angry with Ali when he discovered that this was not to be the case, and that if the company were ever restructured, it would be Ali's extended family, not the new freelance employee, who would be on the board. Danny spent weeks of wasted research on this silly pipe dream of his, at Ali's instigation.

What it all came down to, finally, something I tried to point out to Danny when he was living with me, was that Ali had cheap labour on this deal which Danny had been so proud of. While his time should have been spent only on securing new orders and making sure that the orders were as good as promised, in fact most of his time was spent in the office, answering the telephone, working in the vegetable preparation, organizing Health and Safety, trying to plan expansions, doing the accounts, babysitting Ali's child, going to markets, bringing in new products, finding new suppliers. It was a full-time job, and more. In effect, he was acting as a managing director and financial director. And for this he was being paid, in commission, less than half the salary that the job was originally advertised at, well below the poverty line.

To be fair to Ali, much of the work Danny did was not required. It was Danny's ambition and his misunderstanding of his role and the responsibility he assumed which allowed Ali to use him like a full-time worker for up to seventy hours a week.

The serious discussions I'd had with Danny when he set out on his very wrong-headed assumptions about his role had to be conducted with finesse.

'Why are you going in today? Is Ali paying you to work?' is something I could say once as a dig in the ribs, maybe twice as a reinforcement, but any more than that and he would have perceived the reservations I had about his job as interference and my comments as nagging.

And that's a real problem when dealing with Aspergers like Danny (not that they're all as pig-headed as he was!) who make a decision, then stick with it, and who refuse to listen to anything they don't want to hear.

I had to be very careful that in any advisory capacity I didn't give him direct instructions when he was feeling alienated by my suspicions. There was in him an element of Oppositional Defiance Disorder, a behaviour sometimes given as a co-diagnosis to children with Asperger's. This shows itself as a refusal to comply with an instruction, and isn't given as a diagnosis in adult Aspergers, although a few do have traits of it, as Danny did, from time to time, when he was set on doing something.

A woman who wrote to me about her Asperger father-in-law, said, 'When he comes to visit, if I say to him, "Would you like to take your coat off?" he refuses to, and will sit, sweltering in it, all the time he's in the house. But if I don't say it, he'll take it off when he's ready to. I've had to learn not to ask.'

So I had to leave it to Danny to find out how badly he'd misinterpreted those who exploited him at work. Each discovery that he'd been let down, or duped, was so painful for him that I just wished I could have transferred my cynicism into his head while he was asleep one night, rather than have to witness the dreadful effect that enlightenment or revelation had on his innocence and trust.

But from that day when he came back for his CV and I was able to confirm, gently, some of the fears that he had for his future, we began to work on the project to find him a new job. He wanted one which preferably supplied him with a car, was certainly a full-time job rather than commission-only self-employment, and one which took him on daily trips to explore new leads. It had to be a sales job.

I asked him what he wanted from work, and those were the criteria he specified. So, from being his lover, I had now been demoted to careers adviser. Actually, I felt happier in the role.

We worked for hours, shaping up his CV so that it looked more appetizing. It had looked quite good, but had no punch, no prioritizing. Everything had been given the same status, and somehow it didn't hang together. Weak central coherence again. When we'd finished, it sounded as if he meant it.

'I'm seeing an agency this week,' he said. 'I'll let you know what happens. I'll take this along.'

'No,' I suggested. 'Send it. Let them read it before you show up. They'll be impressed.'

I knew that they would be, now that we'd included details of his impressive rugby career, the qualifications in Health and Safety, accounting, and quantity surveying that he hadn't thought to include, his interests in wine and his chess championships. It made him into a more rounded person. It made him sound more like the exciting vibrant Danny I'd loved but couldn't live with. It made him sound in control.

He sighed as he left.

'I've got to get out of that flat, you know. I can't stand it.'

Oh dear. Was this a request for help? And if it was, did I respond? No, is the short answer, and I know you'll be with me on that. As the psychologist had said, I had to fight against being his caretaker.

He phoned during the week. He'd sent his CV to the agency, and had been telephoned immediately with a number of possible job offers. Everything was looking good.

'I'll call in and see you after the interview,' he enthused. 'If that's OK with you?'

I agreed, and he was bubbling when he arrived, certain that he'd be offered one of the multitude of jobs which had been mentioned.

But, as the week went by, nothing happened. The agency had gone cold on him.

'What went wrong?' he asked me on one of his, by now, all-too-regular visits. It was clear to me that he neither wanted to work for nothing for Ali, nor did he want to return to the pristine cell that was now his home. 'Do you think it's my interviewing skills?'

'Could be,' I said.

I wondered if he'd sounded diffident, detached? I wondered if he'd started to twist his hair as he spoke? I wondered if he'd managed to keep some eye contact? Interview techniques can be a problem for Aspergers.

From the questionnaires I included at the end of the last chapter, it was clear that I had a self-selected group of intelligent people married to intelligent Aspergers. As I explained, I'd found many of my participants on the Internet, and that suggests that these are couples who can afford a personal computer, who have educated computing skills and who are resourceful enough to discover and access support groups through internet use.

So I wasn't surprised when most of the Aspergers were in professional work. Both husband and wife were educated, often to post-graduate level. But there was a wide range of careers. Many of the Aspergers were in computing, one was in farming, some in engineering. There was an Asperger pianist, a piano tuner, a telecommunications expert, a bibliographer, librarians, many academics, especially linguists and historians, a teacher, and one, just the one, minister of religion.

This is the one I found fascinating. American, originally Jewish, like the woman he married, both had converted to Christian Protestantism before meeting. She had been a member of the congregation at his first church, and they had both been involved in the intellectual, philosophical area of the religious experience. He, however, was an Asperger with an unfortunate stimming habit – picking his nose when under stress. She wrote:

> He once picked his nose throughout a job interview with a research committee, and I was certain they would just write him off, but they invited him to more interviews and he came very close to getting the job.

But he didn't get the job. The nose-picking really wasn't a great habit in a clergyman.

Beyond the interview, even if they survive it, Aspergers often are found out, suspected of being weird or odd, noticeably out of step with the rest of the workforce, and excuses may be made to sack them. Others may feel uncomfortable around them. Jane Meyerding writes:

> My next job was at the bottom rung of the clerical ladder at Encyclopedia Britannica – the only employer who ever fired me. The official explanation for the firing was that I had proven myself 'unable to adapt to an office environment'. I had done fine in the AFSC office environment, but at EB employees were expected to look and act 'right'. My clothes were not 'right' and my body language was definitely 'wrong'. I did not know what to do when I ran out of work (which I did every day, because I didn't know enough to work slowly), and I was observed to be 'lounging' at my work table. The two women who told me I was fired acted as if they were afraid of me. That makes me think that I probably was seen as 'weird' by the other people who worked there – possibly because I never talked to them. I didn't know how to talk to people spontaneously, and no one I overheard was ever talking about anything of interest to me.

Karen Rodman, the inspirational woman whose marital experience compelled her to set up FAAAS – Families of Adults Afflicted by Asperger's Syndrome – met her husband, who had a degree in psychology, when she went to the bar where he was the piano player. Like Danny, he had opted out of the effort of being employed, and chose to earn his living as a gifted pianist. He plays still, and teaches piano, but has never used his many academic qualifications.

Many Aspergers are employed at below the levels of their skills, making do with any work they can get in order to survive. One who carved out a career very different from that which he imagined was Larry Arnold. He had attended university, but had dropped out before qualifying. Drifting and adrift, while his father was too inept and violent to cope, his mother became wheelchair-bound, and his job was determined by circumstances:

> My mother, who had not been well for a long time, became diagnosed with rheumatoid arthritis. I remember her tears as she came home from the doctors that day. I had arranged to be at the family home as she needed someone for support. My dad had a personality disorder of some kind, and he had a particular outlook on life that was not real.
>
> My dad could not really cope with the concept of disability, in a world where he wanted a perfect wife and perfect children. That conflict often led to terrific violence. On more than one occasion my dad smashed the house up in frustration. That was what led to his various stays in mental hospitals. The worst of it for him was that he took it out on his most prized possessions, his collection of vintage jazz 78s, his prized guitars which were worth a lot of money, and, worst of all, his wife, whom he genuinely loved.
>
> Naturally there came a time when she could not cope with that and a disability and had to leave him, although he could never understand why till his dying day. My mother was a remarkably tolerant woman, and gave back more than she ever took from society. My brother (who had by this time dropped out of university and returned to Coventry to live in digs) and I alternately put her up. The rest of the time she spent in a battered wives refuge where she became a counsellor for other women in her situation. On Good Friday 1981 she received the keys to her own flat and moved in. From that time forth my life changed too, as roles changed and I became her carer.

Larry's mother was a tireless campaigner. Although he began as her live-in helper, she began her campaign for disability rights, and he was called in to assist at every level, helping to set up a disability rights group, writing newsletters, attending council meetings, demonstrating, and finally writing a consultation document about transport for the disabled which was presented to a government committee. He had discovered his life's work. After she died, he tried his hand at photography before finally enrolling on a media course.

One US Asperger woman chooses to work as a temporary administrative assistant. Many Aspergers are particularly well ordered, because of their love of routine. She likes an occasional change of scene, but also fears the disorientation of a new office. Her strategy in dealing with this is unique.

> When I go to a new place I feel very confused, but I know how to get round it. I always say, 'You know what this place needs? A proper inventory and some

schedules!' So I find where everything is and I label it or make a plan in my head and another for the office staff. They think I'm wonderful, an organizational genius, but what I'm doing is plotting my routes. Then I can feel comfortable.

According to Kevin Phillips, these Aspergers with jobs which suit their skills are rare. He spent two years after leaving school collecting glasses in a night club. Yet here was an extremely intelligent man who at the age of thirteen had stunned his teachers and classmates with his detailed knowledge of the Suez crisis. And that's quite apart from the strange calendar calculating skills. Now, finally diagnosed, he's doing what he should have done years ago, taking A levels in history, psychology and English.

I talked to him about suitable jobs for Aspergers in his area.

'Postman,' he suggested. 'It's a routine job, which we like, and there's the sorting and the organizing. Or warehouseman. If an Asperger had a job in a warehouse he'd know where everything was without having to check it up. But some of us have real problems with noise levels – I can't work when it's too noisy. I have to drown out the sound of voices by listening to music.'

And that's an odd thing he said about the music, because it took me back to Danny and the buzz he got from noisy pubs. When I thought about it, the music was always drowning out the sound of voices in the places where he drank. And that gave me yet another idea for a suitable job for Danny.

He'd found the flat he was looking for, an unfurnished Georgian ground-floor apartment right in the centre of the city, with a small courtyard, and a cellar for his wine. Of course, his wine never made it to the cellar, but was proudly displayed all over the kitchen and living room.

A useful tax rebate enabled him to move in, but I helped with some furnishing, while he improvised beautifully with junk shop finds to make the place feel like home. There was an angry blip on our friendship when he was missing on the morning he was supposed to take delivery of the sofa I was buying for him on credit. That morning he was delayed, as he'd spent the previous night with four girls who had, he said, 'kidnapped' him. The sofa delivery had to be re-arranged. We didn't speak for a while, understandably enough.

I think that until then I'd imagined that we were living in my dream scenario, apart, but lovers, rather than in Danny's original scenario, together but parallel. I had secretly thought that my way was always the best way to preserve any romance there was between us. This 'kidnap' taught me that we were only close friends. If I was truly as honest as I pretended to be, we had never been very much more, except when I got caught up in Danny's fantasies. From then on, I had to accept that if I wanted him to be free to be happy, then he had to be free to make other relationships, play The Game, and go back to his roistering ways. Sad, I know, but true.

I suppose I'd always had an instinct that what he needed to do was to have a bolt-hole of his own, and although I'd tried to encourage him to move out and find his own place, I'd never realized how frightened that made him feel. It was fear alone which kept him at my side for all that time.

He'd moved from living with his mother to, at sixteen, finding a flat with Heather, then the sumptuous house which she'd totally refurbished. When she left and he was alone, the first thing he'd done was to take in student lodgers. When Heather offered to buy him out, so that she, her new husband and their new baby could return to the house she'd loved, he'd moved in with his father. Then he'd moved in with me. I'd been a fool to miss that, hadn't I? He'd never fended for himself.

Of course, the brief interlude in the box within a box which he and Ali had chosen for him, too far away from the excitement of town, had scared him more. But at least it had given him a period of reflection, time to consider whether he actually could make the transition, at thirty-six, to living alone.

Aspergers always find change difficult to contemplate and even more difficult, given their passivity, to seek out. But the flat, chosen with love by Danny, was exactly what had been missing from his life – somewhere to escape to that was totally within his control, an environment in which he could be whatever he fearfully chose to be. I saw the change in him as he settled into his own secret place. He kept it perfectly neat and wonderfully organized, except in the bedroom where his clothes were heaped on every surface as always. He grew up. He blossomed. He was earning some money, not enough as yet, but enough to keep him ticking over with the frugality that came as second nature to him. He loved entertaining me there, cooking for me, but was happy when I left him to his own routines.

The move motivated him. I knew that it would signal a change in his entire outlook on life. It was exactly what I'd imagined for him.

So, reconciled to a different kind of relationship, I was sitting in Danny's living room, responding to his invitation to coffee, when I noticed an advertisement for a job which would solve several of his problems at once. It was a vacancy for a barman in a local nightclub, on Thursdays, Fridays and Saturdays.

'Look at this! You can get the buzz and you don't need to drink!' I said, passing it over to him.

His face lit up. 'I'd make some money instead of spending it!' he squealed. 'Oh, I'd like to do that.'

Naturally he was offered the job – a mature, so they thought, male applicant in the rush of students. Within a short time, he had made his mark here too.

He was still looking for full-time work, still working for Ali, but less enthusiastically and less obsessively, but the job in the bar was perfect for him. On his first night at work he set out in his dress shirt and a bow tie, and was put in charge of the VIP bar where the impeccable manners in customer service which he had learnt from the public school wine merchant were immediately noted as both rare and rather wonderful, an ironic postmodernist note in a noisy crowded disco. And he loved the work. He loved the brash non-stop music, the fact that he could get people drunk, and control them, the fact that no one noticed that he was a little odd, and, although he remained abstemious for the most part, he enjoyed sneaking a drink occasionally.

'But I don't need to!' he told me, amazed. 'For the first time in my life, I don't really need to drink!'

Visiting him there was a bizarre experience. I had to fight my way through crowds of schoolchildren and students to reach the bar where he worked, tucked away at the back of the club. There, although music pounded, there were rarely more than the club bouncers, the club managers and their wives and guests, and a few local personalities, all heaping praise on him.

'Best barman we ever had in here,' said the owner's wife to me. She was very drunk and didn't know who I was, but this was nevertheless a testimonial.

I was going on holiday, and had a message to give to Danny before I left the next morning. So I sat at his bar while he poured me a free drink, and spoke to the manager. Danny introduced us.

'She's my friend, and she's on the radio,' he boasted.

When I said goodbye, he asked me what time I was leaving the next day.

'I'm catching the eleven o'clock train. I'll call you from Spain,' I said.

But he surprised me with the most unexpected and spontaneous thing he'd ever done. The next day, as I waited on the station platform, he turned up.

'What are you doing?' I asked.

'Came to see you off,' he said.

He lifted my case on to the train, kissed me, waved until I couldn't see him any more, and I haven't to this day worked out why he did that, or what gave him the motivation to get up, early for him, on a Saturday morning, to do no more than reassure me that we were still close. Thinking about it, even now, leaves me confused and very deeply touched.

When I returned from holiday, he was still in an upbeat mood. He invited himself round on the night I came back, to help me drink the bottle of wine I'd bought for us, some rare, rare Ribero Del Duero, very special indeed.

'Stunning,' he kept saying.

He was still applying for jobs, wanted me to trawl the internet to find out if there were any sales jobs in the area, and he'd been promoted at work. He was now temporary bar manager, for all the bars in the club, and he had a special date the next night. He didn't know what it was, but the club manager had told him to turn up early, and that they would be going round to another club together. It all sounded very promising. I told him I'd cross my fingers for him, and he told me that he was going to dress up, specially, in his designer suit.

In the early hours of that morning there was a ring at my doorbell. He stood on the doorstep swaying, his suit filthy.

'What happened?' I gasped.

'Can't remember, but I lost my keys so I'm here,' he slurred, taking off his clothes as he stumbled towards the bed. He fell down on it, and immediately into a deep sleep at my side.

The next morning, I checked his suit. It was muddy and torn, the front bearing the stains of vomit. Ruined. It had cost more money than I cared to think about.

Slowly, as he briefly struggled out of unconsciousness, fell into it again, and finally woke at four in the afternoon, begging for coffee, water and orange juice, he pieced together the story. The manager had decided to open a new cocktail bar, with Danny in charge, and had taken him to another bar, owned by the same company, for Danny to demonstrate to various staff the lethal cocktails he'd been serving in the VIP lounge. They had then drunk the concoctions, every one. Danny remembered crawling back to his own club, and falling asleep in an alleyway behind it. He thought that for part of the night he may have slept in a bush outside the cathedral which was opposite his flat. Then he discovered that his keys were missing, as he tried to open the front door with a two pence piece, but he knew that I would know what to do. I instructed him to phone the management company of his flat to get someone to let him in.

'Your suit's ruined,' I told him.

'Hmmmmmm,' he agreed, inspecting it. 'It'll have to be cleaned and mended. It'll be fine, just fine! Anyway,' he added, 'I'm a hero. I remember the manager telling me I was the best cocktail barman he'd ever known.'

'Not great if one of your clients from the restaurants saw you in that state, though,' I reminded him, keen to put a damper on this re-emergence of his drinking culture.

He thought for a moment or two.

'I can't afford to do this if I'm looking for jobs, can I?' he asked.

'No, you've got to get your act together.'

'But,' he said, 'I'm a hero anyway!'

It was very hard for him to unlearn the rule taught to him by his rugby team-mates, that heavy drinking is a manly thing to do and earns you admiration. Once a Rule had been entered into the book, it was cast in cement. But I found it almost impossible to understand that this intelligent, wonderful man, whom I loved, could sit for an entire evening, sipping slowly from a bottle of the best vintage wine, savouring every mouthful, yet could also see it as not only acceptable, but a mark of honour, a signal that he had won over his peer group, when he had ruined a good suit, acted like a buffoon, fallen asleep in a bush like a vagrant, and tried to identify what he'd drunk by the colours of the dried vomit on his lapels.

Am I being judgemental here? Or am I being, as Danny lovingly described me in his inimitable Asperger way, logical?

Still, custom being what it is, he did indeed earn accolades for his cocktail night, his job as bar manager was assured, and promises were made to him that the idea of the cocktail bar, featuring his own inventions, would be put to the next meeting of the owners. And, the manager had invited me and Danny to his home for dinner and to play chess. I don't play chess. But Danny did, and he was very excited by the invitation.

'He told me to bring my partner. So will you come?' he asked. That was quite a surprise.

Meanwhile, there was something promising at last in the search for work. An advertisement I'd found – why was I the one who searched for jobs for him? – sounded perfect. It was for a sales manager, with a nationwide remit, travelling to various outposts of a chain of greenhouse manufacturers whose head office was in a nearby town. There was a car provided. Danny knew as much about glass and UPVC as he did about wine, fruit and vegetables, and while he was reluctant to go back to selling windows, selling greenhouses and conservatories was far more acceptable. Cool, in fact.

We set out on the furious task of trying to get him an interview, and trying to make sure he impressed. I played with his CV until it looked even more enticing. Danny kept his mobile phone turned on, just in case they tried to contact him, and as Ali was now being given the same treatment I'd been used to for years – the phone was never answered if Ali's number showed on the screen – the phone was always checked when it rang.

The company not only phoned, but also wrote, inviting him for an interview the following week. It was a family firm, well established, looking to extend its base of operations, and needing someone to co-ordinate the sales team, and attend board meetings to offer new marketing ideas. The job was exactly what Danny could manage, and the long hours of driving, the necessity to spend many nights away from home, were unlikely to attract a family man of his age. We worked out that any other applicants would probably be older (while the firm was looking for youth and dynamism) or be younger but far less well qualified. He was certainly in with a strong chance, provided he could come through the rigours of an interview, not an easy task for an Asperger.

Interviews involve very fast attention-shifting, moving from answering one type of question to another seamlessly, something Aspergers find difficult. They involve being under scrutiny, something most Aspergers hate. They involve deep concentration, which some Aspergers have problems with, especially if they're also trying to fight against the blank expressions they sometimes adopt when thinking deeply. They involve being judged, sometimes by those for whom they may have little respect, and perhaps being directed, too. This can be a nightmare for the more arrogant Aspergers like Danny.

In many ways, interviews represent all that they might hate about the proposed job, and Danny hadn't had a real interview for years. We'll discount the interview with Ali which was merely an example of Danny taking control. This time he had to be careful not to overwhelm but to respond, thoughtfully.

However, I knew that Danny was more capable than most of modelling and scripting, picking a mode which he felt would impress, and being able to stay in role, no matter what happened. His cheerful smile, even when he was feeling wretched – remember I mentioned this in the first chapter, and remember Joel doing the same? – was a clear example. He was able to mask feelings which he thought others might find unacceptable. It was the way he had survived.

All I could do for him was to encourage him to think positively, and make sure that he looked the part. With his desperate need for respect and acceptance I knew that if he looked as good as he could, he would feel more comfortable.

'You can't wear your suit,' I told him. 'Not with a darn in it. It doesn't look professional.'

So, it was off for retail therapy once more, a joyous experience I'd seriously missed since he and I had been living separately. We found him another designer suit, offered at half price in a chainstore sale. And with alterations, this looked both elegant and tailored, almost as if it had been made for him.

'What about a pink shirt?' he asked.

This was a new venture for Danny. I'd once tried to persuade him into a pink shirt, explaining that with his dark colouring and blue eyes it was just the right choice to wear with a dark suit. He'd resisted strongly. Now he had come round to the idea.

'I saw a Frenchman wearing one the other day,' he explained. 'He got out of a Porsche and he was wearing a Rolex.'

That was my Danny, ideas above his station again! But the pink shirt was bought, with cuffs for the silver links I'd bought him some time ago, and a dark lilac tie in raw silk. He certainly looked the part of an executive sales manager.

The day before the interview he surprised me, turning up at my flat in full interview outfit, in a mood which he always described as 'boisterous'. It was one of his favourite words, another childhood word, one you normally use to categorize small hyperactive children. He bubbled with excitement.

'Know what I've been doing?' he asked. 'I've been practising my body language and eye contact! I got the big mirror down from over the mantelpiece, and put it on the floor, then I put these clothes on and sat in front of it and tried to act natural. What do you think?'

I was stunned. He had, throughout our time together, accepted my guidance as to his Asperger's Syndrome, he had talked over with me some of his problems, but he'd never before acknowledged that this had been the basis of his life's difficulties. He'd never before, if you like, owned his condition. It was a huge breakthrough.

So I watched while he demonstrated.

'I thought this was the best way for me to sit. This way I look focused, but relaxed. I don't look intimidated, do I? And see, I'll just turn like this, and look at whoever asks a question. Does that look right to you? Am I doing it right?'

It was so disingenuous, so touching. I felt honoured to have been used as consultant in this way – private body language tutor, now, in addition to careers adviser.

'It's perfect,' I told him, and it was. Nothing could stop him. His mind was fixed on this job. I hoped that nothing would happen to disappoint him, as I could see this would be a devastating blow which might put him back a long way, just when he'd taken this giant stride towards accepting who and what he was, and had seen and understood the impact this might have on others.

I was barely able to settle to anything on the morning of the interview. Danny had borrowed Ali's 'boy racer' car on some pretext to drive himself to the nearby town. He phoned from the car. He was on time.

Two hours later, he called again, breathless with disbelief.

'I start on twenty-two thousand, and a company car in a fortnight's time! I'm driving over to see you right now! Right now!'

I cried with happiness, raced out to meet him when the car pulled up, and we hugged and jumped around together on the patio like two demented pogoing bunnies. Neither of us could speak for ages. He made most of his little noises, one after another, happy to let them out at last.

'Hmmm, oooohhhh, pshhtttttt, oooohhhh,' he sang, and then, finally, as he managed to drink his coffee and return to some sort of self-control, he boasted, 'I didn't make any of my sounds, and I didn't pull my hair once! I was so good, you would have been proud of me!'

'I am proud of you. I really am,' I said, hugging him again.

'And you know what the MD said to me? He said, "Some of the others wanted another candidate, but I insisted on you. There's something about you. You're different!" ' He squealed with pleasure. 'He doesn't know just how different, does he? Well, no one does except you!'

I took him out for a celebratory lunch. He was working at the nightclub that night and all weekend, and I warned him not to get overtired, suggesting gently that he might like to resign from the nightclub.

'I'll be fine,' he insisted. 'Just fine!' The use of his favourite masking expression sent shivers down my spine. Just fine usually meant trouble.

As the week went on, the sheer exhaustion of making that two-hour effort was telling on him. If I saw him he seemed dazed and out for the count, but he did arrange to meet me on Friday evening, to taste a wine he'd bought, phoning me out of the blue.

'Are you sure you're OK?' I asked. I knew he was due at the nightclub that night.

'A bit tired. But come down and meet me,' he said, arranging we'd meet in a café halfway between our flats in half an hour's time.

Unusually for me, I was a little late. I'd dashed out and forgotten my mobile phone, too, so I couldn't phone him to warn him.

'Seen Danny?' I asked one of the people in the café, after I'd searched in vain for him.

'He just left,' he said. He'd long ago grown out of the habit of disappearing on me once he made an arrangement, so I found this difficult to understand.

I reasoned that tiredness had got the better of him, as I suspected it might, and that he'd returned home to sleep. I collected my mobile phone, and raced round to his flat, phoning on the way.

There was no reply. I arrived at his flat and rang the bell, then banged at the door and his window. Nothing. I was very worried. It was only an hour until he was due at the club, and I wasn't sure if he'd gone straight there. I had to find out if he had bumped into someone from work, and gone along with them, or whether his old narcolepsy had returned.

It wasn't true narcolepsy, just the Asperger tendency, which you'll remember, for him to fall asleep in an instant and be impossible to arouse. Is this what had happened? If so, he'd be likely to sleep until the following morning. He certainly wasn't answering his phone. Increasingly concerned, I made my way to the club. He'd said something about meeting one of the staff, Toby, a medical student, who worked alongside him in the VIP bar, and who was due to stay with him that night.

When I arrived at the club, it was opening. Staff were pouring in, but I couldn't see Danny, or the manager whom I'd met once and who had invited us to dinner the following weekend, or the club bouncer we'd spent many evenings with. I went in to find a crowd of strangers setting up for the night. I looked round helplessly, not knowing who else I could entrust my sinking feeling to that Danny wouldn't make it that night. I'd been introduced to Toby in the frenzied darkness of the club, and a couple of the others, too, but wouldn't have recognized them again. Nor, I suspected, would they remember me.

There was a woman who seemed to be in charge.

'We're not open for another fifteen minutes!' she said.

'I know, just looking for Danny. I'm a friend of his. He was supposed to be meeting me but didn't turn up, and I'm worried.'

'He's not in yet,' the woman said, deeply suspicious.

'Is Toby here?'

'Upstairs,' she said, gesturing with her head.

'Could I have a word with him?' I asked. Danny trusted Toby.

'Go on up,' she instructed, so I did.

There was only one person upstairs. I assumed he must be Toby, and when I asked he nodded. As I'd thought, there was no recognition in his eyes.

'Have you seen Danny?' I asked, repeating my story. 'You were supposed to be seeing him tonight, apparently.'

'Change of plan. I let him know I wouldn't be staying with him, a couple of hours ago. He should be in now,' he said, sounding surprised that Danny had given me this information.

'I think he's fallen asleep,' I said.

It was all rather surreal. Obviously no one here knew who I was. Some were staring, aggressively. Toby offered to phone Danny for me, as if I were some girl he'd stood up, but told me that he couldn't give me Danny's address. Just what was going on?

'It's OK, I've got his number, always have had it, and I know where he lives. I've just been round there,' I reassured him. I didn't tell him that I'd chosen the place with Danny, furnished it, and lent him part of the rent each month, although by this stage I certainly wanted to. 'It's just that he's not answering the door or the phone. You can try if you like.'

So he did. Still no answer.

'I'll go back there, try to wake him,' I said.

The club had opened. Some customers were wandering to the barn-like main room. I walked down the stairs, and just as I emerged from the club, Danny appeared, red-eyed, zombie-like.

'Thank God!' I said. 'You fell asleep?'

He nodded, too tired to speak.

'You should have waited for me, as arranged. You didn't answer your phone and it's ages since you did that to me. I've been panicking.'

'No need,' he said, and he was right. I felt a fool. I didn't dare tell him about the stupid fear that had gripped me, that maybe, just maybe, he'd had another bout of serious depression, and couldn't face the prospect of starting the job. I knew that he wasn't suicidal, but it's a thought that had entered my head. As had the possibility, which I saw recorded on the faces of those work-mates of his, that he'd been bedding someone else. I still couldn't quite cope with that idea.

'OK, I'll see you on Monday,' I said. 'Try to wake up!'

It was a passing trivial incident, totally forgotten by Monday when he turned up for dinner looking as bright as ever, having slept all the previous day. I cooked, and we started to eat. He was staying with me as we were leaving for a celebratory London trip early the next morning.

'The people you work with seem a strange crowd,' I grinned at him, just sharing idle banter. 'Some of them must have seen me with you before, but they weren't terribly helpful on Friday.'

'No,' he said, 'but I sorted that out. I just told them you were mad.'

I laughed, 'I was mad! I was furious. You asked me to meet you and then disappeared!'

'No,' he corrected. 'I meant the other kind of mad. Bonkers.'

'What?'

'Well, I thought that was the easiest thing to say. You shouldn't have come into the club.'

'Why not?'

This conversation was getting dangerously out of hand and was rapidly turning into one of those AS/NT misunderstanding discussions that I just didn't want to have, and that I didn't think we'd ever have again.

But, you see, that's one of the problems with Asperger's. It isn't something that ever goes away, even though we in the NT world are trained to believe that once a problem has been talked through, and the message received, then the issue is repaired. It just doesn't work like that.

'Because that's where I work, and you shouldn't come in to where I work.' He'd invented a new Rule. Or was it an old one which had been reinstated? I didn't know.

'But I've been to the club lots of times. And I came to the wine shop when you worked there. And you used to come to work with me. What is all this?'

'I didn't tell anyone about you and me,' he said.

Suddenly I was reminded of another Asperger partner I had interviewed. Doris. Her husband's work-mates in all the years they worked with him didn't know that he was married and had children, so when he had a wedding invitation from a colleague, it was for him alone. The single man. And, what's more, he went to the wedding and thought nothing of it. She could never explain to him that this was breaking the rules of accepted and conventional social behaviour.

'Ah, so that's why Toby didn't know I knew where you lived or that I had your mobile number?'

'Yes,' he said.

'But the manager knows I'm your best friend?'

'Not really.'

'Well, how come we're going round to his house together next week?' I asked, more and more mystified.

'I didn't tell him I was taking you. I told you, but I didn't tell him. You shouldn't have come to the club. You just shouldn't have come.'

By now Danny was becoming more and more entrenched in this Rule and more and more sulky.

'So you found it easier to say you didn't really know me, that I must be some mad woman you were trying to get rid of?'

He refused to reply. He refused to look at me. Then he grabbed his coat.

'I can't deal with you when you're angry,' he announced. 'I'm going home.'

'Good,' I said.

I was outraged and the outrage wouldn't burn itself out. My NT perceptions of what had happened were naturally based on human psychology, as yours would have been, I think. I just worked out that he'd wanted to present himself as young, free and single, a wild-oats salesman, ready for any bit of fun in a skirt that took his eye, and that my appearance at the club, purporting to be his closest friend, must have embarrassed him in front of the young people he worked with. I saw it as a form of rejection of me, and what I'd meant to him, in that company. And it was more than that. By inventing this story, he had now made certain that I could never go into the club again.

So when he drove round to show me his company car ten days later, during which time he hadn't attempted to make contact, I wouldn't let him in.

'Go and show someone else that you care about,' I said. 'There must be some old friend that you haven't insulted.'

Childish, wasn't it? I admit. He drove away and I didn't see him again for weeks. Nor did I miss him, much. I was seething.

Now I think differently. I realize something I'd perhaps discounted, although Danny did tell me this over and over again. He told me from the first that I was the only person he had ever spoken to about life, love, the things that matter, since his divorce. He'd told me that he was an intensely private person. And that's exactly what he meant. Being Asperger, he was literal. Being NT, I'd heard the expression 'intensely private person' before and thought I knew what it meant when people described themselves thus. What it meant to Danny was that no one ever knew anything he did or thought, except me. With no other person, ever, was he forthcoming about his true self, and if he had shared any information with the men in the wine shop, it had been inappropriate, but not insightful. He just didn't pass personal information around to others. The Danny I knew was someone no one else knew, no one, and no one else was allowed to know. He was the genuine article, the Asperger, the private person. And he didn't want me to share what I knew about him with anyone. He hadn't told anyone about me, merely because he never told anybody anything.

The next time he contacted me, he'd calculated carefully that he wouldn't have to see or speak to me. I arrived back from my Sunday night show, six weeks after he'd started his job, to find a letter, hand-delivered, through my door. It was from Danny. Two hundred pounds dropped out of the envelope when I opened it.

'I'm sorry I haven't been in touch', it said, 'but this job is very hard. I've been working a fourteen-hour day, every day, and I'm still doing what I can for Ali on Saturdays. I've now had my first month's pay, and commission from Ali, so this is the first instalment of the money I owe you. I'll try to pay you back like this regularly. My mobile is always switched on these days, and if I can, I'll answer it. Please call.'

He could always find my weakest spot. I suppose that's because we always were so close. I understood him, and gave him no credit for understanding me, but he did. He once told me that he'd learnt about my anger, and that he knew that if he left me alone until it subsided, it would always subside, where he was concerned. True. I'd promised him unconditional love. Funnily enough, he knew exactly what that meant, and he gave it back to me, in his often messy, but always honest, Asperger way. So, within a day or two we were back to being secret best buddies. As, I suppose, we always had been.

This time, despite regular phone calls, our meetings were less frequent. We were both busy. But I welcomed the times when, impulsively, he'd just turn up on my doorstep, his smile in place, a bottle of wine in his hand, and march in as if he belonged, calling over his shoulder, 'You wouldn't believe what a bargain this was! Just wait till you taste it and tell me what price you think I paid for this '95 New Zealand Sauvignon. I thought of you as soon as I saw it!'

Sometimes we'd go out for a meal. Sometimes he'd invite me round. Once we went to a university dinner and dance, and convinced everyone that he was a lecturer in philosophy, which, in his own idiosyncratic way, he was. Sometimes he'd stay the night, and once he asked if he could do that the next Friday too. He'd missed me. The following Friday he called to check whether he could leave his car in my drive for the night, if he came straight from work.

'Course you can,' I laughed. 'Like you did last week.'

It was the same old same old. That night I cooked, then tidied his coat away as I served up dinner and he opened the wine. He'd become calmer. He'd learnt ways of taking responsibility and living alone. He was almost the man I knew he could be. Getting that job had transformed him. I loved having him around.

'Shall I leave your mobile here in the kitchen with us?' I asked.

'Oh, yes, please!' he grinned, taking it from his coat pocket. 'Toby's phoning me at nine.'

It was eight now.

'OK,' I said.

'And then I have to go back home. I'll leave the car here and walk, so that I can have some wine.'

'Go back?' I asked.

'Yes, I forgot. I promised I'd go out with Toby tonight and he's staying at my flat. So I'll have dinner with you, and then I'll have to go.'

He was still smiling, but he'd dropped his eyes. A giveaway. We both knew this was wrong.

'You couldn't tell him you had a prior engagement, could you?' I asked quietly. 'You always did say yes to whatever anyone asked you to do.'

'I'm sorry,' he said. It was genuine. I knew he was apologizing, but I was tired now. I'd needed to talk to him about my new job, a demanding four nights a week, three-hour show at a new radio station. I'd been the victim of my own success, and this new programme was too much for me. I didn't have time to make the fine adjustments necessary to keep a relationship with an Asperger functioning smoothly at the same time. It was, to use an expression Danny used all the time, 'too much hassle'. I knew exactly what he meant. It was the attention-shifting I couldn't manage, either, just at the moment. And, more than that, I couldn't take the emotion-shifting either. I wanted to opt out and recuperate. It was my turn, surely?

'Tell you what I'll do,' he said, in a rare attempt to repair the damage, 'I'll come round every Friday from now on. Then we both know not to do anything else on Fridays. Is that all right?'

'No, love,' I said. 'I'm away in London next Friday. The Friday after that you have your firm's Christmas party. The Friday after you'll be elsewhere, or I will. Lists like that just don't work in the run up to Christmas, do they?' You'll have noticed that attempt of his to set up an Asperger routine.

'No, I suppose not,' he agreed.

As he left he said, 'I'm sorry. I haven't been fair, have I?'

Later, I went out and kicked his car.

The next day I heard the car engine start, and through my curtains saw the squat dark blur of his head, and the rapid wriggle of fingers, and a gesture that meant busy busy busy as he drove away. He was just a shape that moved inside a kicked moving shape.

I never saw him again. Ever.

We spoke the following week. I said I was tired and stressed, I had problems with a book I was writing, and with the tantrums of the narcissistic presenter of the radio show, but I asked him to get in touch near his birthday, and reminded him that he'd said he'd come for Christmas Day. He promised that he would.

My son brought his girlfriend home for Christmas, the one he'd spent the previous Christmas talking to on the phone. I'd known it was serious, even then. It was good to see them both so happy this time. He put his arm round me just before we had our lunch and said, 'He's not coming, Mum.'

'I know,' I said.

We pulled crackers, and didn't set that extra place.

It's strange. We live only half a mile from each other in this village of a city where you see everyone that you'd hoped you'd never again bump into, every day. But I've never caught sight of Danny, though I've looked for him, often. I sometimes ask after him. People are vague. They can't remember whether they've seen him or not. He was that kind of man.

He was not the kind of man you fall in love with.

Aspergers and employment

Most of the Aspergers in my survey were employed or self-employed. This, though, is not statistically average.

In a pamphlet 'Ignored or Ineligible' published in 2001 for Autism Awareness week, and written by Judith Barnard and colleagues, the true face of Asperger employment (in the UK) was revealed.

Bear in mind that those who took part in the survey were Aspergers who had been diagnosed and therefore the results do not take into account the many Aspergers who have not had a diagnosis. But these results are very much worth considering.

- 12 per cent of diagnosed HFA/Aspergers are currently in full-time paid employment.
- 6 per cent of diagnosed Asperger Syndrome adults are in part-time employment.

So why is this?

Danny's experiences on the employment front highlight some of the difficulties encountered by Aspergers in their efforts to find a job, and keep a job. These are the problems I identified in Danny's search for a job.

Job-seeking

- The CV can lack central coherence and is poorly organized.
- There can be problems with referees – confidential reports often contain references to the Asperger's 'oddness' or 'difference'.
- Autistic inertia can make it difficult for the Asperger to motivate him- or herself to look through job adverts.
- The dislike of change means that Aspergers prefer to stay put, even in a difficult or non-productive job, rather than look for one more suitable.
- Job-seeking demands the frightening prospect of job interviews.

Interviews

- Those Aspergers with eye-contact problems can appear in interview to be shifty and untrustworthy.
- It is difficult for an Asperger to avoid stimming at times of stress (remember the nose-picking clergyman?) Central Auditory Processing problems can mean that questions asked at an interview are poorly understood.

- Aspergers tend to dress badly or inappropriately for interviews.
- Interviews demand quick attention shifts between various questioners – an exceptionally difficult task for an Asperger.
- Unless the Asperger is well 'scripted' and prepared, the language he or she uses may sound stilted, formal, or overly familiar.

The workplace

I am indebted in this section to Roger N. Meyer, author of the *Asperger Syndrome Employment Workbook*, published by Jessica Kingsley Publishers, 2001. In an appendix to that book Roger identifies many of the Asperger characteristics which can cause problems in the workplace and many which can be an asset. A selection of both negative and positive characteristics are noted below.

Negative characteristics in the workplace

- difficulty with 'teamwork'
- tendency to 'lose it' during sensory overload, multi-task demands, or when contradictory and confusing priorities have been set
- difficulty in starting projects
- discomfort with competition, out-of-scale reactions to losing or failure
- low motivation to perform tasks of no immediate personal interest
- oversight or forgetting of tasks without formal reminders such as lists or schedules
- great concern about order and appearance of personal work area
- slow performance
- perfectionism
- difficulty with unstructured time
- reluctance to ask for help or seek comfort
- difficulty with writing and reports
- stress, frustration and anger reaction to interruptions
- difficulty in negotiating either in conflict situations or as a self-advocate
- very low level of assertiveness
- difficulty in handling relationships with authority figures

- often viewed as vulnerable or less able to resist harassment and badgering by others.

Positive characteristics in the workplace

- perfectionism – yes, it works both ways! In many jobs it is highly valued
- hard-working
- punctual
- pays little attention to office politics or gossip
- often highly skilled in his or her particular area of expertise
- unlikely to bully others
- persevering
- honest
- stoical in difficult conditions
- highly organized in keeping personal records and files
- excellent memory
- will happily act as 'gopher' – making tea, taking messages, collecting lunches, although apt to be a little clumsy
- is not easily distracted once a job has been started
- often has an instinctive understanding of computing
- is happy to learn the rules of the job or task
- believes in a good day's work for a good day's pay
- often able to provide a lateral solution to a practical problem.

6 Breakthrough

Now, you may be wondering whether it might have helped if I had managed to obtain an official diagnosis and counselling for Danny, early on in our relationship.

The easy answer to that question is no. Danny would never talk to anyone but me, as I've said repeatedly. As far as he was concerned, I had solved his puzzle, and that was enough for him. He trusted me, he talked to me, he expected me to counsel him, he struggled to fight the symptoms I had identified. Danny was ultimately a conformist. He wanted nothing more than to slide into acceptability and from there to rise to respectability.

His case was unusual, highly idiosyncratic, totally unresponsive to coercion or control. But, on the other hand, it illustrates the difficulties that diagnosis entails for adults. Some adults just don't want to know. On a practical level, some adults feel they don't need to know as they cope fairly well in their loner but successful condition.

For other adults, confused by their lifelong difference, a diagnosis is the key to peace of mind and a new, more positive lifestyle.

For them, the discovery of naming is a moment to savour, something to relish, a proof that what they have is a difference, which puts them in touch with a wider group of other, equal group members. It is a validation, an explanation and a light through the fog of their confusion.

But it isn't only their own confusion which is the enemy. The diagnostic criteria for Asperger's Syndrome were only validated in the last ten or fifteen years, and the lack of knowledge of the syndrome persists. Remember, too, that these criteria are mostly decided on with schoolchildren in mind.

One of the earliest diagnostic tests, that of Gillberg and Gillberg in 1989 (see page 202) is still considered by many world experts, including the leading authority, Tony Attwood, to be the most inclusive and clear.

The criteria are divided into six sections: social impairment; narrow interests; repetitive routines; speech and language peculiarities; non-verbal language difficulties; and motor clumsiness. This is the only list of criteria which specifies dyspraxia as being part of the syndrome, and this is the one feature which Tony Attwood insists is a constant feature of the Asperger's Syndrome cases he has seen.

The criteria by Szatmari, Bremner and Nagy published in the same year are less detailed, and they do have a separate criterion for one of the most noticeable symptoms of Asperger's Syndrome: 'solitary', with the subheadings 'no close friends', 'avoids others', 'no interest in making friends', 'a loner'. I think that this section might be useful in first identifying Asperger's Syndrome in children but may be less useful when looking at adult Aspergers, where these traits may be adapted into some kind of socially acceptable networking. Danny's apparently easy sociability, for instance, was only an adaptation. Underneath, as I've pointed out, he was unable to make many of the deep, confessional friendships which NTs see as an integral part of life.

In 1993 a World Health Organization classification, ICD-10, was adopted (see page 203). This again is very much aimed at children, including ages at which they might be talking, as language is not delayed in Asperger's Syndrome, and those who do have language delay are more likely to be diagnosed as High Functioning Autistic, like Temple Grandin, and Marc Segar. These criteria also state that motor clumsiness is usual, although it's not a necessary diagnostic feature.

The criteria in DSM-IV (Diagnostic and Statistical Manual of Mental Disorders) published in 1994 and upgraded recently (see page 201) are those in most common use. These are more easily used in diagnosing adult Asperger's Syndrome. They include six sections – impairment in social interaction; restricted and repetitive behaviour, interests and activities; significant impairment in social, occupational or other area of functioning; no language delay; no significant delay in mental ability, and, finally, that the patient cannot be classed as having another Pervasive Developmental Disorder, or schizophrenia. No mention is made of dyspraxia.

Now can you see, as I do, what problems there might be in identifying adults with Asperger's Syndrome? Some of those criteria can't be checked easily without knowledge of childhood development. Diagnosis, ideally, also involves interviews with the parents of the patient, as well as the patient. And how easily can this be done in an adult? Which of us, for instance, can remember whether we talked easily and on time? I can't. Can you? And do you remember whether you played comfortably with others? Of course, some of us can remember. For those of us brought up in homes where contact with other children was negligible, and where early friendships can't be recalled, there are gaps in our perceptions. I led a particularly lonely existence, for instance. Many other NTs will have similar recollections which have their origin in parental choices and decisions. I was rarely 'allowed' to play with other children. But many Aspergers and autistics, with their often keen memories, can recall precisely their childhood play, and playmates, and their own dysfunctions.

I've recently read of one Asperger's memories of not speaking. She says that at five she was wrapped up in a constraining zipped puffa suit, and given an ice cream which she then dropped inside the suit. She couldn't remove the ice cream, and couldn't tell anyone that it had fallen inside. She knew that she had words, but had no idea how to use them to express her needs to others.

That's a very odd case, similar to that of Marc Segar, whom you'll remember. Possibly, if she'd been diagnosed in childhood, it would have been as HFA, rather than Asperger.

For diagnosis of an adult, then, there has to be a strong memory of childhood or parents have to be consulted.

Another, less obvious but nevertheless very important problem is that Asperger's Syndrome is not as yet fully understood or accepted by some psychiatrists and psychologists. The reasons are obvious – that it is a recently diagnostically described condition and therefore, if they qualified before the 1990s, it may be something that their training omitted. But there's also the plain fact that most psychiatrists and clinical psychologists are trained in dealing with mental health problems, not in developmental disorders which is generally the preserve of paediatric or educational psychologists. Many of the symptoms which define Asperger's were even delegated, in the 1970s and 1980s, to speech and occupational therapists. They were not considered to be mainstream psychology.

In some cases there is clearly an unhelpful ignorance, even in those reputed to be qualified, and even in the recent past. Just look at this extract from a report in *The Times* of 3 July 2001. This opinion piece, published in a reputable broadsheet, was an analysis of the possible mental condition of an alleged murderer, by a professor of psychology who directs a University Centre for Investigative Psychology: I have italicized the part of the text which worries me.

During the trial various experts offered a number of pseudo-medical terms to describe the sort of person Barry George is. Personality disordered and psychopath are the favourites. These terms are summaries of how the patient deals with other people, but their medical patina implies that they are explanations of what the person is 'suffering from'. Another fashionable term is Asperger's syndrome. This has been taken from the world of autism, a complex and varied set of ways of being unable to operate in normal society. Those autistic people *who are also violent from time to time, have large mood swings, but who do not inhabit as separate and private a world as the severely autistic, are defined as suffering from Asperger's.* But as there is no satisfactory explanation and no actual medical markers for it, *all it amounts to is the recognition of the coexistence of a bundle of disturbing behaviours.*

This piece caused a furore, and it isn't difficult to see why. Twelve years after the appearance of the first diagnostic criteria for Asperger's Syndrome, here is an academically qualified and highly respected professor of psychology refusing to believe there is any such thing as this condition. He calls it a 'fashionable term', he describes Aspergers as having large mood swings, being violent from time to time (apart from in meltdowns, which many Aspergers don't have, Aspergers are exceptionally non-violent). The professor claims that there is no explanation for Asperger's and there are no medical markers. I suppose he means such things as blood tests and definitive brain scans but he has obviously not read his DSM-IV. I mean, is there a medical marker for depression? This is hardly the level of expertise one would expect from a man in his position. The piece brought a letter of complaint from the National Autistic Society. I would have signed it too.

Ignorance like this is patchy, but it does exist in medical fields in the understanding of Asperger's Syndrome.

Kevin Phillips certainly crashed into an edifice of ignorance when he finally plucked up courage to see his GP about Asperger's. He knew that this was exactly what he had. He'd bumped into a friend of his one day who gave his opinion that Kevin had AS, as he himself did. (It was curious that Kevin had not thought along those lines himself, as he had always been interested in autism, and had done a sponsored swim to raise money for the National Autistic Society.)

We talked about generalities for a while, then he suddenly changed the tone of the conversation by dropping a remark which I immediately challenged him about.

'You know, I think you are one of us.'

Puzzled, my reaction was… 'What do you mean, one of us? Who are us?'

'By saying that…er…I think that…erm…you have got Asperger's Syndrome.'

'What do you mean I have got Asperger's Syndrome? I only performed a sponsored event two and a half years ago to raise funds for the NAS. What do you know about Asperger's Syndrome anyway?'

'I have got it myself. I was diagnosed with it at the beginning of this year.'

'OK, fair enough, but what makes you think that I have got Asperger's Syndrome?'

'Well, I have seen your behaviour and the things that you are interested in. The calendar calculating skills that you have gives it away. I also remember the time a few years ago when you bluntly approached me and asked me to help you with this mathematical equation you were doing for your studies. You just barged in. Plus there are the things you talk about, all of which make me think that you have got Asperger's Syndrome. In fact I think that you are nearly as obvious as I am, and I stand out like a sore thumb!!!'

'I'll tell you what, I shall look it up on the internet and research it. I know a lot about autism but not very much about Asperger's Syndrome to be honest. If this is true, well…I don't know what to say.'

It took Kevin another few years to pluck up courage to admit that what his friend said was true. By this time he was twenty-four. Prompted from time to time by television programmes and newspaper articles which confirmed his friend's diagnosis and his own reluctant conviction, he made an appointment to see his doctor at the beginning of 2000. It was his millennium resolution to try to solve his difficulties by getting a diagnosis.

The GP I saw at my local surgery refused to grant me a referral point blank. I dwelled on this and four days later I went to see her again to try to bring about a change of mind but all to no avail. She wouldn't budge, and said that it was likely I had Obsessive Compulsive Disorder and then went on to say that there was a chance I could even be 'schizophrenic' but it was more likely that I had OCD.

In reply, I said that she was a 'schizophrenic' for suggesting I could be a 'schizophrenic'. All the way through the meeting she wouldn't budge. The only thing I gained was when she said I would be referred to the psychiatric unit of my local hospital, as that would be best 'suited for my needs'. I retorted that I wanted to see someone who was an expert on the subject, whereas the person I was to see at my local hospital may not be. She wouldn't have any of it and was unmoved by my protest. Perhaps out of frustration, I let fly with an angry outburst and stormed out.

In another way it was a good thing I got diagnosed later in life I suppose. What I find deeply disturbing with the 'schizophrenic' suggestion in January 2000 was that if this had happened ten years earlier, I could have been taken to a psychiatric hospital and drugged up to incapacity, if someone else in a white coat agreed with the suggestion. I could be walking round like a zombie now, so I suppose I should be grateful in one sense that I got diagnosed when I did.

Does this make you as angry as it makes me? Here is a rational coherent young man who shows no signs whatsoever of delusions, being given a possible diagnosis, by a medical practitioner, of schizophrenia.

Perhaps the doctor's tentative suggestion of OCD, Obsessive Compulsive Disorder, is fairly understandable. Sufferers with OCD have similar rigid and repetitive patterns. But, as was carefully explained to me by an Asperger, and as I've pointed out before, the rituals and routines in Asperger's are of a totally different quality and arise from a different need. Aspergers find their rituals and patterns happily reassuring, but can resist them if need be. Those with OCD, on the other hand, are unhappy with the control exerted on them by compulsive thoughts or actions which they find almost painful to resist.

But Kevin persisted, thank goodness. He could easily have been so angered by his doctor that he never sought again to have his condition properly recognized. But then, we are talking about Asperger's, with their powerful sense of justice and an ability to persevere, aren't we? Kevin was determined to have the truth verified. He went to see another GP who referred him to a psychiatrist, who could pass him on to the consultant he wanted to see, Professor Digby Tantam, who works in Sheffield. He's one of the few Asperger experts in the UK. Kevin had researched the condition well.

On Monday 3 April I fortunately saw a doctor/psychiatrist who was understanding and open minded. He listened to me talking about the problems and difficulties that I have faced in the past and will face in the future. He took time to read the report that I had painstakingly written four days before. The doctor said he wasn't in a concrete position to say whether I had got Asperger's Syndrome or not but stated he had never come across behavioural habits and problems that matched mine in all his years spent in the mental health profession, which has amounted to over thirty years.

The doctor stated outright that I don't appear to have any form of mental illness which people have been admitted and detained in psychiatric wards for. He himself referred me to Professor Tantam immediately.

On Thursday 20 April I got the breakthrough I had sought and wanted. I received a letter telling me that I was to see Professor Tantam on Wednesday 31 May at 2 p.m. at Sheffield Northern General Hospital.

Just after this, on Thursday 11 May I was evaluated by a clinical psychologist in a two hour session. It took place at a building near where I live. The report stated that the 'Patient doesn't appear to be psychotic. He stated that he has never in his entire life suffered from auditory hallucinations. He showed no delusional symptoms and certainly didn't show any traces of behaviour or thinking that could be described as schizophrenic.' It went on to say that my speech was 'Clear and coherent', but the tone of my voice was, 'Sometimes flat and often abrasive sounding.' It also added however that my voice had some 'bounce' to it and was not monotone, as the Asperger stereotype always portrays it to be.

On the night of Tuesday 30 May, I filled in a long questionnaire which was sent by Professor Tantam. I also showed him the report that I had written at the end of March. My mother was asked questions first and then I followed. I asked him his date of birth and told him what day of the week it fell on. I still remember that it was a Monday!

He said that I 'Clearly have got Asperger's Syndrome'. Prof Tantum also diagnosed that I have some degree of dyspraxia and agreed to refer me for an EEG scan. He said he would be very surprised if there wasn't any brainwave disturbances. Professor Tantam said my reflex reactions were 'lightning sharp' but some of them were very clumsy.

He said that I also have savant abilities typical of Autistic Spectrum Conditions.

If Kevin had to fight against one kind of ignorance to obtain his diagnosis, George Handley, who wrote the poem about Hans Asperger, was up against historical mis-timing.

Referred, as Danny was, through the School Educational Psychology services when he was approaching his sixth birthday, the deficits outlined on his report card, read in the light of what we know now, point exactly and precisely to Asperger's Syndrome. But at that time, in 1984, it was almost unheard of. He slipped through the net, and it was another twelve years, after a school career in which he was bullied mercilessly, before the diagnosis of Asperger's Syndrome was made.

But just take a look at these extracts from that report on him as a six-year-old. You know enough about Asperger's Syndrome by now to have made the diagnosis yourself. But this little boy lost all those years when he might have achieved something through schooling.

Date of report: Friday 18 May 1984
Report on George Handley

George was transferred at the age of five years and seven months by the school medical officer. At this time there was concern that his speech was not normal, he showed odd movements of his arms at times and had difficulty fitting in socially with the other children.

Medical Assessment

Dr K looked at previous medical notes and asked his mother about him. He was far from slow in his early development. At the age of three years he was seen by Dr F in the City Hospital.

The infant welfare clinic doctor had noted uncontrolled jerking of his limbs, which he had in fact been doing for years. This was not thought to be due to any illness.

George was in the nursery class at Infant School and is now in the Infant class. His parents do not feel that they have any problems with him at home. However he does like to have his own way and gets bored quickly.

Dr K examined George medically. He did show unusual movements of his arms, which are thought to be a habit and appear when he is excited or concentrating hard. He was able to do most of the things expected of a child of his age except that he was not able to dress himself and is apparently usually dressed by his mother. He is not usually given shoes which require laces, or clothes with buttons.

George was also seen by Dr M, the paediatric neurologist. Both doctors found a degree of clumsiness. It is not felt that this is due to a disease. It is not going to get worse but will tend to improve. He has not got any medical illness.

Mobility and Hand Skills

The physiotherapist looked at what George was able to do on his feet and his control of body movements. He seemed to have difficulty in understanding her instructions and she had to show him what she wanted him to do. He could just manage to hop and was overall a little clumsy but had no real disability.

The occupational therapist, Mrs B, looked at what George was able to do with his hands. She noticed that at times he became excited, laughed, talked loudly, lost his concentration and showed odd hand position. George was right handed. He found it difficult to thread small beads and do other things with his hands but managed to do them. He had no difficulty copying shapes and block patterns or using a six-shape jigsaw. He had an immature grasp of his pencil. He drew a slightly immature man. He needs to be encouraged to dress himself and it would be helpful if he held a pencil in a normal way now he is a big boy. He finds coordination of his hands a little harder than most children and appears to have to make more effort than most, which on the whole he does successfully.

Speech Development

Miss W, the speech therapist, tested George's understanding of speech and spoken instructions. Rather surprisingly George only performed at a four-year level. She also assessed what he was able to say. He pronounces his words satisfactorily apart from a small lisp. He uses the kind of sentence length you would expect of a child of his age.

However he does sometimes make mistakes, leaving out words, occasionally putting words in the wrong order. Sometimes he mixes up 'we' for 'they' and 'you' for 'they'.

In conversation he sometimes says unsuitable or inappropriate things, for example when asked, 'where's that house?' he replied, 'well it isn't really'.

Sometimes, when asked a question, instead of listening and answering the whole question he makes an answer which refers to only one word of the question. It can be seen that this can be rather unhelpful to George. It can make it difficult for him to understand what he is asked to do, particularly in school. It can make it difficult for him to join in games with other children. When his mistakes are pointed out to him he is able to understand what is meant and to answer the questions correctly. It is important that this should be encouraged.

Nursing Report

Nursing staff found at times George tended to avoid looking at people or things.

He also showed the odd behaviour when excited of flapping his hands, jumping up and down, laughing and giggling. He ate his meals satisfactorily and could go to the toilet on his own although he needed some help in arranging his clothes afterwards.

Developmental Assessment – School Health

Dr G from school health had originally seen George at the Centre at the age of four years nine months. At this time she gave him a standard intelligence test for preschool children and his score on this was average.

At the time he was cooperative and showed a delightful sense of humour. He was noted to be slightly clumsy.

When Dr G saw him again on the occasion of the present assessment at the age of five years seven months he was not so cooperative and seemed very quiet. He did not do much more on the intelligence test than he had done on the previous occasion. He was not cooperative and therefore it was not possible to score him.

After the assessment those who had seen George met to discuss him at a case conference. His teacher, the school nurse, and the educational psychologist were all present.

His teacher said that he did not have any problems with schoolwork, but did find it difficult to mix with the other children who on the whole tried to be helpful to George.

He was not naughty in school but had been noted at times to misbehave when his father fetched him.

We feel that George at present has some mild problems. These are:

Difficulty in using speech to communicate with meaning and some difficulty in understanding spoken instruction.

Clumsy Child Syndrome. This does not stop him from doing anything but does mean that he has to make more effort to coordinate his body.

Difficulty in mixing with the other children; sometimes his behaviour appears difficult to control at home.

Now could there be a clearer picture of Asperger's Syndrome? Clumsiness, a failure to understand spoken instructions, social and verbal inappropriateness, normal intelligence, difficulty in playing with other children, hand-flapping, odd gestures, eye-contact avoidance, problems with personal pronouns (Danny, as I told you, still did that occasionally at thirty-five) – it's all there, and perfectly clear.

I give you now the coup de grâce. Enjoy it. This 1984 diagnostic test which could not access and classify this unusual range of symptoms came after the tests on Marc Segar. But the irony is that the county in which George was examined has some of the best diagnosticians in the country for paediatric autism spectrum disorders. One of the specialists now working there was the one who diagnosed Marc Segar.

Of course, Marc, who was clearly more severely deficient in some features, and more skilled in others, had traits which were closer to the pattern which had been noted by Hans Asperger. He was middle class, gifted, strikingly unusual. George was just an odd, clumsy child, who sometimes couldn't understand language. He seemed to have no exceptional skills. But if you look carefully at that report you'll see that no questions were asked about any special interests, were they? Was this a class issue? I hope not. George was a very ordinary little boy from a very ordinary background, with elderly parents. Kevin Phillips, fiercely proud of his working-class roots, is certain that, in those days, only middle-class children were diagnosed. It was Catch 22. The parents who were educated enough to realize that there was something fundamentally wrong with their child were the ones who pressed for examinations and more examinations to discover a name for this condition and some help for their child. But the children most in need of the help, the parents most in need of explanation, never got it.

George was eighteen when he finally managed to track down the diagnosis he needed. Kevin was twenty-four. At this age, diagnosis can right some of the wrongs done by a missed education, perhaps. But diagnosis for the older adult can be a long haul, and we may have to question its worth. Some adults come to diagnosis through problems which can increase with age.

Larry Arnold, for instance, always had dyslexia, dyscalculia and dyspraxia, and learnt to live, reluctantly, with them. In some ways he was protected from the worst side-effects of these by the position he took as his mother's carer. Larry had his mentor, a strong, amazing woman, on whom he could rely, and who, in her turn, depended on him. It was a perfect arrangement. Through her interventions he was valued. The work he did at her side gave him experience and knowledge of work skills, and of people skills.

After her death, however, he plunged into depression as the hopes he had for various careers or courses were damaged by a condition which he found confusing. In his forties, what mattered to him initially was that his handicaps

became more disabling. It was in seeking help over his life-long practical difficulties with words, numbers and motor skills that he discovered a diagnosis
which had eluded him.

> It is at this point that my learning and cognitive disabilities begin to assume a
> more prominent role in my life. I had in fact got an inkling of something when I
> advocated for a child with ADHD, as part of my voluntary work. I found
> instant recognition of my own school days in a lot of his problems. It was also
> the first time I came across DSM-IV (the diagnostic and statistical manual of
> psychiatric disorders). I did not think to take this line of enquiry any further
> as regards myself, only to note that, if this was a problem considered severe
> enough to warrant the high levels of benefit we won for the boy, then my
> parents must have had a hard time bringing me up too, not to mention my
> brother who had his own difficulties. However whilst looking for work it
> became apparent that, although I might not think I have any difficulties
> employers do not share that optimism. It was during one job application in
> particular where I was required to take an aptitude test that all the old
> bogeys returned to haunt me. I failed at it spectacularly. Not only was my
> co-ordination slowing me down, but my reading ability, particularly where
> figures are concerned. I decided I needed to do something. In fact I
> approached the Dyslexia Institute (I was aware what dyslexia is, though I was
> still in denial) and they informed me that co-ordination difficulties are due to
> something called dyspraxia, which I had never heard of. At this time, having
> access to the net, I found out the Dyspraxia Foundation, and discovered the
> description to fit my childhood like a glove. There are however good reasons
> why I did not go rushing off to my doctor demanding a diagnosis, as that is not
> how the health service works over here. It is a low priority, if the doctors
> have even heard of an adult diagnosis of dyspraxia, which is mostly seen for
> the first time in children. Well the next stage on my journey of discovery was
> doing a business course. The upshot is that my learning difficulties made
> some parts of this course difficult, particularly with regard to forecasting
> costs and revenue. It was then I needed to make the PACT (placement
> advisory counselling team) aware of the extent of my learning disabilities, and
> it was they who sent me for a psychological assessment. What I did not
> know, was the extent to which my social skills were impaired, which is what
> got me into looking at Asperger's Syndrome. How had I heard of Asperger's?
> Well, it seems that this is something which is discussed amongst other
> dyspraxics and it is through the dyspraxia mail list that I came across others
> on the same path. Well, I might have been content to leave it at that but
> during a visit to London I took the opportunity to visit the National Autistic
> Society and asked them how I could secure a diagnosis. They were very
> helpful and actually had the names of consultant psychiatrists in Coventry
> who I could get a referral to, though that would be up to me how to go about
> it. I took away some leaflets and contact numbers for the West Midlands who

said much the same. I was very nervous of how to approach this with my own GP; however, I had been waiting to get an appointment for counselling for some time. I am afraid there are aspects of my behaviour which do no credit to me, and the counsellor was convinced I needed a psychiatric referral of some kind. I showed her the Autistic Society literature and explained that an evaluation for this might be more appropriate. She agreed and offered to mediate with my doctor to suggest this. The upshot is that my doctor raised no objections to this and referred me to a clinical neuro-psychologist who subsequently confirmed Asperger's Syndrome.

It should be more obvious to you now why so many Aspergers have remained undiagnosed. How many more Georges are there, who had an obviously Asperger's Syndrome report as a child? How many more Kevins are there, who have a GP who has no clue about the range and variety of autistic spectrum disorders? How many more Larrys are there, accepting their disabilities and lack of social skills as something they've had to live with and work round? Probably hundreds of thousands in the UK alone. It will take decades to find and diagnose them all, to construct a database, to come up with any figures about the prevalence of Asperger's Syndrome. Those who have been found and diagnosed have often been sparked into action by some random media coverage of the disorder. Some may have been having various psychiatric or psychological investigations for years, or counselling sessions, because of behavioural problems, without any useful outcome.

Before we knew what we now know about autism, and developmental disorders in general, most behavioural problems were thought to have a basis in childhood trauma. It's fair enough. Many do. I used to think, in the early days of knowing Danny, that there may have been some abuse in his childhood which made him behave as he did. I knew that he was closer to his father than his mother, and that his father used to stroke his back each night to encourage him to sleep, and it's that kind of thing which makes one think the unthinkable. Because, let's face it, that's our first reaction always, isn't it? We've been conditioned to think that there are childhood sexual and psychological reasons for everything. It's very difficult to shift our Freudian perceptions to understand neurological disorder as the primary possibility. Yet a psychiatrist friend of mine says that his rule is that where cause is unknown, always look for a physical reason.

The extent to which we shift, first, to psychoanalysis is demonstrated in the original belief that autistic spectrum disorders were caused by 'refrigerator parents', mothers who rejected their new babies by refusing to make eye contact with them, the theory propounded by the discredited Bruno Bettelheim back in the 1970s. And the tendency to shift 'blame' to the psychological profiles of those with whom we interact, parents and partners, has been responsible for some grave and almost unbelievable errors of diagnosis, especially in the Freudian analytical years of the 60s, 70s and 80s when we talked through our pains, endlessly.

This is what happened to Beverley, whose partner was eventually diagnosed with Asperger's Syndrome, but only after a series of blunders by psychiatrists and clinical psychologists. She was the one who found out about Asperger's Syndrome, and passed what she knew to those who were treating her husband, whose psychiatric problems baffled everyone.

Relatives say that as a child he was peculiar and his behaviour was appalling and extremely rude. According to reports written by his child psychologist, he was registered with the London Institute of Child Psychology when he was six and was under the care of various therapists, psychiatrists, a child psychologist, etc., until he was at least fifteen. He spent some time at a boarding school for 'problem' children. His local council paid for him to go to various private schools until he left after a recommendation from his doctors.

The childhood psychology reports describe him as having a severely inadequate personality, severe maladjustment, driveless, anxious, vulnerable, solitary, brittle, requiring care and support for some considerable time after leaving school. He didn't say forever, or that I would have to provide it. Also he had an exceptionally severe stammer and mild dyslexia.

He'd been seeing a psychiatrist attached to the local hospital here for eighteen months before I suggested to her that he might have AS. Just before I started reading up on AS on the net M discovered these psychiatric reports in his medical files written when he was fifteen which his GP hadn't bothered to pass on to the psychiatrist (or the other three psychiatrists, psychologists, social workers he'd seen in the previous twelve years or so).

Before I discovered AS I was absolutely frantic. I thought I was going mad. His doctor and the psychiatrists he'd seen earlier had misdiagnosed him with depression and anxiety brought on by the stress of being married to me. He was the poor long-suffering husband, and he played it to the hilt. Along with a bunch of other mental health 'professionals' they gave him intensive 'talking' therapy for several years, during which time they managed to convince each other that I was seriously mentally ill.

They referred to me in his psychiatric records as being 'very abnormal' amongst other things and twice mentioned the possibility of having me sectioned, even though none of these people had actually spoken to me. It was an absolute nightmare for all of us, so discovering the reason for his sometimes bizarre and disruptive behaviour was a tremendous relief for both of us. By the time I first discovered AS I had become pretty hostile, and my son hadn't talked to him for years.

My perceptions have changed considerably over the past three years, since the diagnosis of Asperger's Syndrome. I no longer expect him to relate to me and our son 'normally', so there's far less pressure on him. We've both become far more considerate of each other. He's also stopped blaming me for all his problems. The down side is he's a lot less confident than he used to be, perhaps because he can no longer blame me for his problems. Knowing there's no cure has been pretty devastating too, especially for him.

Beverley's experience is common rather than unique. Partners are often the first to realize that the difficulties they've been experiencing in their marriage may not have a psychological cause, as they resist all psychological interventions, and all efforts to work this through by relationship counselling. Neuro-typical women, in particular, look for explanation of motivations in others, genuinely want to heal rifts in their failing relationships, and are often under considerable pressure culturally to do so. Just look at how hard I worked as an amateur detective to find out exactly what was wrong with Danny, sieving through all the alternatives until I'd uncovered the puzzle that was Asperger's Syndrome. Women are specifically programmed to care, socialized into believing that anything that goes wrong with a relationship must be somehow our fault, or that the reason must be out there somewhere.

For Doris the reason didn't appear until after her marriage had broken up. She had struggled to make sense of her wonderful but strange husband throughout the time they were married. It was therefore extremely painful for her to discover that he had been having an affair. He moved out, taking none of his belongings with him, and without even a backward glance. Was he unemotional about what he did? It's unlikely. It's far more likely that in a Danny kind of way he was just saying yes to his girlfriend, detaching himself from the entire experience of marital infidelity and the pain it causes. Aspergers are rarely unfaithful. Afterwards, he and Doris somehow re-established their friendship, although she was still very aware that there was something seriously different about his behaviours.

It was the very small things I noticed. I thought he was shy in new situations, socially immature and had a vulnerable quality I couldn't put my finger on. He is seven years younger than I am. I thought that as he grew older and had more opportunities he would grow and mature. He didn't. I put it down to an emotionally deprived childhood with a mother who was not too good at showing affection, though cared for them OK, and a Roman Catholic schooling and strict religious upbringing.

After a few years I realized that we never sorted out our problems, I tried to discuss things and thought we had reached a new level, but then found we were right back at the beginning just going round in circles. I realized that as far as a marriage partnership was concerned, ours was not 50:50 but more like 75:25. I felt I was doing all the input, all the planning, organizing, worrying, etc.

After five years I asked him if we could go to Marriage Guidance, but he refused because he did not think there was anything the matter. I was crushingly disappointed in our relationship. I had by then noticed his obtuse reasoning and bizarre thinking, I wondered if he had something really 'wrong' with his brain, but no-one else seemed to notice.

Ten years after we broke up I saw Donna Williams on a Channel 4 TV programme on 6 December 1995. She was talking about her first book, *Nobody Nowhere*, and about her diagnosis on the autistic spectrum. Suddenly it clicked. I recognized the behaviours she described as being similar to my husband's.

I contacted the National Autistic Society to ask if there was any doctor who could give us a private diagnosis, and I set out to find out all I could about Asperger's Syndrome.

The NAS gave me the name of Dr Ben Sachs at Charing Cross Hospital and we made an appointment for June 1996. I told my husband that AS was hereditary and if he had it our children had a right to know. If he hadn't got it, nothing was lost and I would have egg on my face. He agreed, because he was absolutely sure he hadn't got it. But, of course, he had. Dr Sachs confirmed what I'd suspected.

The diagnosis helped me enormously. I knew it wasn't my fault, and that he couldn't help it, he hadn't done it deliberately. Finding out all I could about AS and stopping expecting him to behave normally helped me to heal.

In the United States, at approximately the same time, Karen was making the same discoveries. Remember, this was 1995, a year after the main diagnostic criteria had been published and put in use. This was the beginning of what we can call the 'discovery' phase of Asperger's Syndrome, when information was filtering down from those in the know to those who needed to know. In the UK, it was still necessary to contact the NAS, as Doris did, to find a consultant who knew enough about the newly defined disorder to be able to diagnose an adult. It took Karen some time to locate a doctor who could help her understand the problems which had dogged her marriage.

Her husband by this time had experienced some psychotic episodes. It's very hard to say why these might have occurred, but we can only imagine how devastatingly isolating it must be to live with a disorder which has no name, and no apparent pattern, to know only that you 'feel' different, and that situations which seem to cause no difficulties for others hurt and distress you.

Karen, also isolated, had been undergoing counselling. She couldn't understand her husband, she couldn't understand her own loneliness, but she continued to search for an answer.

> A marriage counselor first used the term AS to me in 1995. She said she thought my husband had the disorder. This was on a Friday. I spent the entire weekend reading about Asperger's Syndrome at local bookstores – not that there was much to read about it in those days. A lightbulb was definitely lit.
>
> I then spent a year locating an MD who could or would diagnose him, at Beth Israel/Deaconess Hospital in Boston Massachusetts. After actually listening to me, reading the reams of papers I'd written over the years of his odd, hurtful behaviors, and the poem I wrote about my loneliness on our thirtieth wedding anniversary, he was diagnosed with Asperger's Syndrome and Tourette's Syndrome.
>
> Diagnosis has helped me in understanding the whys of AS behaviors. He is now taking medication for sleep, depression/anxiety/OCD and he is no longer psychotic as he was before the diagnosis, and with no medications.
>
> I am relieved to know that it is not me who has the problem…for years I was told it was me, not my husband. Knowing the truth of AS behaviors has liberated me to find myself again. I became 'lost' in his behaviors for years and years.

For many wives, the discovery of their husband's Asperger's Syndrome comes when their child is diagnosed. This is the most clear and obvious route to understanding a husband who has always appeared a little odd or strange. The child may receive the diagnosis through the school, although Asperger's Syndrome is famously difficult to detect, and almost half of Aspergers are beyond school-leaving age when their diagnosis is made.

Having had this diagnosis for a child, eventually, a mother might think, seeing the criteria, 'This reminds me of her father…'

In Elle's case the diagnosis of Asperger's Syndrome that her stepson was given when he was twenty-one made her realize that her husband, who had been given medication for Attention Deficit Disorder, fitted into exactly the same criteria.

> My stepson was diagnosed with AS at 21. I started reading about AS on the internet, I figured out what he was and brought him to a doctor. We had brought him to many doctors in the past but no one could help us. He was either mis-diagnosed or not diagnosed. As I read about my stepson, I realized my husband was AS. The doctor figured out my stepson's grandfather was, but somehow didn't acknowledge my husband.

So, my husband doesn't have a diagnosis. Not officially. He did go to a doctor and told him he suspected he was AS and the doctor laughed at him and said no way.

The unofficial diagnosis has helped us because now I don't take things he does and says as personal attacks but rather the AS. I have become more accepting.

I've only told a close friend and therapist about this and they believe me. I have talked to the kids (adults) but they don't want to believe their father is AS. They say no way he could marry and have children. Yet, they are supportive to me and deep inside, they know. I choose not to tell family or some friends because I feel strongly they would not believe me or be able to give me the support I need. His family still doesn't believe his son is AS. They say if he wasn't diagnosed until he was twenty-one, then he must not be AS – the doctors would have found it earlier.

Elle, like many who finally track down the reason for a partner's difficult behaviour, has fallen victim to what Tony Attwood describes as the 'Cassandra Phenomenon'. Cassandra was a prophetess in Greek mythology, celebrated for the astounding accuracy of her predictions. But she was cursed by the gods, who decreed that although they could not take away her incredible clairvoyant powers, they would ensure that no one would ever believe what she said. In Asperger's Syndrome the wives and lovers of those whose baffling behaviour has been explained by the symptomatology of the syndrome are rarely believed.

It happened to me too. Danny's mother, the Asperger parent who had brought up two very different AS sons, insisted that Danny's problems arose from the breakdown he'd had after Heather had walked out on him. Yet Danny's brother, quiet, unassuming and obviously passive and inert where Danny was an impulsive and hyperactive Asperger, had the same difficulty with eye contact, the same mysterious disappearances, the same inexplicable behaviours. He was a sought-after computer programmer, who had a relationship with a university student he saw very sporadically. She never knew where he was, or what he was doing. Danny and his brother were never close, but I was amazed, when I met Carl, how similar his conversational style was to Danny's. The two of them seemed to converse almost in silence with each other and never contacted each other by telephone. Carl had an unhappy knack of never turning up at family gatherings, even when he had assured everyone he would be there. I think that, like many Aspergers, family social occasions were just too much overload.

None of my friends, no matter how carefully I explained, ever accepted that Danny had Asperger's Syndrome. My closest friend was the most critical, describing him as manipulative, scrounging, devious and cruel. 'He can't help it,' I'd sigh, going into the details of the syndrome yet again.

'Wise up,' she'd say. 'That's just an excuse.'

'It's not actually his explanation for his actions, though, is it? It's mine. So how can he be using it as an excuse? He never even mentions it.'

'Ah, but he knows you believe it, and that you'll let him off because that's what you think, so he plays on it,' she used to say. It got too much for me eventually.

And here is Solveig, a Scandinavian woman, who has faced the same credibility problem, and lost a friend through it, as I lost mine.

> I have lost the confidence of my best friend through all this, after trying to explain to her what it is all about. She is in the health profession herself, and I think she finds it offensive that I do not necessarily agree to her interpretations and recommendations of treatment for what she sees as a lunatic deviation on my part. But I have a couple of other friends who have seen my husband more closely during the last years, and they know what I am talking about.
>
> Losing one lifelong friendship has been painful. It is very hard for me to see that the person I liked to see as my best and most intimate friend, shuns me now. I realize that I may have exploited her, that she was not strong enough in her own right to be able to cope with my bitterness over all this.

This attitude is exactly what I've spoken about, earlier in the chapter. Most of us are led to believe that behaviours are determined by psychological dysfunction. It's very difficult to allow ourselves to make that huge leap to dissociate ourselves from the conventional psychoanalytic theory which has dominated the text books, the media and the personality quizzes for a century and turned us all into armchair psychologists instead of armchair philosophers. Now, if only we could be turned into armchair neuroscientists, that might help a few Aspergers to shed their invisibility and become more open to rational interpretation. Even Heather, the love of Danny's life, responded negatively when I spoke to her about Danny's condition.

'No,' she said, 'you're getting too complicated and analytical. I had a friend like you, once, who was always trying to work out what was wrong with him. Danny was just immature, that's all. He was just like a small child. He never understood what life is really like.'

Even 'experts' tend to be sceptical about the condition. They, too, have read the books about typical male behaviour, and unless you've had any experience with Asperger's there's always a tendency to explain it away in the traditional format of 'this is the problem with men'. Asperger's Syndrome has been described as 'extreme male behaviour' and 'as far as you can go on the macho scale', but that's just another way of expressing the egocentricity that is present in all Aspergers – men and women. It's facile pop psychology. It does no one any favours to stereotype the genders in this way. Yes, masculine or left-brained behaviour can appear far too logical and self-interested, but all of us neuro-typicals have both masculine and feminine qualities, and can choose which to access when necessary. Aspergers just have deficits, neurological differences. They actually can't switch between being pragmatic and being over-emotional. Over-emotional isn't available to download.

Liza, an American academic, married to a professor, is all too aware of the Cassandra phenomenon too.

> Counselors that we met with together were never really given the full picture. They were told of little annoyances. There really was no way they could have guessed at the seriousness of the situation. To them it was just typical Mars/Venus stuff.
>
> Counselors that I have seen for my own needs advise me to get out! Recently, I sought help specifically for AS (as I had finally begun to understand the situation). I looked for therapists who said they knew of AS, and that was a real joke.
>
> I was told that my husband could not possibly be AS because people with Asperger Syndrome cannot function in society and certainly do not get married. After I described my relationship with my husband, they did have to think twice about it. (After picking their jaw up off the floor!)
>
> How do you tell people that your husband has this strange disorder that makes him not care about others? Most people can't begin to comprehend. Some say, why doesn't he get help, why don't you leave him, can't it be cured?
>
> Those people that know my husband think he is a great guy and would never listen to my stories without thinking that I was an ungrateful, demanding, complaining wife. Those people who do not know my husband can not believe I would even consider staying in this marriage. The truth lies somewhere in between. Until I met other wives in my exact situation there was absolutely no one who understood where I was coming from.

So, these are experts? It makes you want to weep. Aspergers don't marry? They don't have families? This is obviously an appealing myth, as this is the second time we've heard this in two accounts. So come with me back to basics, and the second chapter of the book, and let's trace the logic, as Danny would advise.

It's clear, from all research, that there's a very strong genetic component in ASDs of all kinds. So, that being the case, where do we think this genetic link comes from? Oh, what a surprise! It comes from people with ASDs marrying and having families, and having some likelihood of passing on the genetic material which is common in this disorder.

That genetic link is more and more evident the more it's researched.

When I began writing this book, I was interested in talking to parents who believed that vaccination was the primary and only cause of autistic spectrum disorders. I did this through message boards and mailing lists on the internet. And yes, I did come across people with this very powerful conviction that their child might have been damaged by a vaccine, and that this was the sole cause of their autism. There was no autism, they said, in the family. I explained about ACs, Autistic Cousins, those with some Asperger traits, but insufficient perhaps to put them on the spectrum. I explained about Sula Wolfe's category 'schizoid personality' which she believes is a higher form, even, than AS, and might represent where the spectrum fades into typicality. The 'schizoid', according to her criteria, is the typical loner: odd, eccentric, the person who avoids others, but is regarded as a 'character' or just 'strange'.

The more I asked about relatives, the more positive responses I got. Yes, there had been Uncle John, he was like that. And there was Aunt Kate, who used to wander off, in the middle of conversations. More in-depth questioning gave flesh to the bones of memories.

'Now you mention it...' most of them would say. 'Come to think of it...'

I asked one man if there was an engineer in the family, as Asperger's has been called 'engineer's disorder'.

'Yes,' he said. 'I'm an engineer.'

Later he wrote back to me. He had been looking into the AC category that I'd mentioned. He'd also looked at Asperger's Syndrome. And he'd realized that his child, although diagnosed with classic autism, was actually very similar in many of his behaviours, skills and deficits to himself.

'He's actually just like me,' he said, 'but disabled by it.'

He's now modified his view, once very rigidly held, and admits that autism may well be a genetic neurological condition.

Whatever the outcome, after diagnosis, or discovery, the benefits outweigh the problems. It can't be easy for many of the undiagnosed Aspergers to calculate the time they may have lost on their educational progress or their employment prospects, by losing the period of their life when they were different, frustrated and confused, but most are happily relieved by the burden of anxiety lifted when the diagnosis is confirmed.

Diagnosis can also have practical benefits. It carries an entitlement to benefits, the Disablement Living Allowance in the UK, and social security payments in the US. It's these initiatives on disability which have allowed Kevin Phillips at twenty-six to return to higher education so that he can fulfil his ambition of becoming a historical researcher, an ideal occupation for an Asperger. They've allowed Larry Arnold to return to university to take a media course and to turn his talent for computing and photography into a future of video-making.

While many, me included, prefer to think of Asperger's as a difference, rather than a disability, there's no doubting that it does cause, for many, problems sufficiently complex and serious to warrant a helping hand. Sixty-two per cent of parents of Asperger's Syndrome adults felt that their son or daughter would not be able to live independently without support.

And partners of Aspergers are unanimous in their belief that it is diagnosis, or discovery, of the disorder which has helped them clear the 'blame' from their relationship. They found out, as I did with Danny, that when you understand all, you forgive all, even yourself, even the friends who desert you, even the family and the experts who don't believe you.

The greater the level of diagnosis in this current generation, the greater will be the understanding of this condition in the future. Once children are properly diagnosed some of us can stop banging our heads against the wall, and start banging a few drums instead.

But I'm going to stop thumping my tub now, and leave the last words of this chapter, instead, to someone who has the magic touch, and the clear, logical, lovable directness of the irrepressible Danny.

Here's Kevin Phillips to tell it like it is:

> Nowadays I divide my life into two sections. The first section is my life before the diagnosis and the second is my life after it. To be honest, I don't like talking about hardly anything that happened in my life before I found out I had AS. Now I know I have it, I can try to, and I mean try to, identify the areas where I was going wrong and at least endeavour to prevent repeats. It's not going to be easy. I will never get it right entirely, but I am not looking for sympathy. To me everyday life has never been easy. It still isn't. On the positive side though something had to give, because my life was like walking around in circles.
>
> When someone with an ASD throws a temper tantrum because something in their bedroom has been removed or the furniture in their house has been arranged in a different way it is for a reason. Some may argue 'Don't we all have obsessions and routines. There is nothing wrong with that'. However, what differentiates the routines and obsessions of those with ASDs from others is the intensity and length of the obsessions as well as the frequency and disruption that the routines can cause.

I suspect that in the past many people with ASDs were locked away in mental hospitals, drugged up to incapacity and left in a corner because the local authorities didn't know what to do with them. In the old asylums they even could have been brutally beaten constantly to make them change their behaviour. They were also labelled mentally ill due to ignorance or bafflement at many aspects of their behaviour and conduct.

When I think of some people with ASDs being locked up in mental asylums all their lives, I think of some of the special abilities and talents which may have gone to waste through nothing but pure ignorance. Simple as that really.

Much can be argued for and against the 'Care in the Community' policy of the early 1990s. Undoubtedly the act has many detracting points and it isn't perfect, but for many people with ASDs it has been a good thing. As awareness of ASD increases (not fast enough but improvements are being made), many people who have ASDs have been reassessed by professionals. As a result it has emerged that they weren't mentally ill at all.

Misery and suffering are what many people with Asperger's Syndrome and autism have been through in life. Much of this has been needless. They have been punished when their only crimes are to have been different to the masses and to have these conditions.

Despite the increased levels of awareness, shocking levels of ignorance still prevail in society at all levels. Parents, children, society and schools all have to be made more aware of ASDs.

And lovers, Kevin. Let's not forget the ones who love you and want to spend our lives with you. How do you think it is for those of us who love or who have loved someone with Asperger's Syndrome?

Asperger's Syndrome diagnostic criteria

DSM-IV Diagnostic Criteria for Asperger's Disorder (reproduced by permission of the American Psychiatric Association)

A. Qualitative impairment in social interaction, as manifested by at least two of the following:

1. marked impairment in the use of multiple non-verbal behaviours such as eye-to-eye gaze, facial expression, body postures, and gestures to regulate social interaction

2. failure to develop peer relationships appropriate to developmental level

3. a lack of spontaneous seeking to share enjoyment, interests, or achievements with other people (e.g., by a lack of showing, bringing, or pointing out objects of interest to other people)

4. lack of social or emotional reciprocity.

B. Restricted, repetitive and stereotyped patterns of behaviour, interests, and activities, as manifested by at least one of the following:

1. encompassing preoccupation with one or more stereotyped and restricted patterns of interest that is abnormal either in intensity or focus

2. apparently inflexible adherence to specific, nonfunctional routines or rituals

3. stereotyped and repetitive motor mannerisms (e.g. hand or finger flapping or twisting, or complex whole-body movements)

4. persistent preoccupation with parts of objects.

C. The disturbance causes clinically significant impairment in social, occupational, or other important areas of functioning.

D. There is no clinically significant general delay in language (e.g. single words used by age two years, communicative phrases used by age three years).

E. There is no clinically significant delay in cognitive development or in the development of age-appropriate self-help skills, adaptive behaviour (other than in social interaction), and curiosity about the environment in childhood.

F. Criteria are not met for another specific Pervasive Developmental Disorder or schizophrenia.

Gillberg's Criteria for Asperger's Disorder (reproduced by permission of the Association for Child and Adolescent Mental Health)

1. Severe impairment in reciprocal social interaction
   (at least two of the following):

   a) inability to interact with peers

   b) lack of desire to interact with peers

   c) lack of appreciation of social cues

   d) socially and emotionally inappropriate behaviour.

2. All-absorbing narrow interest
   (at least one of the following):

   a) exclusion of other activities

   b) repetitive adherence

   c) more rote than meaning.

3. Imposition of routines and interests
   (at least one of the following):

   a) on self, in aspects of life

   b) on others.

4. Speech and language problems
   (at least three of the following):

   a) delayed development

   b) superficially perfect expressive language

   c) formal, pedantic language

   d) odd prosody, peculiar voice characteristics

   e) impairment of comprehension including misinterpretations of literal/implied meanings.

5. Non-verbal communication problems
   (at least one of the following):

   a) limited use of gestures

   b) clumsy/gauche body language

   c) limited facial expression

d) inappropriate expression

e) peculiar, stiff gaze.

6. Motor clumsiness: poor performance on neurodevelopmental examination.

(All six criteria must be met for confirmation of diagnosis.)

Asperger's Syndrome: ICD-10 (1990) Diagnostic Criteria (reproduced by permission of the World Health Organization)

A.   A lack of any clinically significant general delay in language or cognitive development. Diagnosis requires that single words should have developed by two years of age or earlier and that communicative phrases be used by three years of age or earlier. Self-help skills, adaptive behaviour and curiosity about the environment during the first three years should be at a level consistent with normal intellectual development. However, motor milestones may be somewhat delayed and motor clumsiness is usual (although not a necessary feature). Isolated special skills, often related to abnormal preoccupations, are common, but are not required for diagnosis.

B.   Qualitative impairments in reciprocal social interaction (criteria as for autism). Diagnosis requires demonstrable abnormalities in at least three out of the following five areas:

1. failure adequately to use eye-to-eye gaze, facial expression, body posture and gesture to regulate social interaction

2. failure to develop (in a manner appropriate to mental age, and despite ample opportunities) peer relationships that involve a mutual sharing of interests, activities and emotions

3. rarely seeking and using other people for comfort and affection at times of stress or distress and/or offering comfort and affection to others when they are showing distress or unhappiness

4. lack of shared enjoyment in terms of vicarious pleasure in other people's happiness and/or a spontaneous seeking to share their own enjoyment through joint involvement with others

5. a lack of socio-emotional reciprocity as shown by an impaired or deviant response to other people's emotions; and/or lack of modulation of behaviour according to social context and/or a weak integration of social, emotional and communicative behaviours.

C. Restricted, repetitive, and stereotyped patterns of behaviour, interests and activities (criteria as for autism; however it would be less usual for these to include either motor mannerisms or preoccupations with part-objects or nonfunctional elements of play materials). Diagnosis requires demonstrable abnormalities in at least two out of the following six areas:

1. an encompassing preoccupation with stereotyped and restricted patterns of interest

2. specific attachments to unusual objects

3. apparently compulsive adherence to specific, nonfunctional, routines or rituals

4. stereotyped and repetitive motor mannerisms that involve either hand/finger flapping or twisting, or complex whole body movements

5. preoccupation with part-objects or nonfunctional elements of play materials (such as their odour, the feel of their surface, or the noise/vibration that they generate)

6. distress over changes in small, nonfunctional, details of the environment.

Diagnostic statistics

The following are extracts from the report 'Ignored or Ineligible', published by the National Autistic Society in 2001, for which research was conducted into the living conditions of diagnosed Aspergers and autistics:

'Late diagnosis is a significant pattern for people with autism across the spectrum. Only 43 per cent of lower functioning adults were diagnosed before the age of five, despite having urgent needs which could be addressed through early intervention. Eighteen per cent of lower functioning adults were not diagnosed until over the age of sixteen.

'Longer delays were experienced by some at the higher end of the autistic spectrum where 29 per cent of people were not diagnosed until over the age of sixteen. The figure was much higher for people with Asperger syndrome where 46 per cent were not diagnosed until post sixteen.'

'A strong correlation exists between satisfaction at school and diagnosis... where diagnosis took place after the age of twenty satisfaction levels were only at 21 per cent at primary level and 13 per cent at secondary level.'

'Thirty-two per cent of parents reported that their son or daughter had experienced mental ill health. This rose to 50 per cent of those whose son or daughter was not diagnosed until after the age of thirty.'

'Of those experiencing mental ill health 56 per cent had suffered with depression, a further 11 per cent a nervous breakdown...and 8 per cent felt suicidal or had attempted suicide.'

'Adult psychiatrists in particular should be targeted for training to expand their expertise in developmental disorders. This will avoid the treatment of people with autism and Asperger's Syndrome for acquired conditions such as mental health problems without reference to their underlying diagnosis.'

Getting a diagnosis

Here are some tips and guidelines on getting a diagnosis:

- Clarify in your own mind the reasons why you would like an official diagnosis. Is it to settle your own mind? To help you find identity? To enable you to get the help you need? Many successful adults may feel that an official diagnosis is of little help. Others find it the answer to a life-long battle for understanding. Bear in mind that an official diagnosis may not solve the problems you want it to solve.

- GPs (in the UK) and physicians (in the USA) may be of little help unless they have been trained to recognize developmental disorders. Many psychiatric and psychological services fall in the same category.

- You may like to telephone the National Autistic Helpline (in the UK) for further help and advice about finding a specialist diagnostician in your area. The number is 0870 600 8585 and calls are taken between 10 a.m. and 4 p.m., Mondays to Fridays.

- Search out diagnosticians on websites. The website in the USA which carries lists of diagnosticians is Online Asperger's Syndrome Information and Support – OASIS – at www.udel.edu/bkirby/asperger. This site is a wonderful mine of information on all aspects of Asperger's Syndrome.

- Remember that some of the diagnosticians listed may be unwilling to diagnose adult Aspergers.

- If you're looking for a diagnosis for a partner you must be even more certain that your motives are sound, and that your partner understands the implications of diagnosis and has clarified his/her own reasons for wanting diagnosis.

- Remember that help for Aspergers lies uncomfortably between learning disabilities statutory bodies and mental health organizations. The benefits system in all countries has not yet caught up with those diagnosed as having a developmental disorder. Advocacy help should be available, and counselling should be offered, if required.

7 Nuts and Bolts

A little over a year ago I made contact with an old school friend, Martin, through a school website. I don't know whether you've ever taken that walk down Uniformity Lane, into that past, which for me, I admit, was one of the parts of my life I'd rather forget. I don't even know why I did it, but I was glad that I did. Because on the site I found someone I'd genuinely liked when I was in my teens, and I contacted him again.

Our lives, in all those years, had run in strangely parallel courses. He, as I did, had studied English for his first degree. We'd both done post-graduate psychology, we'd both worked successfully in the media. After his Masters degree in psychology, he'd been the director of a treatment centre for addicts, before returning to his first love, music. He was a gifted actor, a songwriter whose work had been top of the charts when he was just graduating from university. We started to talk, regularly, both by email and on the phone, comparing the lives we were now leading, and filling in the gaps. He lived in the part of the UK where Danny had come from, so naturally I told him about Danny. He told me about the woman he was currently seeing, a strange elfin woman, Louisa, in her late thirties, whom he adored. He was confused by her as she gave out what he thought of as mixed signals, and, as we NTs do, we discussed at length whether there was really hope for their relationship or whether he was looking to catch a bowl of mist.

I don't know whether you've noticed how much of our chattering lives is taken up by this obsession we have about relating, but it certainly seems to be the leading topic of conversation within my circle of friends. We just love the questions that arise from the attempt to graft one lifestyle, emotional baggage, mental state and physical attributes on to another. Will this graft take? Will it turn into the statue of Eros? Will some of the leftovers from the operation be swept into the mortuary, or will they survive to turn into a pieced-together nasty gremlin which will haunt us for the rest of our lives?

As he recorded her behaviours and passed them on to me, dissected, to make into neat piles, I almost felt that I knew this woman who confused him so. Then they went on holiday together, briefly, to France, as she'd been ill, and he wanted to help her recuperate. When he returned I asked him whether this attempt at bonding had succeeded.

'It was a nightmare,' he said. 'She didn't speak at all as I drove along. She gave me the silent treatment.'

'What did you say?'

'Oh, I pointed it out, of course,' he told me, 'and you know what she said? She said, "Well, you could have talked to me!"'

I was suddenly Charles Laughton in Notre Dame, shuffling across a black and white movie, and shouting, 'The bells! The bells!'

Yes, you've heard the bells too, with this justification for silence, haven't you? You heard it in Chapter Five. You heard it through Danny's voice – 'You could have talked to me.'

I didn't know what to say, but the neat piles carefully re-arranged themselves to spell out the words Asperger's Syndrome. Should I tell my old friend, Martin? Actually, during that conversation, I didn't. I slept on it for a while. I'd known, of course, that there were women with the syndrome. I'd seen Danny's mother. It was just that I hadn't thought there might be a softer, more passive version of the harridan, a gentle sensitive woman who shared a place on the spectrum with The Bitch From Hell.

I know more now. I've met, spoken to, corresponded with so many AS women. I've also learnt that the disorder presents itself in a number of totally different ways. Deficits in some can be almost unnoticeable, in some can appear exaggerated. Some people mask certain aspects of the syndrome very well. But it was in examining the evidence for my old friend's lover, that I made that cognitive leap from thinking all male Aspergers are Danny, all female Aspergers are Mother, to understanding the variety of patterns that can be formed by this kaleidoscopic condition.

Before I shared my suspicions with Martin, I went through the triad of impairments, and thought about what I'd been told about Louisa's behaviour. The social impairments seemed particularly marked, although all the impairments were mild. If he came into their pub and she was with friends, she wouldn't acknowledge him by word or signal, but would continue with her conversations. He once drove her to deliver something on their way to an evening out. She went into the house when invited and stayed there for twenty minutes, leaving him sitting in the driveway in the car with the engine running. She was being inappropriately polite to people she hardly knew.

As for communication impairments, she misinterpreted a lot of what he said, taking the literal meaning only. In her understanding, 'Do you want to go to bed?', even when asked in a lascivious way, always meant, 'Are you sleepy?' She enjoyed being read to but, despite her post-graduate level education, had to keep asking what words meant. She had difficulty keeping in touch with Martin or letting him know where she was, how long she would be, when she would see him.

She stimmed. When stressed, she sucked her thumb while wrapping her fingers round her nose, making little sounds, and always rubbed her feet together before falling asleep. She slept heavily. She was a textile designer with a particular skill at mosaics, too – that concentration on parts rather than wholes. She would continue with any task she was doing if he called to see her, not even welcoming him until she'd finished. These are all impairments of imagination.

And did she have the Asperger facial features and the immaturity? She had a beautiful child's face with, in Martin's words, 'a rosebud mouth'. Martin had described her to me as 'vulnerable', 'innocent' and 'endearing', and she had had a recent relationship, one of the few she'd had in her life, which sounded exploitative and perhaps abusive.

There were some deficits apparently missing. She wasn't, for instance, clumsy, but only a little gauche. She organized things quite well too, although she always made lists to help her. But generally the pattern was there.

I decided to ask Martin to check it out, rather than burst in on him with a 'Eureka' diagnosis. And this is what I did.

'You remember I told you Danny had Asperger's Syndrome?' I asked him, the next time he phoned.

'Yes…' he remembered.

'Why don't you look carefully and find out exactly what it is, search the Internet?' I suggested. 'It's a possible explanation for Louisa's behaviour. But then, what do I know? It's just a stab in the dark.'

Within 24 hours he'd phoned me back.

'That's it!' he boomed, 'that's exactly it!' He'd checked out every website he could find, he'd ordered a pile of books from Amazon, he'd signed on to an Aspergers and partners mailing list, and he was absolutely certain, even at this early stage. He was in the same position as I had been, deeply in love with someone whose behaviours and emotions confused him as much as they confused her.

'Shall I tell her?' he asked me.

'Not yet. Find out more. Get some advice from some women aspies. You'll know when you're ready to tell her, and when she might be ready to listen.'

I warned him about overloading her with too much information too soon. But when he chose his time, and passed on a little of what he knew, she slowly accepted it. He read her extracts from books, she listened and nodded. He asked her if she'd ever been thought of as aloof, distant, a daydreamer.

'All my life,' she said.

She recalled, too, how upset her parents were when, as a child going on her first school holiday, she had walked out of the house, with her bags, without saying goodbye to them.

Women, as Tony Attwood points out, are much better at adapting than men, and the Asperger traits are less likely to be noticed at school. He says that the common experience is that women Aspergers are the passive type, whereas school referrals to the psychological services are likely to be of the more active and aggressive boys, who have tantrums, like Danny, and draw attention to their difference by rowdy behaviour. Girlfriends, too, tend to gather round and help out those with fewer social skills, protecting them and concealing their shortcomings from others.

Martin's going into this relationship with an Asperger woman with his eyes open. He knows, as he's researched the condition, what is likely to happen. He has a generous, thoughtful nature, is naturally protective and mentoring, and his psychology background will come in useful. Above all, when there's a breakdown in his communication with her, he has support to fall back on – me. Speaking to Martin, listening to what troubles him, reminds me so much of what I went through, but I can, at least, say, 'she isn't rejecting you, she just needs time to de-stress', or 'of course she's going to say that she finds another man attractive, if you ask her. Aspergers are literal and honest. She won't know how to make the effort to lie so that your feelings won't get hurt.'

So many of the reassuring gestures which NTs are used to may be missing when you love an Asperger. One Asperger told his mother, 'Why do I need to tell you I love you? I told you last year, and I haven't changed.'

Martin, then, is fortunate. He understands. He can make allowances. But let's have a look at those who were less fortunate, and exactly what information might have helped them.

In this huge group are women who've been married to men with Asperger's for many years. Neither partner may have heard of the condition. These women find that their roles are often reversed within the marriage, and that, far from what they expected, they have had to take the initiative rather than be the one protected.

Aspergers have problems in just coping with domestic duties.

I cover for his lack of responsibility around the home. For years I took control over everything since he would not participate in any household activities. Slowly over these last few years, I've stopped doing that. He has begrudgingly picked up on a few things, like mowing the lawn (hum…can't think of anything else!).

He wouldn't know how to screw in a light bulb if you asked him to! He once asked me to open a package of sliced cheese, because there were no directions. He tried to put panelling up in his den once and placed it right over the top of wall hangers and hardware for the curtain rods. He doesn't even take on responsibilities which are normally considered the 'husband's' chores. I used to mow the lawn, take out the garbage, paint the house, unclog the drains, fix the toilet, and repair the appliances. He uses his poor skills as an excuse to do nothing for the family in this regard. He also refuses to spend a cent for the things which he won't or can't do. Either I do them or they don't get done. I used to do them...now they just don't get done.

These are comments from Liza, an American married to a professor prominent in his field, yet incapable of opening a packet of cheese. It has to be said that dyspraxia is partly to blame here, and she was not to know that he actually was incapable of doing many of the chores which wives expect husbands to do.

When Danny and I separated I bought him a flat-pack bedroom suite consisting of a wardrobe, desk, chest of drawers and a bedside cabinet. I didn't know, even after almost four years of intimacy, that he was far less practical than he pretended to be. I gave him an electric drill and screwdriver set and, naturally enough, expected him to be able to construct the suite. One weekend he actually managed to put the wardrobe together, in a makeshift kind of way, but had to prop it up with a piece of wood. The rest of the bedroom remained in the boxes. It was still there the last time I looked.

Heather did all the house refurbishment, decoration, wiring and plumbing. As you'll remember from the first chapter, he couldn't even take radiators off the wall without causing a flood.

As well as clumsiness, a serious problem for most domestic Aspergers is inertia. They rarely can motivate themselves to do those jobs which seem either difficult or boring or, as Danny would say, 'too much hassle'. As the effort of living and working socially is so draining, those things which might more easily be delegated to others, or just neglected, they refuse to even think about. It's an overload. So Liza's complaint that 'he uses his poor skills as an excuse...' is not so much an excuse as a reason, something she would have known about if she'd been aware of Asperger's Syndrome before she married.

And this is Abigail's experience of her husband's efforts at woodwork.

He often strips screws, breaks components when he is assembling things, because he fanatically over-tightens. He is so precise he makes simple jobs very complex and time-consuming. He washes every particle from the dish before placing it in the dishwasher, so that it takes an hour to load.

She has identified another difficulty that Aspergers can have, perfectionism, and this is also implicated in their refusal to do very much in the home. They can be highly critical of something that isn't done properly, or, like Abigail's husband, spend hours getting something done rather too well.

Muriel, a Canadian farmer's wife, has discovered, as all the partners have, the power that routine has over an Asperger's life.

> I have got him to make his own breakfast – toast and instant coffee. Up in the morning and the same old habits every time – put on the kettle, take out the toaster, and put in four slices of bread. I once said to him, 'why don't you surprise yourself and do something different?', which was the wrong thing to say!!!
>
> Also if I am not at home for supper, he will fry up potatoes and an egg! Oh, yes, he has made a salad twice when he thinks about it!

Cooking and eating seem to give rise to many routines and repetitive behaviours. This is Beverley's husband.

> When we first started going together unless someone else fed him he ate nothing but eggs, which he'd boil a dozen at a time whenever he was hungry.

And this is Abigail's:

> He rejects my cooking now, and eats tortilla chips or squirt cheese for dinner every night. He eats out at lunchtime every day, even though it is not in our budget. He won't drink coffee from our house, but will buy a cup from the store.

And Liza's:

> 'Fad' is the word for it. Once he decides that he likes something (or has read that he should) then it must be available at all times for him. He goes bonkers if his latest food trend is not available in the house. Some fads last for years and years, others come and go. He once read that spinach had something bad in it and didn't touch it for about ten years. Then he read how good it was for you and started liking it right away.
>
> He has set notions about what is considered food and what is not. Fruit cannot be served with dinner; it's not dinner food. But then fruit is not an acceptable salad or dessert. Whatever he grew up with is the only way things can be prepared or 'the right way'. He cannot ever say, 'I don't like these.' It is always, 'These aren't good.'
>
> He also had strong preferences for mealtime routines that could not be compromised. Most of these routines were out of his control after I became

too busy with kids to worry about his every little whim. So, many are no longer followed.

If he likes a particular restaurant, we eat there regularly (on our routinely once a week dinner out) until another restaurant catches his interest. Food and eating habits fulfil most of his ritualistic obsessions.

Everything is a routine. Many are not worth worrying about and therefore have continued to a point that I doubt he could change them. He finishes his dinner leaving one bite of each food item on the plate. I doubt that he even knows he does this. But, it never fails, ever. He must leave his last bite of dessert (a dinner requirement) until he has been given his third cup of coffee. At restaurants he has been known to throw a fit if the waiter tries to take his dessert plate away with that one bite left, or worse yet, if he doesn't get that cup of coffee.

I hope you're taking all this in? It's truly amazing, even for me, and I lived with an Asperger. Not all are so set in their ways about food, but do you remember that Danny was? I told you how he masked his preferred rituals, gravy or mayonnaise on everything was his favourite one, until he took charge of a meal, or when he was picking his midnight snacks. He wanted what we NTs might call 'comfort food', high in carbohydrates. His eating habits had been established in the boarding house his mother owned. Despite thinking of himself as a man of the world who had actually eaten a sheep's eye in Turkey, he chose boarding house food when stressed just like Liza's husband and 'what he grew up with is the way food must be prepared'.

Routines comfort Aspergers. They actually need them. They're not being rigid in order to annoy everyone else in the house, it's just that the familiar provides stepping stones over the river-flow of time and events. Without the familiar, they become disorientated. Here are a few more examples which might appear designed to irritate those who share living space, if you didn't know that your partner had an incurable neurological condition.

He showers for a full twenty minutes, using tons of soap, scrubbing every part of his body over and over again, completely draining the hot-water heater. He then spends the next half-hour drying and styling his hair, shaving, and dressing. He cannot skip any steps or alter his pace. Each step must be done precisely, no matter how late he is, or who is inconvenienced.

Abigail

He used to dress in our office in the apartment, where his clothes were… when we moved into a house with a master bedroom and walk-in closet, he still dressed in the office.

Jasmine

He adheres to the Book of Common Prayer, the Daily Order, must do laundry every day, must shower in the morning and before he goes to sleep. He has a weekly routine, also.

Linda

He has a routine for after work. When he comes home from work, he re-parks the family van in the garage so that it is precisely the correct distance from the wall, etc. He then begins to tidy up certain areas of the house, placing items very precisely. He can tell instantly if something has been moved, and he obsessively replaces anything that has been moved to another location.

He goes around the house checking to see that all the pens and pencils are in their proper places, and gets very angry if they are missing.

He drags the dusty outside trash-can into the living area to open the mail. He rips open and reads all the junk mail every day, noisily crumpling it into balls which he throws onto the floor, and thoroughly rips up any confidential material. He then gathers all the trash from the floor and puts it into the big can.

Abigail

The adherence to routines is probably the feature of undiagnosed Asperger's Syndrome which most distresses partners. In the long term this may mean that the Asperger develops a pattern of behaviours within the marriage which are totally rigid and unbending. Marriage should be organic, growing over time, adapting to changing circumstances, but if one partner insists on an inflexible daily routine there's little option for development as a couple, and the relationship atrophies.

Another factor which scores high on the distress scale of women married to Asperger men is the impairment of communication in Asperger's. If you have a relationship which is dying, you need to have some means of rescuing it, and that, according to every text book, counselling service and woman's magazine is 'Talk about it', isn't it? But what if your partner either can't talk easily, or can't understand what you're saying, or misinterprets, or would just rather be left alone?

Doris's case is unusual as her husband, helpful in the house, funny, attractive, rather like Danny, sometimes just misunderstood what she said to him. Deficits in auditory processing or verbal understanding when under stress are a feature of Asperger's Syndrome which was highly marked in her strange husband.

He gave a different meaning to words so we ended up arguing about something we actually agreed about. Sometimes I thought he agreed with me, but he actually didn't. It caused a lot of confusion, and misunderstandings.

This strange use of words is a problem with Abigail's husband, too.

> I noticed that he had difficulty calling objects by their proper names. He has never been able to call sheets anything but *bedspread*, and a blouse, top, or skirt, is a *dress*.

Some problems can be caused by Aspergers' literalness. Irony and sarcasm can be lost on them, so when Beverley needed her husband's help and sympathy, but gave a pained sarcastic reply to his question, this elicited a response from him which must have sounded almost unbearably cruel.

> His behaviour deteriorated markedly when I had a series of miscarriages. He was totally indifferent and appeared not to notice. By the third one I was frantic. The evening before I miscarried I asked him to stay with me. He said he'd like to but there was something he wanted to watch on the TV. When the miscarriage actually happened he woke up and asked me if I was OK. I said, 'Yes, I enjoy having miscarriages.' He said, 'Oh good, that's OK then,' turned over and went back to sleep.

Can you see exactly what happened there? Her Asperger husband believed her to be fine, because that's literally what she told him. Her 'reassurance' enabled him to go back to sleep, comforted. Yet, as she had no idea that he had this disorder, remarks like this chipped away at their marriage. Her husband's language difficulties were very marked in all ways.

> He appears to have very little idea how his words impact on people. Goes in for wild exaggeration, though nowhere near as bad as he used to be. He definitely interprets words differently. When we talk to each other I often feel we're slightly out of sync. He says we're always talking along parallel lines. Occasionally when extremely tired he appears to speak gibberish – as though he's talking in tongues and is totally incomprehensible.

Had she known about AS, Beverley would have been able to understand that his speaking 'gibberish' was a symptom of excessive stress, and an element of Tourette Syndrome, and that he needed to sleep or to find time on his own so that his speech centre, disrupted by his disorder and exhaustion, could settle and recuperate. Solveig's husband shows his stress by making, as Danny did, small vocalizations and hesitations.

> What's noticeable is his flat intonation, hesitation, pauses, eehrs and aahrs, a long pause or sigh before the last word in a sentence, as if it is a great effort to finish a string of thoughts.

The 'flatness' which she mentions is often said to be a feature of Asperger's speech, although I've spoken to many whose speech, as Kevin's does, and as Danny's did, for instance, has bounce and vitality. Danny's voice was unusually light, high-pitched for a man, but all Aspergers have some unusual vocal quality.

Most partners say that their husbands speak at them, rather than to them, but this is not so much a language disorder as not understanding the social rules of communication, taking turns and responding to what's just been said, rather than the Asperger tendency to smother someone with a thick duvet of facts, commentary, obsessional thought. This is Liza's husband's habit, too.

> Now we don't communicate. There is only the occasional comment about the weather or politics. If there is a need to connect with regard to schedules, mine or the kids, then we state our information and that's it. It has come to this because I quit trying to form communication bonds after years and years of rejection.
>
> Early in the relationship I remember discussions about feelings and futures, but that did not continue for long. Soon after the wedding the kindest words were only in writing, letters or cards. Phone conversations could be far more personal than face-to-face conversations. The more he rejected my attempt to converse, the harder I tried to draw him into my life and activities, and the more he rejected me still. Once he told me that my voice bothered him and he couldn't stand to hear me talk.
>
> However, if he wanted to carry on a conversation with regard to an interest he had 'we' could 'talk' for hours. It barely simulated a conversation. No matter what my responses were, he continued the discussion as though I had made no contribution at all.

There's an interesting tip inside Liza's heart-rending (for an NT) description of the communication difficulties she has with her husband. It's the reference to writing things down. I found this very useful in my own dealings with Danny. Listed bullet points work very well when trying to convey facts, instructions or requests, and many Aspergers can express their emotions in writing rather than in face-to-face meetings. Many are responsive to poetry, and can write it, movingly (remember Wendy Lawson and George Handley?). Some have telephone phobia, but some do feel easier when talking on the phone. It's worth trying all forms of communication to discover how to get through to an Asperger most effectively.

Another strange habit which Aspergers often have is, as I've mentioned before, echolalia – mimicry or repetition. Sometimes when talking to an Asperger, you can find your own words echoed back at you. Sometimes your gestures are included, too. They might silently repeat their own words or rehearse them by mouthing before they speak. Or they might adopt the tone and content of something they've heard elsewhere. You'll remember that I said this arises from a need to model, to take on characteristics of whatever they see to be good, funny, or admirable behaviour.

This is what Menthes, a Dutch woman, says about her husband's 'copying':

> Oh my, does he ever copy me and others, and he's sooooo crafty at it, I didn't even realize for a long time. That's got to be one of the weirdest things. Another thing he does, is repeat his own sentence. Like he can say, 'How are you doing' (out loud) and then right away the same sentence but now only his lips move, no sound! When I ask him what are you doing? He says, yes…strange…I know…I just do that, always have.

Others back this up:

> He likes to think that he imitates funny things that others have said. But, it seldom comes out all that funny.
>
> Liza

> He'll watch others and try to copy their reactions, although doesn't quite come off. Often vastly exaggerates mannerisms, to the point where he appears quite ludicrous. He appears totally unaware of this. Will also sometimes repeat the last few words of sentence. Before AS we (me and son) used to think he was mocking us, which could be intensely upsetting. He'll sometimes copy entire phrases from something he's seen on TV, especially soaps.
>
> Beverley

> He parrots what I say in an argument. It's as though he can't think of anything original to say, but he wants to counterattack me, so he just says, 'Well, you _____.' He also watches sitcoms and whispers the lines of the script to himself after the character finishes speaking. I have never heard him repeat the dialogue verbatim, but I suspect he has learned most of his 'small talk' and the 'sense' of what is funny from watching television.
>
> Abigail

> Sometimes if I have accused him of not doing something he will use my words (which he would not normally use) later on to prove that I am wrong.
>
> Doris

> He does not copy me, but other people who he admires.
>
> Karen

I think he copies words and phrases that he has heard without much regard for the actual interpretation. He says what he believes he is 'supposed' to say.

Linda

He says things I say and thinks it's original. If he's around someone of a different nationality, he will pick up their accent and start talking like them.

Elle

I've mentioned this feature partly because of its curiosity value. It rarely impinges on normal relationship issues, but a positive response to the question of copying came up so often in the questionnaires that I felt it might be useful to see how widespread it is. As a tool for survival and a proof of the way that Aspergers use adaptation techniques in order to fit in, this aspect of behaviour demonstrates that a total withdrawal from the social world is not what AS is all about. They recognize, and use, strategies to allow themselves to function within an alien environment, and this is, however small, an example of willingness to conform, which may be useful for partners to bear in mind. Your aspie partner is not closed off to flexibility, and can learn when motivated!

What grieves most partners, though, is the way that Aspergers need and even demand their own space. I've described this in detail, and how it affected my own living arrangements with Danny, even though I fall at the top end of the 'get out of my face!' range of space-lovers. I've also told you why this space is essential for recuperation, de-stressing, and attention-shifting. Even so, it remains one of the least understood, and most bitterly resented behaviours of Aspergers when they're in a relationship with an NT. Liza wrote:

He has always needed his own private space in our home where he can hide away from everyone for hours at a time.

And Beverley, while agreeing, mentions one of the ways in which Aspergers can create the space they need – they merely fall asleep:

He has the ability to simply switch off. Will actually fall asleep in middle of conversation, especially if there is emotional content. Sometimes he looks as though he's in a trance.

Muriel's husband does the same:

He sleeps when he sits down at any time in the living room, but he used to sleep at table even when we had company.

For Solveig, this apparent remoteness from the family is a major issue in the breakdown of the relationship:

> He needs space in the sense that there is no place for me or our sons in the house, outside of his own needs for space. Silence is what we are used to enduring.
>
> Sometimes I think of him as those pioneer explorers of the Arctic, where getting enough and regular sleep was crucial to surviving. His sleeping hours do not have to coincide with the normal rhythm of life. He likes to sleep late in the morning, to get up when the house is already empty, and keep to his own hours.

Perhaps Doris best explains the feelings which this need for space, this detachment, causes in the neuro-typical partner, a woman who just wants to be loved in a way she understands:

> Before we split up I craved to be together more often as I often felt at arm's length, I wanted to feel close and intimate. I always felt I was scrambling for the emotional crumbs he would throw down to me.

The end result of this can be, in a long-term relationship, an overwhelming loneliness from which, for some, there is no relief or release. It is a feeling I know well, although my relationship was not as long as Karen's, and it's a feeling I wouldn't like to revisit.

> He has had a live-in care-giver, housekeeper, cook, etc. ... for thirty-eight years. While I have been left lonely, sad, isolated, physically ill. This aspect of AS has yet to be recognized or understood by the 'experts'.

Most Aspergers themselves fail to recognize how much others need comfort, togetherness, joint efforts, and the recognition that this is a family which operates as a unit and does things happily in harmony. Sometimes this failure is the result of remoteness, and sometimes it is the result of the lack of social skills which may be more apparent in some Aspergers than in others. This is an example of Muriel's husband's lack of understanding of social conventions and the requirement of married couples to put on a unified front when visitors call:

> He never asks people to come here, and when we have them over, he often goes outside to 'do some work', except when my sister and her husband come, and then he will stay. He usually acts like a guest and leaves everything to me unless I ask him to help, before the company comes. When he does not

enter in to the chat, then I know he'll soon go outside on the farm or is going to sleep. If one of the people is a farmer then he can talk 'shop' and that is OK for him.

One evening we had neighbours come for supper. After supper we were sitting and chatting and my husband just up and left and then we saw the truck drive out of the driveway. The company asked where he was going and I said that I did not know, so they decided to go. Just before that, I was asked if he did this kind of thing often, and it was then that I started to be honest about the problems and said yes. Well they left and E came home and was surprised to see them gone. He asked me why they went so I told him at which he got angry at me and told me that I knew where he was going and so should have told them. I did not know, but had an idea, but this time I was not going to make any more excuses for his bad behaviour.

Social occasions, especially if they're family-based, can be deeply distressing for Aspergers. They're often unsure of what to do, there are too many people around, and the whole thing becomes a huge effort, especially if they can't work out the 'rules'. Abigail's husband is particularly gauche and unhappy in this situation, not realizing how much his behaviour impacts on others' happiness.

He's extremely uncomfortable (won't go to weddings, etc.), especially with my relatives. He shrinks into a corner. I remember when my son (now twenty-seven) was a child he would leave work early to attend his birthday parties, but never joined in. He would just read a book/newspaper. He seemed to think simply being there was enough.

You can see, from that example, that some knowledge of Asperger's Syndrome in both partners could have salvaged those birthday parties. Her husband was willing to obey the rules as far as he understood them: he left work early and he knew that his presence was needed. All that might be necessary to do in this case would be to give him some definite instructions which were clear and unequivocal. Aspergers respond very well to clear instructions. Had he been told that he'd be required to set up a video for the children which would start at a certain time, if he'd been given a list of CDs to play, in order, if he'd been told that he would be required to blow up a given number of balloons at a set time, this would have been within his capabilities, and would have solved some of the problems for his son and his wife. Linda has discovered the 'be clear' solution:

> I am as specific as possible about everything. If I request a task, I must give a deadline. I can get through if I find an example within his experience, and he can understand that.

Elle has also found her strategies for coping, which include finding the right time and place, and sticking to the subject. Aspergers' difficulty with processing auditory information can often make them obsess about the nature of the discussion, rather than concentrate on what is being said. This journal idea is brilliant, an extension of Liza's discovery that writing things down helps, and is one for every partner to include in their 'must-do' list – get a journal!

> In the past he talked in circles and wanted to examine a word I used rather than talk about what we needed to talk about. He told me I didn't feel what I said I felt, he avoided any kind of serious discussion or decision making.
>
> We communicate now in a number of different ways – sometimes we sit down, in times of peace, and talk. He still sidesteps the issue and will want to talk about my tone or choice of words. I have to set up ground rules beforehand. Other times, we write it down, face to face. We share a journal, so we write things in there and tell the other one that there is something that needs to be read.

Some, like Elle, have changed their habits of a lifetime and the tendency to assume an equal ability to relate, in order to accommodate what they now realize is an incurable, but possibly manageable neurological difference in the man they married. Beverley, who has become ill herself, is fully aware now that she has to do things she didn't expect to have to do.

> I have to make *all* the decisions, possibly the hardest part of our marriage, I feel as though I can simply never rest. I decide where we live, what we do, what sort of lifestyle we lead, furnishings, etc. I choose his clothes, tell him what to wear, when to wash, etc. It makes me sound like an absolute control freak but if I don't do/suggest it nothing gets done. Even if we go out to dinner I have to choose what he's going to eat, otherwise he'll become quite agitated. Having said that I often lean on him too. I've developed social phobia so he's largely the one who deals with people. He also does most of the cooking and puts up with my depression.
>
> In the last two years he's begun to open up and will attempt to explain why he reacts in the way he does, as long as I try to keep emotionality out of it.

Doris is now separated from her Asperger husband, and he still refuses to accept, despite diagnosis, that he has this condition. She works round it.

Now I know I don't expect him to behave as a normal person and don't get upset at his shortcomings. I phone him up about family things every other week and he very occasionally phones me. We see each other every few weeks and he always greets me with affection. He seems much more relaxed about being in my company since I stopped trying to get him to understand his Asperger's so he could see how he was hurting me and stop it. Waste of time. Now I accept he cannot see it. I'm better since I learnt about AS, learnt all I could about it, stopped trying to teach him about it, learnt how it affects him. He's now better at planning and organizing so he's more reliable.

I have thankfully reached a stage where I feel balanced, not unhappy but not so far up as happy or even contented, I would say a state of equilibrium.

Counselling did me no good at all, they kept telling me to stop talking about my husband, I was there for myself. They would not listen that *he* was my problem and if they would only listen and tell me what was the matter with him I would then be OK.

I started a partners' network, got the National Autistic Society to print some literature about partners and organized workshops for partners of people with AS with Dr Tony Attwood who has been very supportive.

Doris, as I did, discovered that separation can actually work as a positive force for good, and that if deprived of their caregiver, some Aspergers will happily develop their own executive functioning, and do it well.

Linda's solution is to forget what she's missing, and be more self-sufficient. It's a pragmatic answer, but one that works.

There's a lack of affection, comfort, physical intimacy. My own level of stress has a lot to do with how well I can cope with his limitation.

The greatest help for me has been learning to take care of myself, my own needs and not making him responsible for my feelings.

Menthes, on the other hand, has decided on divorce, although it wasn't her idea.

Trying to understand him is a bottomless pit, I do understand that much. He hates me, I can tell by everything, but when asked, he'll say, you are a good person. And when I say, oh come on, I would like to hear the things you really do not like about me, and everybody has those, you can't say it wrong, and I won't argue, I'll be silent, try it. Then after ten minutes, he'll go, I can't think of anything, you are good looking and you are a good person, but I do think we better get a divorce. For me to ask why? is absolutely useless. So after hearing that for thirteen years, I've had it, and he can have his divorce, I no longer want to be treated like this.

Aspergers don't usually initiate the idea of divorce, and are often very loyal to the point of being rather clinging, as Danny was. They don't, as we know, welcome change. So Menthes' husband is unusual.

So now we've heard about some women's views on their relationships, and along the way picked up a few tips for dealing with the behaviours from the repair point of view. I actually believe that there are many different repair tools available both to Aspergers and to their partners, but that there have to be many more. I also believe that as the diagnostic procedures begin to take account of the numbers of couples there are in this situation, more and better services will be delivered. Perhaps I'm being a little naïve.

The essential service needed is support. I've told you about the Cassandra Phenomenon, the refusal of friends and family to believe the partner's suspicion that his or her other half may have Asperger's Syndrome. You certainly can't count on those closest to you to deliver the help and advice you need. That compounds your feeling of isolation which may have its roots in the thin soil of a problematic relationship, or a relationship which has recently wilted for reasons beyond your comprehension or control.

I've also referred to counselling. This was my first choice. I needed to talk about my despair with someone who knew what they were talking about. Unlike Doris, I actually wanted to talk about me.

Can you blame me? All I'd thought about for four years had been Danny. In that time I'd spent hour upon hour advising others about their problems, in print, on the radio and on television. I was drained. And now I'm going to tell you something I've rather glossed over.

After that dreadful row with Danny over my undesirable appearance at his place of work, I cried for a week. I couldn't stop. I'd loved and cared for him, lavished money and attention on him, found him a home – well, two if you include mine – explained his disorder to him, brought him a newly independent life and the world of steady employment, and right at the end of that he'd rejected me, as I saw it. I know I was wrong to think that. I've made that clear. But it was only my head that knew it. My heart didn't, and wouldn't accept it. That's what happens when you love an aspie. You know they can't respond in the way you'd like them to, but you go on somehow expecting it, or hoping for it.

So the first thought was to get help. And the second thought was, where do you get help about something that you have to explain in detail before you can start on the recovery? No one knew anything about Asperger's Syndrome. Counsellors and psychologists aren't even geared up to understanding Aspergers themselves, let alone dealing with the human detritus of their disordered lives, which is how I thought of myself at that time.

Things have already improved in the last two years. Relate, the UK relationships advisory and counselling organization, has now set up training in Asperger's Syndrome for its counsellors, and the Relate centre at Derby, in the Midlands, can offer support to partners. There's another expert counsellor in practice in Coventry, Maxine Aston, who has written a wonderful guide book on relating to an Asperger partner. We're getting somewhere, two tiny dots on a map of Britain, and how many in the rest of the world? I hope you can detect my irony.

Having had second thoughts, and identified my needs more closely, always a prerequisite of presenting myself for counselling, I realized that perhaps I didn't need to talk so specifically about the disorder, but more about why I felt so heartbroken, what it was in me that had initially taken on this responsibility, then tried to get out of it, then got caught by it yet again.

I made an appointment to see a psychologist. It was a disaster. Some people actually enjoy the type of counselling which starts, 'Tell me about it', then goes into this clinical silence in which a clock ticks and you become nauseously aware that cabbage has been cooked in the building recently, and that there is a dog on the premises. For myself, and I stress that this is a personal preference, I actually don't want someone to listen to my interior monologue. I do a pretty good job of that myself. And I'd had enough silence-for-two to last me a lifetime. I started to wonder what animal the psychologist reminded me of (a badly-shaved ferret), where he'd bought his trousers (a car boot sale), why he thought those glasses suited his face-shape, and why there were railway magazines in his book cupboard. This very nasty wooden mantel clock, a 1950s model (same car boot sale) lacking wit and style in that atavistic room, clucked away each moment until I said, 'I'm in the wrong place,' and left, very quickly.

Then I discovered Transactional Analysis, and that suited *me* perfectly. My advice is to shop around, do what I did, telephone all the counsellors and psychologists, finally settling on one whose voice is pleasant enough, and who appears to have a sense of humour. Replace 'sense of humour' with anything that you prioritize. That is mine.

But it was more than the therapist himself, a partially-sighted man with wit, wisdom and a cheeky laugh, that I took to. It was the fact that TA was rational, structural, clear and calming. It taught me to look at the dynamics of what had happened between me and Danny, without placing blame, without taking a ticket for the next available guilt trip, without being at all negative. I came away from each session on the learning curve feeling stronger, more able to unravel the knot in my stomach.

I learnt there about Drama Triangles, and how easy it is to get involved in them. It was this explanation which showed me precisely what I'd been up to all those four years, so I've decided to let you have a look at this, too, as it might help you.

There are three different characters, positions which we can adopt in a dysfunctional relationship. One (the one I was always most attracted to) is Rescuer. This is the person who is out to save others from themselves, the zealot with the medicine chest and the unerring belief that everyone needs her. Yes, it's usually a woman.

Then there's the Persecutor, the one who's determined to make trouble, a really nasty piece of work, but nevertheless powerful, capable, controlling. That's your typical male character.

At the other corner of this triangle is the Victim, a childlike waif who waits for help, who can't help himself. That's a child character.

And we can all play all three, and do, in an argument, in a relationship, in life generally. We move easily from one part to another. And that's all they are – parts, roles, stereotypical silly behaviours that are unhealthy.

I'd been my favourite, Ms Rescuer, saving Danny. And he'd played to the hilt his wonderful virtuoso Victim. I'd not helped. I'd just patronized him by assuming I knew better than he did how to run his life. He found it easier and easier to let me run it until he became so absorbed in the part of Victim that he couldn't actually help himself. And we'd both toyed with the Persecutor role. His victimhood was controlling. It dominated our lives together. My anger was also part of the issue. The less he would do for himself, the more I became a nag and a harridan, biting his bottom when he wouldn't move. He certainly saw me, in his best Victim moments, as the one who was hurting, not helping him.

And the only thing to do, to stop the game, the fairy story that becomes very Grimm, is to stop blaming, accusing, allowing the role-playing to continue. I'd been quite right to ask Danny to leave. It was best for me. It's what I had to do to help me feel happier. Ultimately, it helped him too. But that isn't the point. TA starts with simply believing that we're all OK – you are and I am. It starts with acceptance of self and others.

After a year, I'd started rewriting the TA literature in my head, finding small holes in it, so I knew I'd come out of the petrified forest, and was back to being my old sensible self, not disenchanted, but merely de-mystified. That's how I managed to juggle work and home and still find time to renew, on a more take-it-or-leave-it basis, the fragile friendship that I still enjoyed at times. It helped me to cope with the final open ending of the love that had broken me.

I'm not recommending this particular line of support or this therapeutic system. It worked for me. And, what's more, it's given me a chance to show you the pattern of what can happen in a relationship with a difficult partner. Drama Triangles are full of adrenaline, but you produce the adrenaline, become exhausted when there's no more left, and feel limp and powerless. I've never played a Drama Triangle game since I learnt how to identify them, and how destructive they are.

Every partner in an AS/NT relationship needs the help and support of an expert, to remain healthy and focused. That's the bottom line. Or find a counsellor, just in order to discover the You who has been taken over by the It, the relationship itself. But if you can't find either, finding a friend who has already developed some expertise is the next big thing. So, I help Martin if and when he needs me. But all three is best. Asperger's Syndrome is tough to live with, for all concerned.

The best resources for all those in this problematic relationship are on the Internet. Why? Because the Internet is where many Aspergers live for much of the time. Whatever their problems in face-to-face negotiating and in some executive functioning, the plain fact remains that many Aspergers, fascinated by and skilled in computing, create the most revealing websites, share online support groups and mail lists, and within the confines of the computing world, flourish and inform each other and us about the differences of their condition.

And the Internet ignores geographical boundaries, and can hook you up to that expert, that support group, that literature in another country. It puts at your fingertips the best information there is about Asperger's Syndrome.

In the UK, or on the Internet, the first source of information should always be the National Autistic Society on www.nas.org.uk. The NAS deals with all autistic spectrum disorders. In the US, or on the internet, there are two major sites, The Autism Society of America on www.autism-society.org, and the Asperger Syndrome Coalition of the US.

These organizations and their websites contain all the latest information on the disorders, can provide help and advice, and have fact-sheets and recommended reading. If, like me, you prefer to start with the most reputable organizations, start there, then follow the links which will take you to some of the more remote outposts, many personal websites, and some very interesting byways.

What you'll certainly notice as you delve into finding some support, or further information, is that there can be a tendency to polarize into NT or AS. Aspies are quite rightly very keen to assert their right to non-judgemental recognition, which does bring them into conflict with the US-based website specifically set up for the partners and families of those who have Asperger's Syndrome, FAAAS Inc. at www.faaas.org.

This website was set up by one of the most interesting women I've met in the Asperger's Syndrome world, Karen Rodman. I've already mentioned her. Tough and feisty, she fought for years to have her problems with her husband identified and eased. He was finally diagnosed with Asperger's Syndrome in his seventies. She came to the UK in 1998 where she met Brenda Wall, another pioneer, and to attend the first workshop for partners of people with Asperger's Syndrome given by the leading authority, Dr Tony Attwood.

The transcripts of the first, and a subsequent workshop with Tony Attwood, are on the FAAAS website, and contain powerful insights into the way some relationships can flounder when AS is involved. The partner and family support offered is second to none. The website offers a refuge for those confused and perhaps dispirited by their experiences with an Asperger partner. There are news items, a mailing list for sharing difficulties, and many very moving stories about the impossibility, at times, of living with undiagnosed Asperger's Syndrome.

But, mention FAAAS to most Aspies, and you'll be able to hear the silence which precedes a thunderstorm. Then it erupts. They have taken great exception to FAAAS. One of the reasons is its title – Families of Adults Afflicted by Asperger's Syndrome. It's the word 'afflicted' that they vigorously object to.

They're not being totally realistic in this objection. The fact is that undiagnosed AS *can* be an affliction within a family. Even Aspergers themselves agree that late diagnosis has, in most cases, held them back, has made them more confused, has led to further trauma – bullying at school, employment difficulties, relationship problems. And if you probe deeper into some Aspies' backgrounds, they will freely admit that if they've lived with an undiagnosed Asperger parent, as some of them have, they haven't had an easy time.

But they still seem unable to grasp that FAAAS is, in some very clear ways, doing a great service not only for the partners who've perhaps had a lifetime of worry and concern, but also for Aspergers themselves. More than one expert in the field has said that it has been largely partners who have brought undiagnosed adult Aspergers to their attention. So, FAAAS should be a solace to partners and other family members, but should be mentioned only cautiously to those Aspergers you might love.

In addition, there's ASPIRES, an international support group and listserv dedicated to the support of AS partners in their marriages and relationships. This group, co-administered by Roger N. Meyer, the author of the *Asperger*

Syndrome Employment Workbook, is a very positive resource. As Roger quite rightly points out, many Aspergers do make and maintain happy relationships, and the support exists for them to discuss any difficulties they may have with other couples, who may be able to suggest solutions.

Having lived with marginalization, misdiagnosis and ill-treatment, many aspies also have their own refuges on the Internet. Some of these are wonderfully informative, hugely supportive, mines of information and help. One of the best is OASIS, which I referred to in the last chapter. It is principally aimed at parents of children diagnosed or suspected of having AS, although there are resources for Asperger adults, too.

Many of these sites have mailing lists and message boards.

But, and this is what I mean by polarization, just as FAAAS is none too keen on Aspergers themselves joining the mailing list, some of the AS sites are none too keen on NTs joining their message boards. I was driven off one Asperger's message board with a very large genetically modified flea in my ear for asking if any Aspergers might like to give me some insights for this book. The owner of the site told me that he didn't want any successful NT writer who'd had a relationship with an AS man coming on to his site while so many Aspergers themselves were both unemployed and had never had a relationship. Another told me very kindly and courteously that all prospective members had to be vetted, and that I wouldn't be allowed on the site as they had had some vulnerable people on it. Hmm. What can I say? I am hardly noted for my evil ways.

Polarizations notwithstanding, those message boards which have allowed me to communicate with Aspergers have given me, and still give me, fascinating visions into a world which runs in parallel. The vitality of intellect, the subtle disabling deficits, the amazing scatter skills, it's all there, twinkling, intergalactically. Sometimes I can see the interface between genius and disorder very clearly. Usually I'm humbled by what I read.

I felt with Danny, I will always feel, that Asperger's Syndrome offers the gift of the alternative. But I know how much he hurt, and how I was hurt by almost understanding what he couldn't offer, but not quite getting there, not quite being the right person to be his best friend for ever and ever.

There's no blame in that, and should be no guilt. But there are memories of champagne and fireworks, involuntary but inspiring difference, trust and innocence, love of a mysterious kind, which I'll always keep in my pocket.

Here, hold out your heart.

I'm handing some of those memories to you.

Negotiating relationships with Aspergers

Here are the major tips (rules, if you like!) for handling the difficulties that might occur in relationships with Aspergers.

Do...

- Do give clear unequivocal messages, whether these are instructions, information or requests.

- Do be prepared to allow time for these messages to sink in. Attention-shifting is a long process.

- Do choose the right time and place for communicating. It's never a good idea to disturb an Asperger who is concentrating on something else.

- Do make it clear what you want or what's troubling you by starting sentences with 'I'. If you start sentences with 'You' these can be interpreted as blame – i.e. say, 'I get unhappy when...' instead of 'You make me unhappy because...'

- Do make lists, write things down, communicate important information through the written word as well as verbally. Some Aspergers have huge difficulty in taking in verbal information in an emotionally charged atmosphere.

- Do announce changes that might occur in advance, allowing the prospect of change to sink in. Aspergers resist changes to their predicted routines and must be prepared.

- Do explain the 'rules' of each social occasion before it starts, so that the Asperger is aware of what's expected and can observe the script or model which you provide.

- Do allow space, time alone, recuperation time, and time for personal hobbies.

- Do get mind and body support for yourself. You'll need a good friend, or group of friends, who understand the problem, to whom you can talk. You need to keep aspects of your own social life intact – a regular leisure time activity is helpful. If you have a computer, join an internet support group. You may need help in the house and garden too. Counselling can be useful.

- Do help the Asperger with analogies when new experiences occur. Be prepared to say, 'This is like the time when...'

Don't…

- Don't go into this with your eyes closed. You'll have to be prepared to understand behaviours which are alien to you.

- Don't overstress or overload the Asperger you love. Watch out for signs that s/he is getting too tired or anxious. Stimming is a useful clue.

- Don't use conventional expressions like, 'Look at me when I'm talking to you!', 'And you can wipe that silly grin off your face!', 'Why aren't you talking to me?', 'Can't you see how that makes me feel?', 'Are you listening to a word I'm saying?' They are meaningless and insulting to Aspergers.

- Don't expect any DIY or much help around the house. Aspergers can be very good at arranging things, but can take hours over a simple task, and are too clumsy in subtle ways to do decorating or home improvement.

- Don't be confrontational. Aspergers fear anger and confrontation and may even accuse you of being angry when you're not. Try to calm down, take your time, be logical during an argument.

- Don't make the Asperger responsible for your feelings. Your feelings must remain under your control.

- Don't get into the Drama Triangle by playing Rescuer. This forces the Asperger to play Victim, and you may find that it's a pattern of behaviour that you can't escape from.

- Don't look for hidden agendas. Aspergers are literal. What they say is exactly what they mean, so you can forget about all those emotionally manipulative games. If an Asperger says, 'I need some space,' this does not translate as, 'I've fallen in love with someone else.'

- Don't drop hints, make subtle allusions, expect your body language or tone of voice to carry a hidden message. Messages of this kind will not be understood.

- Don't expect conventional reassurance when you're down. You should ask for a hug, if that's what you want, and may even have to ask for sex. Your Asperger partner may be able to see that you're upset, but may not know why, nor how to deal with it. You have to spell it out.

- Don't compel your Asperger partner to attend family functions or celebrations. These can cause too much pressure.

- Don't give up trying. If the worst comes to the worst, you may have to leave the relationship, but you will be missed. Aspergers are very loyal, and even clinging.

Reading material for Asperger relationships
Websites

www.faaas.org – Specifically set up to support families, friends and partners of Aspergers by Karen Rodman, an American. A treasure chest of personal accounts, news, expert opinion, help and backup. It is a brilliant site.

http://aspires-relationships.com – ASPIRES, a website support group set up by Linda Newland and co-administered by Roger N. Meyer. It also runs a very helpful email subscription list for those with Asperger's Syndrome, and their families.

www.udel.edu/bkirby/asperger – The Oasis website. Although this is not specifically for partners, there's a great deal of wonderful material.

www.tonyattwood.com.au – The website of the world expert on Asperger's Syndrome. This is the man who knows everything!

members.ozemail.com.au/~rbmitch/Asperger10.htm – An Australian website packed with information.

www.isn.net/~iypsy/autlink.htm – I love this site, possibly the most comprehensive you'll find. It's Canadian, and although it is an autism site, there's a huge section in every category for Asperger's Syndrome.

www.maxineaston.co.uk – The website of Maxine Aston whose book is discussed below.

www.delphiforums.com.au – The home of the message board AS Partners which for me was a life-saver. This is a forum where you can cry your eyes out, listen to others' stories, help others in the same boat, and keep in touch with the latest news about Asperger partnerships. With FAAAS, this is my recommended site.

Books

Maxine C. Aston: *The Other Half of Asperger Syndrome*. National Autistic Society, 2001. This book is written by a Relate counsellor who was in a relationship with an Asperger. It's one of the most useful support tools for those in Asperger relationships, full of sound advice, help and tips.

Christopher and Gisela Slater-Walker: *An Asperger Marriage*. Jessica Kingsley Publishers, 2001. This book, written jointly by Christopher, who is Asperger, and his wife, Gisela, is the story of their successful marriage. They also have a website at www.asperger-marriage.info.

One-to-one support (UK) for Asperger relationships

The Park Counselling Centre
10 Park Road
Coventry
West Midlands CV1 2LE
Tel: 02476 224422
email: maxineaston@aol.com

Maxine Aston is the author of *The Other Half of Asperger Syndrome* and a fully trained Relate Counsellor. She offers a full counselling service to couples, individuals and families affected by Asperger Syndrome. She also runs workshops to increase awareness and offer support. www.maxineaston.co.uk.

Derby Relate
Tel: 01332 345678
Tuesdays 10.30 a.m.–4.00 p.m.

This is initially a telephone helpline for those in Asperger relationships. As a relatively new service, it can be hard-pressed, but this will ease as more counsellors are trained. It is the only telephone helpline in the world for those in partnerships with Aspergers. You may be able to arrange one-to-one counselling in your area.

Index

Lightning Source UK Ltd.
Milton Keynes UK
28 September 2009

144289UK00002B/2/P

9 781843 104728